ESCAPE

THE TRUE STORY OF THE ONLY WESTERNER EVER TO BREAK OUT OF THE BANGKOK HILTON

DAVID McMILLAN

MAINSTREAM
PUBLISHING

EDINBURGH AND LONDON

First published in Great Britain in 2008 by
MAINSTREAM PUBLISHING COMPANY
(EDINBURGH) LTD
7 Albany Street
Edinburgh EH1 3UG

ISBN 9781845963453

This book is a work of non-fiction based on the life, experiences and
recollections of the author. In most instances, names of people, places,
dates, sequences or the detail of events have been changed to protect
the privacy of others. The author has stated to the publishers that,
except in such respects, not affecting the substantial accuracy of
the work, the contents of this book are true.

A catalogue record for this book is available
from the British Library.

Typeset in Badhouse and Caslon

Printed in Great Britain by
CPI Mackays of Chatham Ltd, Chatham, ME5 8TD

ESCAPE

In memory of Michael Sullivan,
1945–2001

PROLOGUE

The young Thai girl with long nails at the check-in desk had just walked away to her supervisor, losing her automatic smile as she gripped my ticket and fake passport. Across the hall, men in dark suits began moving backwards to unmarked doors. At the airport's exits, local police in uniform eyed one another, seeking initiative. Two rows away, I saw an old acquaintance and fellow smuggler at another airline counter. He was on a different mission but had caught enough of what was going on to edge his suitcase away with one foot and step back into his queue with the other. It was a bad airport day and would get worse. Now, after three days in Thailand, and with months of planning and my new identity clearly blown, I had about six minutes to get out of Bangkok airport and disappear completely.

Turning towards the exits, I tried to appear casual, miming thirst when heading for a soft-drink counter. Instead of buying a drink, I took to the nearby stairs, descending to the Arrivals hall. From there, it was out and past the first taxi rank into the gloom of a covered car park where 50 drivers waited and dozed in the fumy heat.

The driver I woke was pleased to get a job out of turn. After we bumped out of the darkness and ramped up to the freeway leading to the city, I was certain no one had followed. The metallic wind of the taxi's straining air-conditioner failed to cool a head ablaze with frustration. Otherwise, I might have given more thought as to the cause of so many police waiting for me at the airport.

An hour later, at the bar of the Sheraton Hotel, I listed my losses and remaining assets. The small bag at my feet held a pristine passport. Even the most zealous investigators would have problems identifying and circulating its name in less than 72 hours. My pockets held $12,000, with a further $32,000 in the bag's lining. At the airport, the Westlake passport had been taken, and was of no importance now despite its link to the Oriental Hotel, where I'd stayed. In the hours before technicians might tap family telephones, I should call to say I would not return for Christmas – then five days away – and perhaps be absent for many more. But then, no one had known I'd left home.

Calling a Chiang Mai contact from a payphone, I reported my fall and hinted that I would stop at a travel agency in Chinatown, from where I might phone beyond the roar of Bangkok's traffic. In open language, I said I'd head for the southern border and then hung up. It was then rush hour, so traffic was at a standstill.

Why was I being so heavily pursued? Plainly, I was a drug smuggler, and those against me were doing their jobs with government agencies. Yet, over the years, the contest had dropped below that elementary arrangement. My stubbornness had heightened their desire for the pursuit, and the chase was all that mattered. The rules were now defined only by what worked. For over a decade on both sides of this war, the costs, the drugs, any worthy cause and even our true identities were unimportant compared with the desire for combat and victory. It no longer interested me what they called themselves, only what they did.

The sun was setting as I stepped through alleyways, rode tuk-tuks and motorcycle taxis towards Chinatown. There, I would spend an hour making calls before the final retreat to a forested house beyond the city.

As I walked the last few feet through a jangling arcade to the glass door of the shabby travel agency, I dismissed those eyes upon me as merely the usual curiosity directed at foreigners. Standing inside before Large Raj, the Indian proprietor, I sensed movement behind me as he spoke.

'David, you're here to use the phone?'

Four Thai men stepped in quickly. One older and confident leading three younger but uncertain. They wore guns close to hand, visible yet undrawn. That meant they were not robbers. They began speaking English but I knew that their words would not be helpful. They were policemen with accomplices outside the shop. A shop I knew had no back door, and Chinatown was where the Thai Narcotics Suppression Division had its headquarters. I was led away, with one man carrying my bag. They took me to an underground car park. There, handcuffed and defeated, I was held against the front of one of their cars while they opened doors. The engine was cool. They had been waiting for some time.

* * *

In the final years of our second millennium, many thousands of men and women, young and old, would fly to Bangkok, that reclining navel on the world map and capital of Thailand, on the underground pilgrimage of the smugglers' trail. They would come from the cities of the Asian tigers and as often from the rich West. Most of them couriers, guided by kind or callous hands, and all hoped to cruise silently from that city, their cargo white and hidden, to thank the gods for their safety and vow: never again. Until next time.

In the departure lounges trembled bachelor gamblers from Lahore, adventurous girls from Leeds, broken fathers from Chicago and alcoholic dreamers from Pretoria. Staring from a chair opposite might be a stoic matron from Kiev, a numbed addict out of Bern or a silent smoker from Nairobi. Soon, they would be airborne, returning home to fair or ruthless settlements. Yet beneath them, in the city barely rising above its watery veins, and confined in the great city prisons of Bangkwang and Klong Prem, were those who had fallen or tripped at departure. Those who would not die in

Escape

confinement would be changed for ever. A few might be released, as grains of sand drop from the grip of a brutal hand. Those who waited in the humidity of sweating concrete for an end sometimes found the energy to dream of escape. This dream would always prove unsatisfactory, though, as no one had ever survived an attempt.

CHAPTER ONE

The bus from the court took two hours to jerk through the traffic and reach the prison. The last of 75 prisoners had been squashed into the van by ill-tempered guards at the courthouse. Now on the road, the prisoners' faces pressed into the iron mesh that served as windows. Their thin brown uniforms were soaked with sweat, and their leg irons pounded bare feet with every lurch. As a newcomer, I was still in civilian clothes.

The bus turned from the airport road through some patchy grass, then over two bridges of a swampy moat. Eighteen-inch pipes curling from the prison wall pumped lumpy brown water into the surrounding canals. This was Klong Prem, the sprawling complex that held 12,000 inmates. I was heading for the drug-remand section called Bumbudt, a name that meant the Cure.

Inductions of new prisoners took place around five each afternoon, when most of the other inmates had been put to bed. After six busloads of returns had been run through, about fifty newcomers waited with their bags on the empty, wide roadway between the three-storey accommodation blocks. I was the only foreigner. One chair was placed in the roadway. As the sun sank low, a rangy, bald-headed guard with a long cane took this seat. Two other guards stood by while a dozen trusted prisoners in short pants fussed at tables nearby, ready to do the drudge work with pens, knives and fat registry books.

Escape

With exquisite boredom, the boss drew long fingers from his eyes, dropped a hand to the cane resting on his lap and tapped the ground for the show to begin. The trusties stood tall and ordered us to remove and pile all our clothes on top of our other possessions. Then, to squat naked and wait to be called to the throne.

A trusty then moved from pile to pile, hacking off shirtsleeves and trouser legs using a rusty knife. Over the next hour, prisoners would present themselves, still naked, before the chief guard, called the Skull, to suffer his welcome while trusties chopped soap bars into quarters, squeezed toothpaste onto torn newspaper fragments and confiscated items of value.

One newcomer half stood to take his newly fashioned shorts. The Skull swatted the prisoner's ear with one practised swipe of his cane.

'Did I tell you to stand up?' Then, turning to his number one trusty, 'I told you we'd have trouble with this lot.' The trusty grinned and nodded at the sagacity of his boss. The troublemaker was then allowed to duck-walk, clutching his rags and dripping shampoo paper, to the guard conducting anal inspections. The Skull began working up a drill-sergeant's banter as he served his next customer.

'So, Ox-head, where do you come from?'

'Klong Toey, sir.'

'Oh yeah, a bit of a sailor, are you?' sneered the bald chief as he used his stick to flick clothes at his trusties.

'No, I— ' The cowering prisoner's response was immediately halted by a wide slap to the back, sending him to the ground.

'Don't argue with me, idiot! I know a sailor when I see one. Now get over there.' The Skull gestured to the roadside, where another guard stood, flabby-faced and leering, hands at his side, and wearing one knitted woollen glove, the tips of two fingers a muddy brown against the original pink colour. 'The doctor there will tell us how much of a sailor you are. Next!'

Next was a young man I'd befriended at the Chinatown police station where I had sat for a week before a brief court appearance.

Escape

His name was Nong, an easy-going junkie with an understanding wife of 40 who worked in one of the lesser massage parlours. Six kids, none of them his own.

'You've been here before.' The Skull, as usual with prison guards, never forgot a face. 'I'm sure. What's your name?'

'Nong, sir.'

'Nong, eh?' The Skull jerked a half-hearted slap to Nong's neck. 'Welcome home. Looks like you've still got the same pants you left with.' The Skull's fingers drew along every hem and reversed every pocket. At a loose seam, he tore a wide gap. 'There, I've given you another pocket. Can't have enough pockets, eh?'

'Thank you, sir.'

When my turn came, the Skull turned to another guard. *'What have we got here? More white trash?'* Then to me, in English, 'Where do you come from?'

The question meant: is your embassy strong? Dead foreigners in jail always resulted in a Thai foreign ministry inquiry. Embarrassment if a consular official called. Embarrassment was much bigger medicine in Thailand than in Europe, where it is mere entertainment.

'My name's Westlake. Australian.' I gave the nationality of the passport taken at the airport.

'Ah, Australia.' The Skull worked his fingers along the collars of my shirts before picking up my new shorts. That morning, I had folded two 1,000-baht notes, made damp, into the top seams. 'Why do you come to Thailand?' His firm grip passed over the hidden notes. 'Drugs?'

'No. I came for the water festival.' I raised an envelope kept visible on my clothing pile, showing a few thousand baht in small notes. 'Can I keep this?'

'No money here. We keep for you.' The Skull waved me over to the bookkeepers. This qualified as a mission ordered by the Skull, so I dressed quickly and sidestepped the bum-prober, who was busy poking through a prisoner's hair with his glove.

The trusties at their registers logged the cash and then asked for my court papers. New arrivals have two: a notice of the next court date and a copy of the charges, stating the weight of the drugs. This second sheet I had shredded at court following a conversation with a Hong Kong Chinese. He'd been wearing heavy chains that were welded around each ankle. While most prisoners' chains were rusty and dragging, his had been carefully polished and were held aloft by homemade metal garters. He looked as though he'd been through most of it, and he had. His advice had been from the deepest shadows, and I took it.

The registry clerk was getting frustrated. 'Your charge paper? Police paper!'

I looked on dumbfounded and half-witted. Shrugging, I said, 'I give to lawyer. No have', using broken English to confirm the Thai trusty's belief that all *farangs* (Westerners) are stupid. Then I fumbled out a lawyer's card on the back of which was written '41.9 grams'. This was entered in the ledger, and I was sent to the bench to await the prison barbers.

Those prisoners charged with more than 100 grams were sent to a bench on the other side of the street. There, each was fitted with heavy leg chains, ankle rings squeezed into a bracelet by a trusty swinging down from a seven-foot lever of a jail-built contraption. These leg irons would remain attached for the years until the trial's conclusion.

By the time the sun had set, the last of the confused, humiliated newcomers in their hacked rags were shorn of the hair of former lives. Scalps reduced to chewed, patchy stubble; the shears having transferred scabies, lice and nematodes through bleeding nicks. The barbers understood that as a Christian I was not to be shorn, a religious observation as new to me as it was to them, having been revealed just as I waited on the bench.

When those newly chained had shuffled back to the bench, greasy aluminium plates were set out. A meal of rancid brown rice and fish-head soup was then ladled out from a battered oil drum. A third among us ate, those with a determination forged in the hardship of street life. As we stood to be led into the dormitories, the prison kit was issued: a small much-used plastic bowl that served as food dish, water-scooper for bathing and to hold chunks of soap and smears of toothpaste. Many searched for bits of string with which to lift the chains from the ground so they might walk with less pain. Some questioned how they might remove their shorts through the ankle rings for washing. Others, once fast friends from their week in the police station, rapidly became shy as they could barely recognise each other, their shaven heads now revealing scars of night encounters and many lost battles.

At the bars of our second-floor dormitory two trusties fingered their neck-sized key rings, discussing the difficulty of housing another forty-eight. The dormitories were long, open cages, with prisoners sleeping on the floor. Some long-termers had bits of cardboard for beds. One hundred and twenty to each cell the size of a family garage. When these were full, the corridors became open cells.

A few minutes after we found crouch space in a dormitory, there was an accident with one of the 44-gallon drums used as a toilet for corridor inmates. The plank seat had broken, wedging a prisoner sideways and overturning the heavy drum. Ammonia, water and shit gushed to the floor, forming a putrid lava that raced for the metal stairway. The toxic mixture of bile, rotting food and slime dropped through the stairs onto yelping inmates unseen.

A trusty locked our cage as we stood with our bowls and clothes, surrounded by current residents squatting on the concrete. Standing on a large square of plastic linoleum in one corner was Lim, the room leader. He was dressed in white shorts, T-shirt, long socks, and had a whistle strung around his neck. Crouching at his feet were his two boys: his lapdog and a housemaid.

'Right! You don't like it, and I don't like it,' Lim began in his provincial Kanchanaburi accent. 'But for one night – I hope – we'll all have to do our bit and share the room. It means some consideration for others.'

Lim waved an arm across one side of the room. 'You lot move to the other side. Squeeze up a bit and you'll just get down. Not on my lino, though. There's a limit! I'll let my boys share my lino.' The boys exchanged a look. 'But,' Lim peered over imaginary spectacles, 'I can't be the only one with his ass in the air, as it were. You newcomers will have to sort yourselves out along one side.'

Although Lim's boys nodded and gestured 'That's fair; reasonable enough', and 'Can't argue with that', it was clear there was not enough space.

'A couple of tips, lads – I don't like to say orders, but why call a knitting needle a chopstick? Now, the trick to sleeping here is to get yourselves head to toe. You know, like those little tins of fish. Got that? And don't wiggle about. Makes one hell of a racket in your chains. Won't make you any more comfortable and it definitely will wake me up. Now that's something we don't want, eh?'

Lim paused for signs of dissent. Someone coughed.

'No, don't go asking me a lot of questions. Save them till tomorrow when you go to your own section buildings. One more thing—' Lim inclined his head and toyed with his whistle. 'One thing I can't stand at night is the smell of piss. Can't abide it! So all of you hold your water'; now wrinkling his nose at an old man in chains trembling near the single hole-in-the-floor toilet. 'As for number twos, don't even think about it!'

Four minutes later, we had found spaces. I had managed a corner with a couple of blankets next to my new friend Tam from the police-station cells. Others found themselves in the narrow walkway next to the toilet. Lim's boys had spread his dinner on placemats across his vinyl, and Lim laughed as he ate.

'Watch that one.' My friend Tam nodded towards Lim. 'He'll offer you dope, then inform on you the next day. He doesn't make much money here.'

One day after my arrest, Tam had arrived at the police station. He'd been arrested on a minor trafficking charge and was facing ten years' imprisonment. This was the maximum sentence for those convicted of trafficking less than 10 grams of class-A drugs, although Tam was sure his friends would buy him his freedom at some point. That day in the police station, I'd reluctantly woken under the greenish fluorescent light to the windowless cell and to the everlasting smells of chicken and cabbage that lived with the sweat in the walls. Sleeping on the next mat was a tall Nigerian arrested at Klong Toey cargo port while signing for locally made water coolers ready for shipment to Lagos. Barely concealed inside the coolers were 35 kilos of heroin. It had been a genuine shock for John, who had been given a ticket to Bangkok with instructions to buy jeans. *And just take five minutes to see to those water coolers, will you?* John was crushed. He had spent the previous day hunched and crying about the loss of his life and planned marriage to a village beauty.

Tam, by contrast, had arrived fully equipped at the cell with bags of clothes, blankets, an icebox and plenty of food, which his girlfriends were to supplement twice each day. Chubby Tam arranged shopping for me, and told me what to expect.

'Seven days here. Good time, police let us buy everything. Then jail. Bad time. But first, you go to court, five minutes, and you'll go back every two weeks for the next three months. Then waiting starts. A year, maybe three. The courts not good. If you say not guilty, they give you full time. You say guilty, they make you half. The African,' Tam looked at John, 'he's the end. Death or 99 years if he says guilty. Your case, a airport case. A problem.'

Tam asked if anyone from my embassy had come. When I said yes, he didn't like it much.

'Never ask for embassy,' he advised.

'I didn't. Several were waiting before I hit the police station.'

Tam said that nothing would make any difference now. Those whose friends could not release them from the police station were going to the jail. And, he added, those who remain in jail are almost certain to be found guilty. Yet the appeal courts, where the lights were lower, could be made more understanding. In those higher courts, cases were rarely reported as they were considered academic and technical, so unworthy as tabloid material. 'But not for you. You're a foreigner.' Tam was about to tell me why my money would be no good in the Supreme Court when I was suddenly taken from the cells to an upstairs corridor for questioning.

Escape

The massive police station was built in the 1930s, and had since been remodelled and partitioned into departments. Its corridors and windows held limited avenues for escape and near-certain recapture for a foreigner. A young police captain found a translator. We took seats at an empty bench. The captain rolled paper into an old typewriter. The translator, a young woman attached to the tourist police, was an avid trinket collector. Her name was Noi, and she was determined to educate the captain on her hobbies. This, then, is the result of Surasak's investigation of the Westlake case. It was our only interview, and Surasak spoke no English:

SURASAK: *Tell him I'll type this interview, which will go to the judge in court.*

NOI [to me]: How do you like Thailand? I work sometimes tourists. This is a nice policeman.

WESTLAKE: OK.

SURASAK: *Ask him who he gave the 250 grams to at the airport.*

NOI: He want to know 250 grams at airport. How much you pay?

WESTLAKE: What?

NOI [to Surasak]: *He says he doesn't want to say how much he paid.*

SURASAK: *Tell him he doesn't have to answer questions, but I want to know about the case.*

NOI: It a lot better you say guilty. Save time. I collect beautiful telephone cards. You have a foreign telephone card?

WESTLAKE: Plead guilty to what? I've got some English telephone cards, but the pretty ones are from Singapore. You can have them if you want.

NOI: OK, give me please. [Then, to Surasak] *He's in the drug business in Singapore. Has his connections in England. I have to meet my girlfriend in an hour.*

SURASAK [while typing professionally]: *Tell him I've been given a travel bag with $12,000 in it. He also had $3,000 in his pockets. Did he bring this money to Thailand?*

Escape

NOI: Did you bring money from Europe? Australia? USA? Is drug money. We must keep.

WESTLAKE: That's travel money. I don't know anything about drugs.

NOI: *He says he's been travelling to buy drugs, but he's not sure how much they cost.* [Then, to me] Can I have your new shoes? You no can have shoes in jail. You go there long time!

SURASAK: *What did he say?*

NOI: *He said you type very well. Very quickly.*

Returning to the cells, we passed an open window. Only three floors to the ground. Too low.

A Chinese–Lao group of seven was now in our cell, already playing poker with lots of smiling curses and easy wins. An old man, clearly their leader, appeared to be calmly losing.

'Not much of a player,' I suggested to Tam as I sat.

'I don't know about that. By the end of the day the old man will have convinced the two younger ones to confess and save him.'

And save him they did. With the police chief's approval, the driver of the car carrying 64 kilos of heroin agreed he was acting only with the youngest member of the group. The old man and another – the real driver – would be set free, and five would go to trial. The police chief then offered to act as negotiator with the appeals court to acquit the three flunkies in a few years' time. The old man, however, preferred to make those arrangements himself. He was released the following day, but not before arranging a feast for those remaining. At that, even the women prisoners in the next cell woke from their continuous narcotic sleep. They surfaced from an igloo of clothes to receive many colourful plates of delicacies from a nearby restaurant. John and I were given a large cream cake decorated with reindeer. My Nigerian cellmate could barely eat, and slipped quickly once more into the hollow carved in his heart. For his life was over, and it was Christmas Day.

With time, I would come to know the future of those in our cell. Tam's generous spirit would not serve his best interests. Once drained of money, those accomplices still free would do little to shorten the eight years he would finally serve.

The old Chinese man returned to his northern enclave to continue bidding and forbidding; those three underlings expecting their freedom to be purchased in the higher courts would remain in prison. With the wisdom of age, their master had decided it would be too expensive to set them free; just as well to pay for their food, clothes and occasional visitors to bring them hope, year after year. More importantly, they had proved themselves unlucky. There was no place for the unlucky in the old man's world.

John from Nigeria was sentenced to death, commuted to life in Bangkwang prison (known as the *Big Tiger*), where he remains to this day. His constitution turned out to be much stronger than anyone expected.

Most of us had settled for our first night at Klong Prem. The newcomers head to toe, trying not to move at the itch of chopped hair stuck to their skin, lest their chains fell. Room leader Lim had stopped moving around under the tent that his boys had made from blankets to shield him from the light. Tomorrow, I would go to the building where most of the foreigners were kept. I was in for a long campaign, thousands of miles away from any reserves, burdened with unwilling confederates and effectively beaten by the enemy. So surrounded, I slept.

CHAPTER TWO

Building Two was just like the other eight of Bumbudt. Three floors of caged dormitories holding 650 prisoners. Perhaps 40 foreigners stumbling among them. Dark, cramped sweatshops were created underneath. A handful of guards trying to extract a living with the help of their trusties.

At ground level, many prisoners had laid mats from which they sold cigarettes and toiletries. Other Thais were working at benches. Clumped around were two Chinese groups, four schools of Nigerians and other Africans, and no more than three small clusters of Westerners. An American with a beard was speaking in easy Thai to a guard. When he turned from the guard's desk, I introduced myself, explaining that I needed to break a large note to buy some toothpaste. 'I couldn't bring myself to scrape back off the ground what some bald-headed guard left me yesterday.'

'Ah, Chazoo,' laughed this thin man with a musical Boston accent that was confidently out of place. 'He likes to give newcomers a warm welcome.'

The American gave his name as Dean Reed, and paid for my toothpaste with a dozen small, flat packets of aspirin powder. When I complimented him on his Thai, Dean told me that he lived in Thailand. Loved the place. Married a local girl who worked for the US Information Service. I suggested that he might not be in Klong Prem for long.

'Oh, my case is a nothing. Silly, really.' Dean stooped at the

21

mat of a disposable-lighter repairman to drop his plastic Bic for refilling. 'Now, you can't change a thousand so easily,' he insisted. 'They don't like to *see* money in Bumbudt. Of course, there's a bank over there in the main prison. Let's see if I can get you a mattress. You'll need one, won't you? You know, that will cost you 4.50, so there'll be lots of change.'

'What's with the aspirin?' Most of the floor traders I saw kept the packets in bunches held by rubber bands.

Dean explained that the aspirin sachets, called *Tam Jai* (strong heart), were the local currency notes, traded at floating rates of around one baht a packet. *Tam Jai* would buy any of the stallholders' goods, including the doughnuts cooked each morning in a giant oil-filled wok. Some of the factory workers, little more than slaves, were paid in *Tam Jai*. At the end of each day's trading, the shopkeepers would lend their thousands of packets to the men who ran the dice games in the dormitories.

'By the way,' Dean advised, 'don't worry if the other foreigners stare at you for a day or two. Some have been here for a long time. Anyway, most foreigners go next door to the big jail if they can fix it. It's better there.'

Yet it was already clear that there would be few big players anywhere. No oasis of foreign luxury. Perhaps only those blown into these walls by misfortune and held fast on the jagged edges.

A group of young Thais were lined up beside a large water tank in the sun. They were to take showers by scooping water. A trusty, dressed as a PE instructor, blew his whistle each minute signalling each step: *Strip off, splash quickly. Stop – wait for it! Now, soap yourselves. You, keep in line. Stop fussing with those chains. Rinse off!* These boys had admitted to taking drugs, and so were being cured. The smallest patient almost fell into the tank. Only his chains brought him back to the ground.

Between the tank and a smouldering heap of decomposing garbage, there was another American. He was muttering curses while washing some shirts in a plastic bucket. When I approached, this short, stocky man with a Beatles-era haircut wiped a hand dry on his arm before extending it and smiling.

'Sorry for the rave. It's been a hard night. My name's Calvin.'

At his table, Calvin gave me a coffee sweetened with tinned milk, and introduced me to the breakfast club. Calvin was from Hawaii, Eddie from Switzerland, Paolo of Portugal, crazy-eyed Saleem from Kuwait, and Mads, a motorcycle fan from Denmark. All were awaiting charges originating at the airport for attempts at exporting a kilo or two each of heroin. All wore chains except for Mads, who had clearly never recovered from a bike accident. His embassy's requests and 15,000 baht had bought a medical dispensation.

Calvin invited me to join his food group. Their cook, Chang, was a hyperactive Taiwanese in his 50s who had been arrested at least once on every continent. Bangkok would be his last, not for lack of smuggler's enthusiasm but because he would run out of years. As for Calvin, he had been arrested with a woman from California in a local hotel the week before Christmas. They had flown over to retrieve a kilo of heroin hidden in an air-conditioning duct of the hotel room a year earlier by their friend's friend. It was to have been Calvin's and Sheryl's big break after two lifetimes of lousy breaks. In a decision almost guaranteed to maintain their losing streak, they recruited someone to hold the ladder steady beneath the ceiling: a Bangkok taxi driver. The cabbie turned informer, and Calvin and Sheryl were arrested that afternoon in the room with the parcel. For Calvin in prison, it seemed he had more trouble letting go of his former sputtering life than others whose lives were more finely tuned. He tormented himself ritually with a thick photo album, drooping over pictures of his wife in Oahu and their six-year-old boy, Nicky.

'I've still got the toy crane I'd bought for Nicky in Hong Kong. Look at the little tyke! It's in my suitcase, still gift wrapped – wherever that is, for Christ's sake. I told his mother I'd be gone one week. God knows what she's telling little Nick.'

Calvin's travelling companion, Sheryl, was in the women's prison, within waving range of Klong Prem's upper floors. 'She's taking it

OK. Doesn't like the other foreign girls. Calls them a bunch of whiners.'

'Wasn't the stuff in her hotel room?' someone asked without prejudice.

Calvin wasn't the kind to leave someone else holding the can, he said. 'She offered to take the rap. But the truth is we were in it together.'

Most of us knew the terrible odds against a judge pronouncing a not-guilty verdict in a Thai court, and the doubling of sentence for those who fought and lost. Calvin, like most Westerners in Klong Prem, had not chosen criminality as a career. Unable to cope with the pressures of taking heroin, he became an in-patient at Hawaii's plush rehabilitation clinic. There too, recalcitrant addicts would have their heads shaved. Eventually, Calvin graduated to the white uniform of a resident nurse, employed to apply the institution's principles. He had been fired six months before tying up with Sheryl.

Before I could learn more, a flat wagon arrived loaded with the market food bought by prisoners. Limp vegetables, strips of chewy meat and fish that drew the flies away from the rubbish heap in a frenzied cloud. Still, mouth-watering compared to official prison food. Once Building Two's cooks had argued and collected, the wagon was used to carry an injured prisoner to the building bearing the sign: Hospital. The flies soon lost interest.

During the eight hours each day prisoners were allowed outside cells, the Cure was busy. Most Thais worked in the small factories, each overseen by a guard who had purchased the concession from the building chief, to whom he paid a fixed commission. If that amount could not be drawn from sales of finished goods, guards would extract the balance directly from inmates. Those without skills made cardboard gift boxes used as funerary offerings. Toxic chemicals labelled Yunbao Crimson Acid Moo 4 from China were used for decorating the boxes and left the workers yellow and seeping with mucus. The most lucrative factory was the one making big, inlaid mother-of-pearl royal portraits finished with fake lacquer.

Escape

Dusty sacks of scallop shells would spill over the ground where workers would stone them to fragments. Once glued to poster-sized boards, grinding revealed a nacreous lustre. Upon this, artists would spend weeks with black ink creating the pictures before clear resin applied a glassy coating. The top sellers were images of King Rama V, upon whom a cult had formed since that monarch's introduction of the knife and fork to Thailand in the nineteenth century. Prison guards could sell the largest portraits for 20,000 baht ($500) apiece, returning a sound profit of 18,000 baht. Hard workers were rewarded with a jar of coffee.

Chang, our Taiwanese cook, had made a fine lunch, my first good meal since arrest. As Calvin was hiding the small earthenware stove and charcoal, there came a sudden hush. Martyn, a middle-aged Englishman, had accidentally knocked a large shell-picture from its drying-stand. The guard had pushed thin Martyn to the ground. Speechless with rage, the guard moved towards this destroyer of income. I looked to the other foreigners. Fortunately, the picture was undamaged, and the Thais, who liked Martyn, pacified the guard. It was clear throughout the tension that the foreigners of Klong Prem would have done nothing to prevent a compatriot being thrashed.

That night I bought bed space in Calvin's 100-man cell. His fellow American, Dean, had brokered for me the sale of a mattress sewn from old blankets. Calvin thought I had paid too much.

'Be careful of that one,' Calvin had said of Dean. 'None of the other Americans will talk to him.'

'I'll talk to anyone,' I shrugged.

'He's been here a year. He refuses to leave the Cure for the main prison. There are people there he owes money to. Apparently, he's made a lot of promises. Kept none of them. Worse, anything you tell him goes back to the DEA. And, he never goes on embassy visits. Leastways not with us. His wife works for them, you know. But it's none of my business.'

The prisoners who had been to court that day were then returned to the cell. One, who had been sentenced to life, was then chained to the floor by a metal ring. Still sandwiched between two others, he was given a plastic water bottle as a toilet. Within a few days, he would be moved to Bangkwang prison, which was equipped for lifers, and there he would be attached to a cell wall.

Calvin had been adopted by a Thai prisoner. Chort was a wiry old bird in his 60s with a permanent smile. He had been in prison for thirty-five years, the last seven sleeping on the same six-by-two floor space of this dormitory. Chort was Building Two's venerated eccentric, and he often selected a foreigner to protect. He was also the custodian of a small shed downstairs behind the toilet block. A valuable piece of real estate, it held lockers and could be rented over lunch by those wishing privacy. Chort dreamed of foreign travel, although he could not point to Thailand on any map. Calvin could not follow a word the old man said, although between us we understood Chort claimed to have once lived in a country called *Grantang-lagial*, apparently somewhere in Europe. Even the few educated Thais of our dormitory were not so unkind as to challenge this, for Chort was a prisoner of wisdom and influence in Building Two. He had no visitors.

While Chort told Calvin another incomprehensible story with great animation, I flipped through Calvin's photo album. Calvin had been married twice, but there was no picture of his first wife. She had been an older woman, and when Calvin had walked out of her life, it was her third dumping. She had then become a Christian and was last seen talking, glassy-eyed, to the foreheads of pedestrians outside Union Station while passers-by ducked her pamphlets.

In the album, most of the photos were of Calvin's boy, Nicky. Calvin could be seen standing to one side at a kids' party; Calvin at the beach at night, startled by the flash; in his white uniform at the clinic, looking sheepish. Calvin had admitted to being a 'joiner'. One who would be surprised when he found himself excluded suddenly from the latest group. Other joiners would know the feeling when they too would unaccountably drive themselves away following moments of self-doubt. As I returned the album, Calvin was speaking of the important songs of his youth. He then sang, '*New York, New York, that tumblin' town*, ah, *East side up, sunny-side down* – ah, fuck it. Can't remember the words.'

'Long time since you've been there?' I asked.

'Yeah, long – well, I've never quite made it. I mean to. For sure, one day.'

The gamblers played into the night. The tube lights sang to the mosquitoes, and prisoners held their chains aloft as they stole towards the open toilet. If anyone should hope to cut through those bars and into the night, he would first have to subdue his 100 cellmates. Inconceivable, it seemed to me then.

First thing each morning, every inmate crouched before a portrait of His Majesty while a tinny loudspeaker broadcast a chipmunk version of the national anthem. Once dismissed, the cooks would begin their fires, and the little stalls would open for business. All watched by 20 prisoners continuously rotating through the row of toilets, trying to balance chains and the scoop to splash their bums.

Despite our shared imprisonment, there remained differences between nationalities. In Bangkok alone, over 700 Nigerians were locked up. Often of the Ebo tribe, they survived with little money and no consular support. While Europeans were often crushed in Klong Prem, most Africans adapted. A few of their bosses were inside, providing a comforting illusion of support and brotherhood. In my second week, I met two clansmen arguing priorities. Both claimed to be Ebo princes. Thailand had become too hot for the Nigerians, and a move to Cambodia was under way. That afternoon, their dispute did not weigh on lost kilos or even money, but on the currency of couriers. Since African couriers were always searched to the toenails, Westerners were now more often employed. A white traveller was more valuable than drugs or even connections.

Prince Nathan wanted payment for a German courier, lost while on loan to Prince Mupara. He dismissed an offer of ten kilos.

Escape

'I know you have fifteen tourists. Five French, another two Germans and Japanese. Japanese, you know! You are a rich man.'

Prince Nathan was modest. 'Not Japanese. Only Americans. Good for one, maybe two times. Just give me two white men, and we'll shake hands.'

Even in this deepest pit of failure, the tradition of their forefathers' slave-trading was being honoured. Perhaps they *were* princes.

As in any prison, expectations are the things that prevent endurance turning to mutiny. Locals knew what to expect, and fitted in. The English felt a duty to be survivors in a foreign land, the French to show independence, the Germans to be organised, the Australians and South Africans to soldier it through and the Scandinavians to be saved by hordes from the north. Few Americans could overcome the culture shock, and were deeply suspicious of any of their countrymen who could. Dean Reed's fluent Thai and cultural immersion was felt as a betrayal, especially as he slept in another building with Thais.

Martyn, the Englishman, and a scientist, had been in the Cure for longer than most foreigners. He was under trial accused of being the translator for a group of Canadian smugglers. One-day hearings would occur every couple of months, and it could be years before any judgment. Martyn was relaxed about the delays, and I found him one morning making a concave mirror for a telescope for someone who wanted to see his girlfriend, who was housed in the women's prison. Martyn had placed a dish on an old record-player turntable. The dish was filled with resin that would harden in a gentle curve, and Martyn was finding 33⅓ rpm too fast.

The operation was interrupted by trusties dragging a small Thai prisoner through the building gate. He appeared dizzy, so it was no effort to throw him before the building chief. He had wandered away from the hospital yard, where he was kept for being 'crazy'. He had climbed over a factory shed and an inner wall, and was pawing the base of the high outer wall when caught. Caught by prisoners whose job is to scoop the sewer moat for plastic bags that clog the pumps. The chief did not dirty his hands with serious beatings, so gave the prisoner only a token caning before having him taken away. Besides, only a crazy man would try to escape. Had Martyn heard of any successful escapes?

'Not in my time. Not from here. A few years ago, a couple of fence workers managed to get to the top of the wall. The electric wire gave them a jolt, and one fell back inside. Hurt himself. The other got to the monastery next door but the monks turned him in. Anyway, things have been quiet like that since the Bangkwang riot.'

A few years earlier in the old Nonthaburi jail, prisoners had briefly taken control. The guards had fled and most trusties were hiding. An army platoon was called in. The activists were cornered and killed by machine-gun fire. Once the army left, and guards once again controlled the prison, a re-education programme was mounted. In the following three months, over two hundred troublesome prisoners were killed by various applications of mistreatment.

Most foreigners misunderstood the interests of the consular officials who came to visit, and lived in hope of royal pardons. Before prisoner-exchange treaties, royal pardons for foreigners were almost standard, granted after eight years to lifers; four years to those sentenced to less. Canada and the USA had effectively changed that with their exchange agreements. Those favoured by their nations could now return to complete their sentences at home. American magistrates would re-sentence convicts before return based on the amounts alleged. It still meant a decade or so in prison, although few Western countries now insisted on the full term. Since prisoner-exchange treaties had become operational, royal pardons were granted mostly to allow those dying to do so away from Thailand.

Even those who cared little for their embassies seemed beyond enacting any alternate plan. Daniel, a loner at Bumbudt, spoke rarely and morbidly. He was someone who seemed once to have had a life somewhere.

Escape

'Westlake, remember Sunday mornings?' he might say without warning. 'Cool, fresh air from a garden doorway. The soft, rising sweeps of music. Gentle light from leaves brushing clear windows ... Heavy blue breakfast plates. A teapot. Glazed brown breads opening their puffed white hearts. Newspapers on a low table spill glossy colour. Duck-down cushions so plush you'd stretch and writhe with happiness?'

Edvart Fleischl from Switzerland had been in a Thai prison before. He'd once been caught stealing from a cheap hotel in Phuket. This time, he had agreed to do a run to Zurich for a local Pakistani outfit. A kilo in swallowed capsules. As Eddie had overstayed his Thai visa by some months, the Pakistanis found it cheaper to give him a doctored passport. Eddie liked that idea, as he had served five years in the 1980s for two kilos at the Swiss border.

Two things worked against the plan: Eddie didn't like the idea of eating over a kilo of heroin, even in capsules. He cut them open and repacked the load in two tins of talcum powder. Locally made Prickly Heat powder that could be useful in the Swiss winters. Worse, Eddie's substitute passport had originally been sold to the Pakistanis by a German flagged on Interpol watch lists. Eddie's arrest at Bangkok airport's immigration desk was rapid and efficient. Plan B had been to kill himself, but despite taking one hundred and forty Rohypnol in the police cells, the only result had been a three-day paralysis on the cell floor. That went unnoticed.

The original holder of Eddie's unsound passport – the most-wanted German Viktor Lehman – was himself now in Klong Prem. Folded and hunched in a corner, he had the posture and complexion of a wet twisted pillowcase. I wondered if he had looked the same in his passport photo.

Compared with the other foreigners I'd met so far, Eddie was an experienced smuggler. Like the others, he had no friends prepared to visit. Yet his willingness to risk escape was no small thing.

* * *

Escape

A few days after my arrival, Calvin's lawyer, Abe Sousel, visited the prison. A fellow American, Abe was the only Westerner operating the criminal-law game in Bangkok. I'd met him during my brief court appearance, when he tried to squeeze a power of attorney through the bars. I recalled only that the red-nosed, baggy-eyed paralegal hack in a wrinkled suit had promised to send through some lunch. He had been unable to arrange a close meeting, and no lunch was sent.

'Abe guarantees me four years,' Calvin said as we walked to the prison's visit cages. 'I hope he brings his phone today, he promised.'

'You know he's not a lawyer,' I said.

'I know that, Dave. He told me he used to sell vacuum cleaners in Hawaii. That was a bit honest, at least.'

While I swatted mosquitoes swarming under our bench, Calvin tapped a small roll of paper through the grille to Abe.

'I'll get this fax off to your mother,' Abe told Calvin, 'as soon as I get back to the office. Now, the 4,000 has arrived. Your mom sent it by Western Union, but I've got to have the balance as soon as possible. Then we can really get to work. My associate office in the States will get all the depositions ready.'

Abe's Bangkok office was a room at the back of his Thai wife's flower shop. The US associate was a cousin who worked the phones to ensure the families of imprisoned foreigners paid in advance. Calvin's mother's $4,000 was just the deposit. Abe's $12,000 fee bought little more than talk and the services of the most underpaid Thai lawyers in town. As scams go, it was fair. The four-year sentence Abe held before desperate clients was simply the minimum waiting period before repatriation to home jails. Understandably, this sounded better than death to those newly arrested.

'I hope you guys are keeping strong,' Abe offered.

Calvin pushed Abe for the promised phone call to his six-year-old boy in Oahu. Even though there was no one near our dark corner, Abe worked up some head-darting before thumbing the numbers into his mobile phone.

Escape

'So, little Nicky is coming now?' Abe winked at Calvin before holding his phone to the grille. After a long minute of shouts and straining, it became clear Calvin couldn't hear a word. Abe took over, while Calvin yelled endearments at the phone.

'Nicky wants you to know he loves his dad,' Abe repeated with treacle.

There wasn't much left of Calvin after a few more minutes of this kind of thing, and Abe clapped the phone shut as a guard approached. Calvin was wanted in the next row. A woman from his embassy was waiting to see him. As Calvin clanked away, Abe looked through the wire to Judy, a US vice-consul. They didn't nod to each other. Many of Abe's former clients in Thai prisons believed he fed the DEA with information from his files. The pretence of he and Judy not knowing each other seemed to confirm the rumours.

'Share a cab on the way out?' I suggested.

'I get quite a few referrals from the embassy.'

'I'll bet. Nicky keeps late hours for a young man. It must be midnight in Hawaii.'

Abe said nothing, so I continued. 'That was a dirty trick, playing Cal's kid. Don't worry, I won't say anything. Calvin might not sleep tonight, but at least he's feeling something.'

Abe wouldn't admit to the pantomime, so moved on. 'I've got some good news for you, Dave. I've been doing a lot of work on your case – but you must've annoyed somebody on our side. And I've spoken to Sharon in Sydney. She says your friends will send the money, you don't have to worry.'

'Abe, you don't want my money. And my friends wouldn't have much to say to you. Just so you know, I met Sharon four months ago. She teaches small children and sings in a band at night. Does both well, and I didn't expect to hear from her. I was more than surprised when she'd asked her lawyer to look for someone here. That was nice, but there's nothing you can do for me. There's maybe three foreigners who've won a case here in the last decade, and even then, they were in the appeal courts for five years. Anyway, your drinking buddies should have told you my dance card's marked, if they've told you anything. I don't want you bothering Sharon. If she calls, tell her what you like. I can't stop you. But don't ask her for money.' I hadn't spoken at such length in weeks.

Calvin shuffled back to our bench and slumped. 'My wife's just divorced me,' he said, looking away. No one spoke for a minute.

'Damn battery's gone dead.' Abe pocketed his phone.

The Americans Andy and Big Bill had been arrested a week apart. Kuwaiti Saleem four months earlier, and an old German, Charley Schweidler, within the last fortnight. All sat at a bench, drinking English Martyn's pineapple liquor from plastic cups, getting to know one another. Each had been arrested at the airport with 2.8 kilos of heroin. None had made it as far as the check-in counter, as the Thai narcotics police were waiting for them. Photographs had been supplied by the US Drug Enforcement Administration. All had stayed at the same evil-smelling guesthouse, and had been put in a taxi by the same Nigerian Joe.

Warmed by the distilled hooch, Big Bill – as visible, yellow and gas-filled as a street lamp – was the first to admit he had told everything to a DEA agent within an hour of arrest. Old Charley, who claimed to be a baron, had gone further: 'I told them to let me go on to Chicago. I'd lead them right to the brutes!' Andy had provided the crumpled guesthouse card. Saleem said he made no admissions but was the first to make the connection.

'Don't you see? They know everything, the fucking Americans!' he said, hastily adding, 'Not you guys, I mean the government of the U-S-A!'

The DEA had 64 operatives stationed in Bangkok. With such numbers, it wasn't long before the narcs got busy with the Nigerians. For a few years, cooperation produced satisfactory results. The princes got their dope to Chicago, and the DEA's usefulness was demonstrated by the growing number of airport arrests. The Nigerians could afford to name every fourth courier, for the supply of poor Africans was inexhaustible. The problem with success was high visibility, and the Thais were soon obliged to arrest every African courier. The princes were unable to recruit enough Europeans, and had threatened to move elsewhere. So for the past year the DEA had been supplying the identities of potential white couriers, often targeting them from the bar rooms attached to US army bases in Europe.

Reactions to this arrangement in Klong Prem varied with nationality. Americans Big Bill and Andy felt no more than cheated, as they readily believed their government capable of any conspiracy. Baron Charley thought the set-up dastardly, but had some admiration for being outwitted. Saleem was wild with outrage, a sense of injustice peculiar to criminals who find police acting criminally. For an Arab, it was of course worse that Americans were playing this trick on him.

Martyn was working nearby on his specific-gravity meters, floating them to measure just the right amount of raw sugar for the next brew. He did not share their outrage. 'What difference does it make that the DEA works with traffickers? One way or another, we all walked into their world, eyes open. Whether it's drugs or peanuts makes no difference. It's like the alpha monkeys say, *Come, climb up our tree, you're welcome. Even more welcome when we push you off!* The vice or virtues of narcotics have nothing to do with it.' Martyn had been well respected within the Anarchists' Society in Britain.

Fortunately, I was called away from this never-ending debate by Kupla, who wanted me to settle with the prison tailor. My court suit was ready. At 250 baht, it was a good buy. The alternative was to select prison uniform from a tub of never-washed brown shorts and T-shirts that smelled like gangrenous bandages. I was due in court the following week.

Kupla was from a once-large family of Chiang Rai traffickers. Chiang Rai was central to the narcotics wild west of Thailand. Two of Kupla's brothers had been shot dead following business disputes, and a third was now serving a life sentence. These days, Kupla spoke with a curvy American accent, having spent six years

Escape

in US federal prisons. Ten years earlier, he had stepped off a plane in San Francisco with two kilos of heroin to find his one contact had lately been arrested. After three days, he had made new friends whose real occupations were revealed only when they removed their long-hair wigs: undercover FBI agents. Following his consequent trial, Kupla had spent his time in half a dozen prisons in as many states since leaving the dispersal jail in Oregon. He returned to Thailand with a fat international address book, and his experiences had encouraged him to expand his small family business. His first new venture led to arrest with five kilos in Bangkok. Yet his enthusiasm had not dimmed. The immediate obstacle was an almost certain life sentence, due to be given some time in the next three years. Kupla was Thai, experienced and not without contacts. As close to a real player as I would find here, yet without any solution to the 40 years he would see in prison before release. He dismissed any ideas of escape from Klong Prem as hopeless. I would later come to know of his life sentence, and his ambition to buy a transfer to a small country prison from where day release could be granted for a reasonable fee. There would be many things I would later come to know, including the fact that Kupla still waits in Bangkwang prison.

CHAPTER THREE

After just one month in the Cure, I saw that not every prisoner in Klong Prem was resigned to his fate.

Four Thais and a Singaporean had managed to control their dormitory long enough to cut their way out to try for the wall. Their attempt failed, but deserved a silver medal for silencing the informers for nine hours. This is what they did.

The escaping prisoners' dormitory was as full-packed as the others of Bumbudt. It held over 100, including some trusties. The rules were clear that any prisoner noticing an escape attempt had to call out. For trusties, a near-sacred duty. Many things in Klong Prem were tolerated mischief: cash-handling; the possession of radios or porn magazines; even drug-dealing and gambling were negotiable as long as kept in-house. Escapes, however, cut to the core of the prison's existence. Mere attempts threatened the safety, incomes and careers of staff, from tower guard to superintendent. For the guards, the consequences of escapes were so fearsome that they saw any attempt as utter betrayal. Betrayal of the loyalty they had earned for allowing some prisoners to eat well and run small businesses. The guards' cut in this commerce was not seen as a bribe. More of a tribute, a token of respect; a share of the food at the table. For any prisoner to endanger this fine cooperation would be madness or treachery. Any officer would sooner answer to the chief for beating a prisoner to death while drunk than account for fleeing prisoners.

Escape

As it was, the night-duty guards usually slept throughout the small hours in peace. Great care was taken by trusties to prepare their beds, linen and refreshment. Should any prisoner's laughing, singing or crying penetrate the guards' mosquito nets as they slumbered under the cool of the buildings, the disturbed sleeper would stumble upstairs to exact punishment. Noisemakers would extend their hands through the bars for caning.

The group's escape plan had been only days in discussion, although Quan had planned it from the day of his arrest. Among the group were three whose cases were sure to bring death penalties. Their leader, a muscled Thai experienced in running street gangs, had practised terrorising others in their dormitory. Another Thai was included not only for supplying a saw and wire cutters, but because of the certainty that he would otherwise talk. Most important was a Chinese-Singaporean: a man with money. Of the five, he had been the last to have his chains removed, just one week earlier. Quan had been buying services and favours since the day he found himself in the New Petchburi Road police station. He had every reason to believe that if anything went wrong, he would be able to pay his way out of trouble. Even so, his earlier failure to buy off the Thai trial court should have told him something.

A week before the big night, Quan had engineered a high-stakes dice game in the dormitory to include the least-trusted trusty, and the keyless key boy. The trusty was a notorious informer and the key boy (the trusty who accompanied guards as they commanded interior doors to be opened or locked) had recently put up his job as stake money. These men would make the most noise if anything rebellious occurred. He'd let them win for a few nights to make them careless. Then, when they lost, they lost big. Quan promised to forgive their 9,000 baht debt, and to reward them with five times that amount if they cooperated. Quan would have said 50 times, but he had feared they might then doubt his word.

All prisoners in Bumbudt are locked in their dormitories by 5 p.m. On the day of the jump, four hours after lock-in, from behind a huddle of blankets the cutting began. With top prisoners, it was not unusual to see a blanket tied to the window mesh and the other end tied at 45 degrees to the floor, making a one-man tent. These tents were more often occupied by two, and dormitory etiquette ignored sounds of straining from within.

By 10 p.m. the mesh had been cut, but it would be another three hours before the second of two bars was hacksawed through. Those few who noticed the five whispering prisoners creep beyond the narrow gap were so paralysed with fear that they willed themselves into sleep.

Over the weeks leading up to this night, Quan had extracted enthusiastic promises of help from criminal acquaintances in Bangkok. More than one promised to drive to Klong Prem and park near the highway flyover to wait throughout the weekend nights. In addition, two of the Thais had promised to arrange a mobile phone to coordinate the pick up. Despite these assurances, Quan felt certain that nothing and no one would materialise. Nothing had, and his private plan was to separate from the others at the first dark corner, then to speed to his girlfriend's house by taxi. He, after all, had the money. The others should be grateful he was getting them out, especially the younger of his case partners, who Quan thought was responsible for their arrest at the hotel way back when.

Yet, there remained the wall.

The group moved quietly behind the prison kitchen. They began crawling over an old two-metre plank that bridged the sewer canal. The heaviest among them cracked the plank, causing the final crawler to fall with a mucous splash into the septic black water. He climbed out, spluttering and retching, with slime and wrinkly plastic bags clinging to his clothes. In his haste to climb from the sewer, the young Thai had waded back to the jail-side bank, so had had to step back through the mire.

By then at the wall, Quan peered up to the electrified runs of barbed wire atop the final barrier. They had brought a blanket to shield themselves from the current. A blanket now wet. A blanket Quan could see would serve only to catch the barbs and make the climb more difficult. The team leader decided to cut the blanket to make their rope longer. He soon gave up, frustrated by the dull knife and wet blanket.

For 15 minutes, the team wandered along the wall boundary, searching for long poles or a ladder. The older among them knew that this was the most unlikely place to find such things. The questions began.

'Quan,' growled the large Thai. 'What time do the kitchen workers begin, mister know-it-all?'

'Six,' Quan guessed. 'Do you think you can take two on your shoulders?'

'Two? Easily. But what about me?'

'Don't worry. We'll pull you up by the blanket!'

The moment soon arrived when the emptiness of promises and assumptions echoed with danger. Such words had once been a comfort. Now, ever so pointless.

With the strongest forming a base, and the combined height of two more shaking and grabbing at air, their human scaffolding reached no more than half the height of the wall. After trying a few more combinations, the five found themselves, breathless and panting, huddled below the last obstacle. One spoke for them all: 'OK. Now, at least we know what we need. Better we get back inside and try again tomorrow night.' The speaker praying for the dull simplicity of a morning doughnut and coffee, as would happen any normal day.

Without further words, the group began walking along the roadway back to their dormitory. The prisoner caked with shit paused near the kitchen to run his head under water from a tap. From the distance came the unmistakable sound of a key unlocking a gate. The group reacted to this without speaking, and oddly slowed in their mournful return walk.

Arriving at Building Four, they saw the night guard sitting up on his night-duty bed, smoking the first of the day. He stared ahead, oblivious to the creatures who should not be there. They looked at the tree they must climb to their dormitory. They should have been thinking about the rope that needed re-attaching to the window ledge, but they were not. They looked at the cut stumps of the bars and thought of the questions and calamity from their former roommates.

Quan kept his eyes on the sleepy guard as he spoke softly to his confederates. 'It's up to you guys what you want to do. I'm going to talk to Samang.' To himself, Quan said: this is going to cost me. He hoped he could now separate himself from the others. Drained by fear, the others would not easily separate themselves from Quan, the one with the money.

'Sounds good,' murmured a voice.

'Looks better if we turn ourselves in,' seconded another.

'I'm with you,' joined a third. 'I've got to wash. I stink!'

A minute later, the five stood silently before Samang the guard. The images of cut bars and twisted mesh faded in their minds, but not in Samang's, whose eyes widened in shocked pulses. He looked at the gang in disbelief, yielding to fear as daylight rose.

'Samang. Something crazy's happened,' Quan reasoned. 'I've got to talk to you. I know you'll want to help . . .'

Samang was not listening. The moment of uncertainty had passed. The guard knew that even after wringing every last coin out of Quan, he would barely survive this treason with his small world intact.

Big Bill got out of bed and dressed. That meant standing up from the floor and pulling on a T-shirt. He then felt under his blanket for the yellow form he had been worrying about as he fell asleep last night. It was a questionnaire from Amnesty International.

'Dave, take a look at this, will you?'

'Just a moment.' I was at the dormitory bars trying to find out why we were an hour late being let out. Trouble in another building, was all the key boy would say.

Bill had put the forms aside as I sat next to him. He was inspecting his ankles for damage, a leper's daily routine. 'Look at those questions. "Can you name the person who tortured you?",

"Give the location and address where this took place." These people want names! I'll bet the Thais would like me giving names. And to think of the trouble I had sneaking my letter out to Amnesty.'

'You weren't tortured, were you, Bill?' Calvin asked.

'No. But you know.'

We didn't, and Bill was disappointed to hear that Amnesty International did not involve itself easily in individual cases. It wanted data for its reports. The lobbyists would not fund his legal representation.

'Don't worry,' Calvin reassured Big Bill. 'If the Thais kill you for sending back the questionnaire, Amnesty's sure to be severely critical in its next report. Every little death helps.'

It was almost eleven before we were allowed downstairs. The cooks began speeding about. Not just to make up for lost time, but in unspoken fear of some sudden end to the day. I found the Captain already lounging on his deckchair. The Captain was a Thai skipper scooped from the Gulf by the navy with his fishing trawler loaded with almost a tonne of heroin. Already five years under trial with no sign of an end. He told me of the escape attempt from Building Four.

'They're crazy guys,' the Captain spoke to the sky. 'They turned themselves in. Better they died on the wire. They're upstairs in the *soi*.' The *soi* referred to the five-foot-long, two-foot-wide steel boxes that lined the corridor of the top floor. The term *soi*, meaning street, came from early days when punishment cages were kept in the jail's open streets. These days, too many outside visitors passed within those streets.

'They give them elephant chains. Then they kick the shit out of them till they no shit.' The Captain let a hand drop to the ground in waves of defeat. He rarely sat upright, and mostly let his arms complete descriptions.

Soi prisoners could spend up to three months in the lightless boxes, trying to survive on a bowl of rice each day with a litre of water for drinking and washing. A one-gallon paint tin was a toilet, supposedly emptied every third day. Rather than the *soi*, most prisoners would readily accept an alternative of even some humiliating, painful and often permanently damaging public torment by cane, boot or truncheon. Such options were not available to these would-be escapers. For them, the very worst of everything was considered too good for those threatening the livelihoods of the guards.

Any fascination with torture is utterly exorcised from those exposed to its reality. Describing its detail becomes an anathema, as prospective torturers listen keenly from a million black corners of the earth. Yet, as with a sudden car crash, the shutter may fall on the images, but the sounds remain. The image carries only haunting dread. On the soundtrack, a warning calls.

That morning, an intrusive quiet rippled through the hundreds massed at ground level. The escapers had been brought to the *soi* boxes above Building Two. We heard the sound of a boot on the thin steel wall of a *soi* box. Then, a rising triple tap with a club on Box One. Then upon Two through to Five. Whose turn would it be? Key sounds; the drop of a padlock, then a steel creak, and the clunking drag of heavy iron links. Links scraping over the doorframe of a box. Some muted words. Silence.

Then, the air being cut with a cane: a wide, low whistle that only the longest sticks create. A breathless pause before the scream.

Down among us there are whisperers. Coffee sipped quietly. Workers working smoothly, not wanting to mask the top-floor sounds with the clatter of industry. I can see pity in some workers' hands. They fold their paper boxes with a special speed and care. There is a system to it, and so there can be an end.

The key boy, a trusty who has given many punishments and witnessed many more, steps lightly downstairs. He sits on a step almost at the bottom. He looks aside, and then inspects his keys. Even he has been sent away.

The sounds of both impact and scream change. The cane no longer makes the handclap, or the slapping sound. It is muted, as though sharply angled, striking with tip into something soft. The report, multiple, divided, close to a mashing. The scream high-pitched, so high it must go beyond our range. But I'm wrong, it does go higher, then becomes strangulated, and then ceases. Now, only blows are heard. A silence arrives, although hard to say when.

Professional boot steps. A kick and a thud at once. Again the same. Then, a last slicing of air from the cane. No scream, although there was some living sound.

I look to Calvin. He is white with rage and fear. I feel bloodless and heavy. The key boy is called up, and springs to his feet. The guard has met him halfway, and whispers instructions. The trusty strides upstairs, his long fingers gripping his keys. I move closer to Calvin. He speaks first.

'Jeeze, Dave. It makes you sick.'

'There's nothing we can do. It's Thai business, they'll say.' It seemed right just to babble at Calvin. A familiar voice. 'This is different from normal. Remember last week with Martyn and the picture?'

'Yeah. Scumbag was gonna deck him, and he hadn't done a thing.'

'Sure. Mostly just happened to be there when the big picture fell over. Only scratched the lacquer. Not his fault anyway. He hadn't touched it. A few baht and all's forgiven. This – this is different. They embarrassed the guards. Holy wars have been fought over embarrassment.'

Calvin stared at me blankly, and then raised his eyes to the upper floors. 'One of them was Quan, the Singapore guy?' Calvin had played a chess game or two with the clever one of the escape team.

'Maybe that's good, an embassy and all,' I suggested. 'Except back home they would have hanged him by now.'

'Fuck you, too, Dave!' But Calvin wrenched a wan smile from somewhere.

Of the five, only Quan would survive. He had begun bargaining and paying from the outset, but only as the others began to die did his keepers listen. Ultimately, all he bought himself was a death sentence in Bangkwang.

Escape

Quan's misfortune provided an excuse to speak of ways out with Dean Reed. With those foreigners who lived in Thailand, the more sophisticated the home country compared to the chosen land of exile, the weirder the expatriate becomes. American Dean was stranger than most. He claimed to have taught at Bangkok's Chulalongkorn University, and he must have been close to someone who had. Dean understood the confusion many Asian students feel when asked to write essays arguing against existing customs, their sense of unfairness at having to devise ideas that have not been taught. Dean's conversations would flutter from tree stump to garden post so it was difficult to steer him onward. Even so, he was the one foreigner I was sure would soon be released. He knew the people of Thailand, and had local contacts – even if they might happily lynch him for whatever blatant swindle he had last pulled on them.

'I try to tell people but they don't understand,' Dean would usually begin. 'That Quan. There won't be much fluff left on his blanket. But anything's possible in Thailand. You know the judges used to drive their Mercedeses to court, but they were too obvious in the car park, so now they have those big, curtained buses for Their Honours. Now don't worry about how guilty everyone looks in court in chains and bare feet. It's who's standing behind you that counts. Be careful about royalty, too. You know even ministers had to crawl out backwards from His Majesty until the 1930s? He was born not far from me in Cambridge before the war. Married in Switzerland, then came back here to the palace and his brother was shot. All the servants locked up, then executed. So, you see? Don't do anything embarrassing. Some tourist was arrested for lese-majesty for spilling a drink on a plane near the princess. Did I tell you I had dinner once with a judge? At the Oriental. French chef, you know, and I'm sure it has two courgettes in the Michelin guide. I know I can fix your case, even bail. It's only money. Not my lawyer, you won't want to use him. You'll need a fixer. Can you be sick? The doctor here can write reports for the court. Doesn't cost much.'

Escape

From the stairs, a thin, grey-skinned prisoner staggered down. Paint tin of shit in hand, he had no energy to lift the chains that dragged around his feet. This sight presented a break in Dean's presentation.

'Isn't that one of the five?' I asked.

'No. Just a *soi*-boy. One of the regulars.'

'Dean, do you know of anyone who's succeeded where they failed?'

For the first time, Dean's pace slowed. 'No, David. That doesn't happen here. There was something a couple of years ago from the court, but that was a disaster in the end. Now, look – don't worry. It's Thailand. Everything's possible with money.'

The *soi*-boy was by then over by the water tanks, cleaning his paint tin. Some of the foreigners were examining him from a distance. His skin was a dry rubber, the tattoos of Buddhist luck phrases faded to a smudged blue. From my compatriots' faces, I could see thoughts of escape had been buried. Eddie came over to remark upon the *soi*-boy declining any food or help.

'He wouldn't even answer me,' noted Eddie.

'Oh, that one,' Dean said of the grey prisoner, 'he hasn't spoken a word for months. I don't think he ever will.'

CHAPTER FOUR

Another day of a court appearance began as usual standing in a queue to have chains fitted. Ahead, a brawny Thai sat on a low stool surrounded by a pile of half-metre lengths of rusting chains. Beside him was a box of C-shaped ankle rings.

Prisoners would sit opposite, looking away as the chain-man hammered tight the ankle ring resting on a small anvil. His aim was usually true, and improved when he was given a few cigarettes.

There was a brief delay in the line while arrangements were made for a one-legged man. A compromise was finally settled, with the real leg chained to the artificial limb, although he was then permitted to use his crutches so that he could walk. Unfortunately, this caused such difficulty he then had to remove the prosthetic leg and carry it under one arm. To the guards, this seemed a stretching of the rule but he was allowed to go, providing he promised to keep one end of the chain attached to the leg he carried under his arm.

A packet of Krong Thip filters bought me a set of polished chains, and by 8 a.m. I was with the others squatting at the internal roadway waiting for transport. I was seated with Daniel, the only other foreigner due for court that day. Daniel, when speaking at all, would talk of distant and irrelevant things. Today, it was of the sour week held in the police station. He was speaking of a small grille that covered a lightless window high in the cell.

'It had some bolts holding it in place,' Daniel said as he stared at his feet. 'Rusted, of course, and unmoved since they were tightened, what, 30 years earlier. They were covered in a fuzz of dust. Held there – the dust, I mean – by the oils from body heat rising over time. Never touched in all those years. Never brushed.'

'Well, they're not big on cleaning in police cells,' I said, before moving back on the guttering to allow a heavy sand truck to pass in front.

'That's not what I mean,' Daniel began.

Whatever he meant was silenced by the sudden action of a small Thai man with a deeply pockmarked face. As the heavy truck slowly passed the old man, he dived forward. Hands flat to the ground, he turned his head sideways to face the twin rear tyres grinding towards him.

From where we sat, a ribbed tyre briefly seemed to spin faster, and the truck rose a little. Then, the sound of a sumo wrestler falling on a watermelon. Eerily quiet, yet powerful. The old man's shoulders twitched, his left arm flipping up from the ground before disappearing. When the truck passed, it seemed his head was facing the wrong way – an illusion caused by his scalp and face having been repositioned over the remains of his skull.

A small group of prisoners rose towards the body and was quickly herded back by a guard, who shouted orders to his trusties to remove the body.

'Bravo! Well done.' Daniel complimented the deceased. 'Did you see that? No fear at all, just concentration on his face.' Daniel must have been watching him for some time.

The judge hearing my case was giving my lawyer, Montree, a puzzled look, as though asking: what's this performance for?

Montree had risen from his chair and swaggered towards the witness like Clarence Darrow. Quaking behind a small podium in the centre of the court stood a Thai immigration officer. He need not have worried. The performance was for me.

'Now tell me, officer. Can you remember this particular passport? I mean, how can you tell if it was the one my client had?'

The Arrivals clerk flicked a glance at Montree before responding.

'Oh, well, that's because it has my number on the stamp. It must be me.'

'But how many passengers would you stamp on a shift? Tens? Hundreds? Thousands?'

'Maybe a hundred. Eighty?'

'So that's just one day. One day from over a hundred days ago. Thousands of people before and after my client?'

'Yes— ' The officer shrank further into his ill-fitting uniform, wishing someone could have told him more of the answers before this began.

'So, since nothing special happened that day, you can say only that this passport has a stamp with your number on it,' Montree then nodded to himself. 'Nothing you can remember tells you that Westlake was actually there that day. The passport and the stamp could both be forgeries. Is that correct?'

'Yes, it's not easy to tell if a passport is a forgery.'

At this, Montree smiled at me in victory. The judge looked to the heavens, and the prosecutor closed his eyes and massaged the bridge of his nose with one finger.

'Anything further, Khun Montree?' The judge reached for the microphone of his dictating machine.

'I think not,' beamed Montree. 'This witness has said all he can.'

The judge then spoke into his tape recorder: 'On cross-examination, the witness said that fake passports can be easily forged. The witness is free to go.' This then became the court's record of my lawyer's most excellent cross-examination.

Montree was a gentle, round-faced man in his 30s. His college training was in microbiology, and, after taking on lawyering, he had contracted for hustler Abe Sousel until a money dispute pushed them apart. I thought it kind of Montree to put on a show for me, even though it would have no effect on the final verdict. He didn't ask for much money, and he was happy to provide as many delays as I needed.

Village folk with flaming torches rampaging behind the high

priest; ivy-league gentlefolk murmuring to gowned nobles at the Supreme Court bench. Between these extremes are the courts we know well, and a Thai court appears as others, with black robes and players working each side of the room. The accused is either damned or dismissed, the judge's way of calling the match. In Western courts, tradition demands an occasional release of the puck to give the contest credibility. Thai judges are not so burdened with any quota of acquittals.

Witnesses' testimony, prosecutors' claims, the defence's pleas and views of exhibits are all transformed into the judge's words as he speaks into his tape recorder. A typist knocks these out while wearing headphones as the trial is heard. Everyone concerned is then required to sign a copy of His Honour's thoughts at the end of each session. After the guilty verdict and sentence (the maximum is always given first, often halved for a guilty plea; the minimum for any amount of heroin at the airport is 25 years), the appeal courts take on the bargaining. In trials with many accused in the dock, some are later acquitted for the sake of economy and convenience. In practice, few executions take place, and death is mostly commuted to life following pleas of mercy to the king.

In less civilised times, the Thai judiciary condemned those found guilty to death. Execution was slow: held in chains, suspended over glowing coals, to be roasted overnight. The twentieth century brought law reform. Capital punishment is now carried out by machine gunners firing at a red cross painted on a cloth hung in front of the prisoner. Even a last meal is available. A feast perhaps only for those with strong constitutions, as the condemned receives 30 lashes with barbed wire before the last supper.

Montree had asked the judge that I sit with him at the defence table rather than, as usual, between court guards. We were able to swap stories of trials we had known. I've never chosen a lawyer on any criteria other than his talent for telling funny stories and being good company. We were both nominating our favourite witnesses of all time, and snickering a little, when the judge interrupted with a question.

Escape

'He wants to know how many witnesses you want to call,' Montree told me, nodding at the judge. 'What do you want to do with your case?'

As I scribbled a list of lesser-known actors, I asked Montree about defence options.

'Ah, the defence case,' Montree capped his fountain pen. 'The *dream*.'

'Is that what you call it?'

'My words? No, that's what everyone in court calls the defence case. The dream.'

The new court building had been built with American government charity. It had a special lift in which guards would return prisoners to the ground-level holding cells. Courtrooms were mostly on the upper floors, so I was often alone with my guards on the way down. The journey began next to a deserted stairwell, and it would take at least two minutes for the small lift to arrive. At that time, floors six and seven of the court building were unoccupied. Even though I was always in chains and handcuffs, this quiet place had possibilities. It would later be the setting for one of my first escape schemes.

The holding cells look like a large underground car park divided into a dozen huge cages with twice as many corridors, all constructed from iron bars and mesh. The sound of seven hundred prisoners in chains moving on two acres of concrete, shouting at visiting families and friends, pounds the ears as if it were a mining site. It looks like a deep-earth excavation, too: everyone in brown, sweating; water dragged across the floor by foot chains from flooded toilet blocks; transport vans growling in and out; guards bellowing, shotguns protecting their cargo, with a steel lift pushing the ore up for processing.

Slumped between two Thai boys, I was counting the lift movements when something caught the edge of my vision. A flash of navy blue and white among the visitors. A woman, slim and small in a knee-length skirt, a white face, a business-like gait. Eyes searching, looking up to thread through a knot of visitors. It was Sharon.

'Sharon. Here!' I called.

'David!' Sharon's eyes widened, then became rounder, pooling. *My God, look at you!* But she hadn't said that. Something else, bright, cheery; lost in the ear-numbing fusillade of lamenting women and children at the bars.

'Wait!' I shouted. 'I'll talk to someone.'

'What?'

Hand-signalling a two-minute delay, I found a guard and settled on 1,500 baht for a visit in the lawyers' room, reserved for counsel–client consultations. Sharon almost looked like a lawyer in her suit. Clanking to the end of the cell rows allowed a couple of minutes to collect my thoughts. But I didn't seem to have any.

Shuffling into the air-conditioned chill of the interview room, I struggled with an opening joke. 'Sorry to call you all the way to Thailand, but I'm sure I left my toothbrush in your bathroom.'

'Oh, David.' Sharon stood, found herself half snared on the bench, and then reached with an arm. 'I just had to come. Didn't you get my message from the embassy?'

There had been no message. As we hugged briefly, and kissed uncertainly, I tried to fit my old, abandoned life to the life of iron around me. No surface matched.

The guard didn't approve of the kissing. 'None of that here. You're supposed to be lawyers, not criminals.'

We sat.

I began talking softly. 'Sharon, when your crooked boyfriend disappears and gets himself snaffled in Thailand, you're supposed to take a powder. But I'm impressed. Thank you.'

She smelled good.

'No one was helping,' Sharon spoke close to my neck. 'No one was doing anything. It was awful. I had to do something. I just got on a plane. Your friends, they wouldn't tell me anything.'

'They're thinking. Watching. Wisely, they submerge to silent running when things like this happen.' Covered only by the thin court outfit, I was chilled by the air-conditioning. 'Experience has taught them that. You look very professional in that white shirt.'

'It was a tough Christmas.' Sharon didn't mean money. 'I was decorating the tree. You'd only been missing for a few days. I opened the box of ornaments you'd brought.'

'Uh-huh.' There was nothing I could do with this.

'The angel is still on top of the tree.'

Okaaayyy.

The visit set-up for prisoners at Klong Prem was bad. A couple of hundred men shouting across two sets of bars that prevented close contact. Arranging something better was real work, especially as Sharon would taxi from her hotel that afternoon. Managing these difficulties was a good task to break the coma of mere observation into which I had settled over the past weeks.

Sharon was at the gate by the time I'd been returned, had my leg chains levered off, showered, haggled and struck a deal with the Skull. We would get a table alone. A table on the kerb of the roadway next to Building Two, but sunnier than the dank cages of the visit coops.

'Was Prompon happy with 1,500 baht?' I asked Sharon once we were seated. Prompon was the jail official in charge of foreigners.

'Hard to tell. His smile didn't go brittle.' Sharon fished in her bag for sunglasses. 'Said, *no, no, no,* as he pocketed the money. Anyway, I had a flash letter from the Oz embassy. Gavin was helpful, as you said. He put lots of rubber stamps on the letter. Look.'

I looked at the visit-request letter from the Australian consulate, blooming with official stamps. 'All different colours. That's a nice touch. Goes down well here.'

'So, David. What happened?'

'I haven't figured it out yet. They were there at the airport. Waiting for me.'

'Who?'

'Thai cops, American spooks, Australian feds – the Salvation Army, I don't know.' I waved a hand in the air. 'That, I can guess at. Some careless calls to my hotel. But Chinatown doesn't make sense. I mean, I didn't know I was going there myself, and even then I moved in faster than they could. Still, they were waiting. A couple of white men at the station when I was taken in. They didn't speak.'

'Do you think you were betrayed?' Sharon's guess would be the usual answer, but I'd always been lucky dodging treachery.

'No. It must have been something very unlikely. As it usually is. I'll let you know if I ever find out.'

This was leading nowhere, so Sharon told me how she had spent Boxing Day. I'd given her a duplicate key to my flat a few weeks earlier. A couple of days after my arrest, she'd let herself in one quiet afternoon.

'I looked in the kitchen cupboards, all your breakfast cereals. Went into the bathroom. Took your soap bar from the shower. Looked at the garden where we once were. Then lay down on your empty bed and cried.' Sharon locked our legs together under the table. 'David, you're not going to send me away now?'

An hour passed quickly at that sun-bleached table. In our minds, we lifted ourselves through the air, table and all, to a footpath restaurant, where the stir-fried breezes added to the illusion.

Returning to Building Two, carrying Sharon's gift bag of groceries, it felt as though I'd been shopping through a stargate. No earthly link between her world and mine. She would return to Melbourne by week's end, so there would be just two more such stargate journeys.

Calvin called me as soon as I stepped back in.

'Dave, come over here. You gotta hear this. Some poor Portuguese guy. He's just come in. He was busted at the airport with a couple of kilos. Not taking it out, he was bringing it in! You won't believe it.'

'I think I will,' I said, giving Calvin some amoxicillin capsules from my supermarket bag. I didn't explain where they'd come from. Calvin had recently torn a toe, and infections often became chronic without access to outside medicines.

Escape

Paolo retold his story as we ate our night food at a table. He had been recruited as a courier in a Spanish resort town. There were Nigerian connections, and although Paolo had made three runs into Europe without problems, he had not been paid in full. After making complaints to his handlers, he was told he would get everything after a final short run to Malaysia.

Malaysia executes drug smugglers surely, routinely and often. While Paolo didn't much like that choice of destination, he needed the money, for he was by then quite broke. His contact, good old Joe from the Bangkok guesthouse, sympathised.

'My friend, we don't want to do this business but we must. In Africa, we Ebo people are enemies within our own country. We are clever, but the stupid, powerful dictators don't let us run our own affairs. So we have to do this thing. It's like the Palestinians and the Israelis.'

As to which side of the walls of the holy lands Joe believed he fell, we would never hear. At that point in the telling of Paolo's story, a factory guard began his daily session of beating those he'd decided were his laziest five workers. With the unlucky five stretched out on the ground to receive their punishment, we moved to a corner of the yard. Paolo picked up the story as he arrived in Kuala Lumpur with his hidden cargo.

It was exceptional enough that he had flown to Malaysia rather than travelling overland, but more unusual that there was no one at the airport to meet him. Paolo scraped up some money for a phone card, and after three hours sitting on his suitcase near the taxi ranks he finally spoke to Joe in Bangkok. Joe was surprised, too.

'Didn't you get on the plane?'

'Of course I did! What do I do now? Who can I call here?'

Apparently, no one. Paolo collected some money quickly sent through a transfer office, then checked into a fleabag hotel while Joe arranged a ticket back to Thailand. It did seem, even to Paolo, that this was losing the opportunity to move the dope onwards to the West. As ever, Paolo was kept too impoverished to make balanced choices.

Escape

On arrival at Don Muang, Paolo was immediately arrested. This time, the phone call to the airport was made on time. A week earlier, a Friday afternoon party at the US embassy had resulted in staff neglecting to arrange Paolo's arrest the first time. Apologies all around. Joe was reimbursed. Paolo was finished.

We all expressed the usual outrage and sympathy. I gave Paolo a Mars bar. Martyn sealed his vegetarian food canisters and added, 'In a perfect realisation of hell, one would not know one was dead. Life would be hellish without even that rare comfort of certain damnation. And the knowledge that suffering can get no worse. In the imperfect hell of the living, things always get worse.'

Within a few weeks I felt I had taken as much of the Cure as would be useful. Bumbudt was so overcrowded, no real privacy could be bought. I'd heard better things of the buildings in the greater Klong Prem jail next door, so began negotiations to move. I'd aired thoughts of escape to Eddie, who advised moving to the big prison, where there was room to breathe. Most of the other foreigners wanted to move, but not all had the means. Greater Klong Prem was for sentenced prisoners, so a transfer required money or light pressure from embassy consulates. Eddie, being Swiss, found immediate compliance with a firm official letter, although British Martyn would have to wait for the weak gravity of imperial support. As I saw things, both men had something to offer. Martyn, his skills, and Eddie, his fearlessness.

Calvin was reluctant to move. We spoke of it one night, my last week in the dormitory. He had been warned by vice-consul Judy that heroin was cheap and available in the larger Klong Prem. 'That Judy, she's like a den mother, and we're her cub scouts. She doesn't want me to get tangled up in the dope again. She's got all this money my mother keeps sending, bless her.' Calvin told it like that, but it was he who had asked the consulate to restrict payments to his prison account, and to leave him in the Cure.

'If I get back on the shit in here, I'm fucked,' Calvin had said.

Escape

Considering this, I found myself absently staring at a tall Thai boy, new to the dorm and being chained to the floor. He had that afternoon been sentenced to life. As the key boy locked him in place, the new lifer caught my stare.

'It's OK,' he apologised. 'Everything all right. This is Thailand. No problem.' He even attempted a smile through some winces as he was held in place. What comparable apology might ever be heard in the West? A convict is being strapped into a Californian gas chamber. Some strangers appear. He feels a need to apologise to these witnesses for his own people's cruelty. What creatures could these visitors be – civilised aliens from Mars? And what did such a convict think of these aliens that he imagined he offended?

Nearby, a small circle of listeners had gathered to watch a weatherbeaten country boy from Laos sing folk ballads. He wore a red-and-white checked blanket draped over his head and shoulders and sat holding a banana for a microphone. His earthy, natural voice carried soft, high sounds across the cell. The dialect was quite foreign to Bangkok ears, and no one translated his simple songs of love and loss. A farmer's son with a face aged by hard times, he added few sentimental contortions and held his notes. When he had finished, his audience applauded, and the tall boy set his plastic water bottle aside to clap as well.

Sharon, too, had met a singer during her brief stay in Bangkok. Her hotel had a bar where a Thai girl sang most nights. Having song in common, they became friends. Some afternoons, May would help Sharon shop. May kept a polite boyfriend who was free some nights to watch her perform for the hotel's customers. On Sharon's last night in town, May invited her to join in a duet on stage. That was when May's boyfriend lifted Sharon's credit card from her bag and stepped into the night to go to work on the ATMs near another hotel.

Using the PIN number he'd been given that afternoon by May, the boyfriend withdrew the daily limit and waited until after midnight to try again. As it was my card, I was unable to have payments stopped for three days. Sharon would never accept that her new friend had pegged her numbers while they'd shopped, and when Sharon returned to Thailand a couple of months later, they resumed their friendship. However, I heard no more of duets in the Kiwi lounge of the Bang Sap Hotel.

CHAPTER FIVE

A last day in the Cure with lots of goodbyes, and more than a few flawed promises.

The one that rattled me most was from Dean Reed. He cornered me as I was rolling half a kitchen into my blankets.

'I spoke to my contact in the courts. He tells me it's best if your judge nominates who should be your lawyer. And the best one is Khun Khanawat. He lectures at the university. Very respected.'

'I don't care if he works in the courthouse toilets checking zippers. As long as he can make a deal.' I hoped I was not falling for all of this nonsense. Dean's pitch was full of last-minute urgency.

'I'll come and see you as soon as I'm out!'

Out?

English Martyn was repairing a Walkman when I bade him farewell. We found ourselves speaking of Daniel. I mentioned Daniel's strange celebration of the old man's death thrust under the sand truck when we had been waiting for court transport.

'He was asking me about suicide,' Martyn said. 'What would be the best way.'

'What did you tell him?'

'Twenty Vesperex and a big plastic bag taped over the head. Only way to be sure, short of a 20-storey building.' There was never any judgement in Martyn's voice.

Daniel was alone when I walked over to say goodbye. He had no plans to move to greater Klong Prem. The last thing I recall him saying was about that moment when babies are getting ready to cry.

'They try to draw in all the air they'll need for the cry. But it's never enough. They are so full of unlimited outrage, they can't stop drawing in. They go purple, suffocating because there is never enough air in the world to do justice for the scream they want to let loose. So, they're just frozen like that.'

Well, I'd had about enough of that sort of thing, and with most of the people I'd so far met in the Cure. Even Dean's vapourware was healthier than the prevailing atmosphere of hopelessness among Westerners in Bumbudt. I left Daniel there, and have no idea what happened to him. I joined Eddie at the gate, where he was tying together pots, pans and bags of clothes. Eddie no longer wore chains, but we still had to hire two Sherpas to help with the long walk through twelve gates to our next prison. There were twenty-one in this transfer, including six foreigners.

Greater Klong Prem was too big to take in at once. Even the reception building, a prison in itself, seemed massive compared to the cramped layers of the Cure. Our last kilometre of pathways leading to KP had kept us busy chasing runaway dinner plates and retying loose clothes to the shoulders of our helpers, so we were all disorientated. Finally, we dumped our bundles at the gate to Building Six, like Bedouins at a dry oasis.

The trusty in charge of new foreigners greeted us. His name was Tanveer, a tall Pakistani with huge feet clinging to the edges of hard leather sandals.

'You guys will be in Six until you go to other buildings. About a month or so. You'll be assigned a factory for work, and must do training in the mornings. This will teach you how to be prisoners.' Tanveer half-heartedly poked through our possessions. He seemed disappointed, but continued.

'Radios are not permitted. Not also are newspapers. I must take away any long pants and contraband items. These will be put in the storeroom until you are released.' A mystified pause followed as we looked among ourselves for any who might have a release date within our lifetime. No one spoke.

'Cash is forbidden. You leave your money on account. Food can be ordered from the outside shop three times a week. You can get cash from the bank here in Building Six, but don't be caught. Books, you can keep.'

While everyone repacked his possessions, I nodded sideways to Tanveer.

'What is it?' he asked.

'I've got a radio. What does it take to get it back?'

'See me in a couple of days.' Tanveer's eyes darted about before he announced to everyone, 'Don't tell anybody.'

At that time in the afternoon, almost the entire accommodation block was empty. We were led upstairs past garage-sized cells, many with plastic flooring, a screen around the toilet and mosquito mesh at the windows. Tanveer stopped in front of a cell. At the door, rolls of bedding and clothes were stacked to head height. A key boy unlocked the door. It was empty, small and had no screens.

'Stack your stuff on top of the others'. You won't have enough room inside.'

This was no exaggeration. After 15 of us had moved inside, the cell was full. With 21, it was packed.

'Sorry, guys.' Tanveer was already walking away. 'You'll have to stay in there until you find someone to take you in. Leave some room for the other newcomers. There's only ten. They come in at two.'

Eddie and I staked some space by tearing blankets from our packs and haggling with the room boss, but he had nothing to offer. Within an hour, every inch of space was taken up with bodies. The rising heat was made worse by the lack of a fan. Only a hook and some bare wires hung from the ceiling.

By nightfall, our best efforts had found us with no more than an eighteen-inch strip, five-feet long. Eddie made some weak coffee from a Thermos of tepid water.

'This is the worst,' Eddie said, snapping at mosquitoes. 'And I've

been in some bad places. You know what it is, don't you? They
throw us in this pit so tomorrow we're willing to pay anything for
a better room.'

'I'm willing now.' I gently kicked aside a fat Burmese who again
lolled his sleeping head on my feet.

We spent the first half of the evening minutely searching the
elastic tops of our shorts, the busiest feeding centre for the hundreds
of bedbugs that swarmed from the rotten floor planking. Until
midnight, I kept my head from the flaking paint of the wall. Over
the decades, a wide black band had formed at head height. A
thousand greasy heads had saturated the brickwork, making an oily
green valley for microscopic blood parasites. The acid from sweat-
soaked unwashed clothes bit at the nose. This excruciating induction
night was unnecessary – we would have been house-hunting on
arrival without this encouragement.

Eddie spoke of his first time in a Thai prison, six years earlier.
'It was all over a poxy hotel television set. I had to check out, you
know, through the window. So I took the set. Eighteen months I
got for that.'

Eddie had been eventually transferred to Bangkok to save the
Swiss consuls travelling south to Phuket. Within days of his arrival
at Klong Prem, pro-democracy riots led to several hundred students
being arrested and taken to the prison.

'They didn't want ordinary criminals mixing with the students,'
Eddie explained. 'Not because we might corrupt them. The jailers
worried the students might turn us political. They put them in
Building Eight. There were thousands of them.' A sweeping hand
gesture from Eddie caught his neighbour across the face. Eddie
immediately apologised.

'Oh, sorry.'

'Asshole!'

'Hey, watch it.' Eddie had his limits.

'Yeah, you watch it,' replied the Thai, although he was too busy
squashing bugs to make an issue of an accident.

'So, I got out of jail after a few months, and went back to Zurich,'

Escape

Eddie continued. 'They tried to put me in the army. Everyone has to join up in Switzerland. But I got out of that. Failed the psychological test. I convinced them I was crazy . . . Fucking bugs!' Eddie leapt up and fell into a wall. While he had been talking, a fresh battalion of parasites had bivouacked in his shorts.

'Eddie,' I managed, drooping on an elbow. 'Tomorrow, please. Bring me the head of Tanveer the trusty.'

Eddie was by then too dazed to respond. At some point, we fell into unconsciousness, and surrendered the dregs of our blood to the insect army.

The following day was taken up with arranging food and finding temporary lodgings. The prison had been hugely expanded during World War Two, after Thailand had declared war on the United States and Great Britain. Then, it was mostly filled with those considered troublesome by Thailand's Japanese ally. The extensive grounds today do not reduce overcrowding, as most of the vacant land is kept for lease to enterprising prisoners. The struggle for a foothold among us newcomers was matched by the daily struggle for survival by Building Six's other inmates. This was the prison's real control. No serious rebellion can occur when people are constantly uprooted, chasing food and using their remaining strength and resources simply to find an untroubled place to sleep. 'You can see why most of the world doesn't give the rich much trouble,' Eddie remarked on his way to the bank.

Building Six's accommodation blocks and factories were at the edges of a wide field of patchy grass where we newcomers were called to assemble.

'This must be where we learn how to be model prisoners,' I advised Eddie.

'I'll give him ten minutes.' Eddie meant the foreign-prisoners' instructor.

Our trainer was a middle-aged Chinese from Laos called Charlie Lao. He spoke half a dozen Oriental languages along with French, and English coated with an Australian nasal rounding, applied during his years in Sydney. Our training was a pitiful version of cadet-school marching and turning. We were also instructed to learn the Thai commands for turn left, turn right, hands in the air and some other expressions of surrender. As soon as we foreigners understood what Charlie was asking of us, we began to walk away.

'Come on, you guys.' Charlie was too reasonable a man to make a fierce master-sergeant. 'Try to march in line. It's only a few minutes. Good eccercise!'

His enthusiasm was met with two grunts and a fart.

'Fellas, the chief is watching me. Maybe we be in trouble. You don't want to end up like those guys!'

Charlie pointed to four young Thai prisoners who were being trained in a more down-to-earth manner. They had been found lazy at work and were now learning to roll from one side of the field to the other, arms and legs outstretched. An acne-faced trusty in uniform was yelling and slapping at them. The approach here was much more lenient than at Bumbudt. As to the chief, he was at his desk, but absorbed in his account ledgers. His office was on the far side of the field, a small open house built in the style of a temple.

We then distracted Charlie with questions, to allow him to make excuses for us all. Eddie had urgent business in the umbrella factory, where he was determined to get to the truth of the allegations that hard drugs could be easily obtained in Klong Prem.

Charlie excused me from future training permanently, fraternally, 'because we both come from Australia'. Charlie had applied for a royal pardon, having already served seven years. The pardon was supported by the Australian consulate, based on a reasonable policy that official support would be given where the time served matched that of average sentences imposed by Australian courts for similar amounts. This policy was under threat for some mysterious reason, but Charlie's application was close to being granted. He was serving 25 years for possession of a few hundred grams of heroin.

Right from our first meeting, Charlie offered sound advice and

Escape

help. Although we were close to the same age – I was 37 – I'm sure it wasn't simply the Australian connection that formed the bond. Charlie was born in Vientiane, and I in London. Possibly, we shared within our natures the characteristic of being servants without masters. I might have long abandoned that search, but Charlie had not. He soon took me on a tour of Building Six.

On one side of the grass field stood an open-sided hall where poor prisoners would eat 'government food', as Charlie called it. The standard was fish-head soup with verminous brown rice. A quarter cucumber for dessert. Before permission to tuck in was given, prisoners waited for some time while a long Buddhist form of grace was chanted.

Inside the hall, an old blind man had set up a cigarette-and-candy counter. Operating by touch, he kept his change tin at close range where its weight and sound provided an accurate accounting. 'He makes more money than you think! He doesn't just pass his time.' If Charlie knew a blind man's profit margins, then he would be someone to keep close.

Charlie steered wide of the chief's hut, tacitly indicating that the sight of us together might excite the boss. Should the crafty Chinese be seen guiding the new white man, we could quickly be called to the chief's office to negotiate a donation to the building repair fund.

Beyond, the roadway led to a gated auto-repair shop. There, officers' cars were tuned and serviced, or those of officers' friends. Some of these cars were in such poor condition that the plates and engine numbers had to be replaced. Factories in Building Six produced army boots, more ceremonial votive paper boxes, plastic fittings for bigger plastic fittings and, of course, inlaid portraits. I was assigned to a large umbrella factory producing pop-up brollies of many colours.

Behind the factories, Charlie took me to the thatch-roofed 'coffee shop'. It sold everything but cups of coffee, yet kept stock adequate for a small-town general store. As Charlie was called away to speak with his Chinese friends who owned this concession, I bought a fried-egg sandwich and sat under a tree, watching the queue at the bank. One window at the coffee shop had been remodelled as a teller's cage, behind which a round-faced man served a queue of 50 customers. With a firm, clean script, he would deduct up to 1,000 baht from prisoners' accounts in return for 800 baht cash. The guards were blind to these transactions during banking hours, but it would be no defence to point to the coffee shop if caught with currency.

'David! Over here.' Eddie was calling through the window of the umbrella factory. 'You want to meet the guy who'll do your work?'

I walked around the water tanks to the factory entrance to meet the Thai boys whom Eddie had arranged to pay 200 baht each to do our work. 'For another 200 we can get deckchairs.' Eddie pointed to a small group of Europeans in a corner under a ceiling fan, reading books or playing chess.

'I don't want to sit around here all day,' I said, but would later buy a chair to establish additional territory. 'Want some lunch, Eddie?' I waved my floppy egg sandwich towards the coffee shop.

'No thanks,' winked Eddie, crossing his eyes. 'I've had mine.'

That night, Eddie and I found temporary lodgings before opening negotiations with the chief for better accommodation. The chief was a short, chubby man who looked like Panama's former master, Manuel Noriega, and smiled at least as often. In his office, he began with the usual discussion of the limited funds available from the Thai prisons department. A deal was struck with the help of Rick, an Englishman who was renting a desk in the chief's office. A dubious tactical location, I thought, too close to the front line. Fortunately, Rick also wanted to share a private cell.

'It'll come to about 10,000,' explained Rick. 'Five for the boss here. And about the same to renovate a cell. We can't get away with less than five or six of us to the cell, but that's better than the ten-to-twelve average for the regular Thais. See if you can scare up some other tenants. We'll split the costs for the chief, and share for the room fixings, OK?'

Escape

Rick had lived in Pattaya for almost five years. He had fled his well-to-do parents and siblings from Southport, western England, before finishing college to find new friends among the British deep-sea divers of southern Thailand. Now, more than nine years later, he had a Thai wife and daughter, and earned a fair living selling grass to expatriates in his area. He had been arrested with 15 kilos of weed a few months earlier, while driving to the capital. His guess was that a man in his employ, another Englishman, had dropped him to the local police. Relatively, this was all good for Rick. A minor case, no foreign entanglements and a Thai wife who would connive to have him released. Rick had money, friends and no serious enemies, so his confidence was justified. Of the more than 100 Westerners I came to know in Klong Prem, he was the only one in this position, especially the having-friends part. By contrast, most Western inmates relied on a monthly grant from their embassies of around $120. Only the British consulate provided no funds; British citizens relied on a little money from Prisoners Abroad, a UK charity. Nigerians, Burmese, Vietnamese and Pakistanis all had to live by their wits, and few lived well.

The three-winged accommodation block stood crumbling in the sun, tiles falling from its roof and external pipes leaking enough water to grow stray ferns and lichen around each barred window. It held almost 180 cells, each no more than a room with a toilet hole in a corner. The chief allocated us a room, which we then concreted and plastered before hiring a carpenter to build a screened shower above the toilet.

'He's an imbecile, but the best carpenter around,' Rick said as we stood on the drying cement. 'Most respected by the old-timers.'

An old-timer himself, our new builder had spent his adult life in KP, and had a permanently curved spine from early years hunched in the factories. He built by rule-of-thumb, one of which was missing, and he measured every strut and plank from the piece last hammered to the wall. When completed, the plastic-covered screen appeared skewed, as though it had survived a hurricane, but it was solid enough, held by 20 crippled roofing nails per plank.

Escape

'I hope he's not connecting our electricity,' I said to Rick. 'I was hoping to put in a light switch. I think we've bought enough trust from the chief for that. My boy says our ceiling fan should be here by this afternoon.'

I was referring to Jet, my new manservant. I'd found him working in the umbrella factory, filling his days drawing large charcoal portraits of prisoners' girlfriends, children and parents from tiny snapshots. Jet was adept at bossing about the humbler factory workers, and attached himself to me to make sure 'nobody cheat you'. This service was in exchange for English lessons. I readily accepted this, as it was unwise to rely only on Rick or other foreigners for financial negotiations with the Thai guards.

Jet's English never improved much beyond the few words he already owned and abused when we met, but as he stepped into the role of head butler, this proved an asset. We learned to communicate almost silently, assume and meet each other's needs without the tangle of long conversations. Jet was minuscule in height and outlook, but rarely abused the power over others that belonging to a moneyed household gave him. He was serving a 12-year sentence for armed robbery. With a pistol in each hand, even a four-and-a-half-foot kid is taken seriously.

Jet arrived at our new cell shepherding a bearer hefting a new porcelain toilet bowl.

'My teacher.' Jet meant me. 'Pornvid want to see you downstairs.' Pornvid was the guard in charge of the accommodation block.

Rick squinted at me through his heavy spectacles. 'I've squared up with the chief. You don't have to give Pornvid anything.'

I disagreed. 'I don't want him feeling left out. Anyway, I've given him my credit card for the day. He should be back from the ATMs by now.' Three things made this safe: I was now a benefactor to the chief; Jet was my witness; and Pornvid believed I was going to be here for ever. Therefore, there was no real risk of my card being misused.

'How much?' Rick wanted to know.

'An honest 10 per cent.'

'Let me go to the chief for you. Only 5 per cent. He collects my money every time my wife visits. For nothing.'

'Rick—' I didn't need to mention the constant demands for donations Rick suffered under the eyes of the chief each day.

'OK. Have it your own way.'

The following day, I found Eddie having his hair cut. The barbershop was attached to the coffee shop. The hut had two surgical chairs salvaged from the *Titanic*, and photographs of a coiffed Johnny Fontane on the wall, now fading to blue.

Taking the vacant chair, I told Eddie of my plans to set up an office in a quiet place in one of the factories. 'Just a desk and some place to do some cooking. Jet's found an ice chest and some cupboards.'

'Kind of settling in, aren't you?' Eddie raised his eyes from under an electric trimmer.

'We want it to look that way, don't we? Besides, it'll take some time to check out the other buildings. Most of the foreigners are over in Building Two, but have you seen the size of their— ' I paused, because one of our cutters had stopped talking, and they would know the word *bars*, '—arrangements? Any ideas for another two for our room here?'

Rick had promised bed space to a Pakistani foreigners' trusty and ledger-keeper from the chief's office. Now that Rick was paying for more than his share, he felt his opinion should count for more. Eddie and I had argued for Jet (it was a rule in any case that foreigners have at least one Thai in their cell), and Eddie had found a South African named Albert.

'He's not much.' Eddie stretched long legs over his footrest. 'But what can you expect? At least he can pay his way.'

'You think he'd be someone who'd want to come along? To take the full pardon, I mean?' A 'full pardon' had long been a code word for escape.

'Wait till you meet him,' Eddie despaired. 'It will be enough if we can shut him up when we want to sleep.'

* * *

Escape

Although not yet 30, Albert's beer gut and puffy, red-lined face told of many sunny afternoon benders. He told me the rest over the next two weeks. Albert dimly remembered waking to a yellow phosphor streetlight and Bangkok traffic fumes gusting in slabs through an open second-floor window of his shabby hotel. For him, it was less sleep ceding to wakefulness than choking out of a coma into a sensation of stunned nausea.

The images that arose in his mind were layers in an excavation of fear: two Nigerians shouting over the racket of a Hillbrow bar in Johannesburg (the details dulled by liquor); then the pale-green Arrivals hall with the sign, Welcome to Bangkok (readable only because of the dilution of in-flight drinks); the cheap girly-bar of the night before his arrest, where he'd asked for his swollen nose, the result of a head-butt or a fall while attempting to dance on a table – fortunately numbed with firewater. And behind every memory a rear-projection of the broken, tired earth of the dorp of his birth and childhood in the South African countryside.

That night, Albert had struggled to remember something recent and positive. Not something he'd actually done, but a firm resolution made: he would demand a greater reward from his employers for the run. Leaning on his elbows, sweat running from the back of his neck, he still could not remember the exact amount of the fee originally agreed upon. Or, quite, with whom.

Stumbling to the window, Albert wiped the sweat from his face with a handful of drapery, stopping to cough and spit when curtain dust coated his mouth. He knew what he had to do, and would waste no time finding a bar where he could strengthen his resolve.

Some time later, perhaps the following day, Albert woke with a jolt as his taxi bounced from a freeway pothole. He smiled at the thought of driving a tough bargain with the Nigerian before taking another step. Albert's new girlfriend from Johannesburg would want him to stand firm. A few miles more, and the sight of Albert's small travel bag at his side, combined with that of the ticket jutting from his shirt pocket, triggered the realisation that he was already on his way to the airport. He was leaving the country, his bag holding 2.7 kilos of heroin loosely taped under its lining.

The taxi stopped in front of Don Muang's glass entrance. Albert peeled himself from the plastic-covered seat, digging into the tight pockets of his stained jeans for some of his few remaining banknotes. He was still arguing for change when two Thai plainclothes policemen moved forward. One held Albert's arm as the other took his bag.

'But how did you get into this?' I asked when Albert had run out of bad memories. We were talking on the third night in our new cell. The smell of paint was still strong.

'I'll show you something.' Albert reached under his mat for a plastic bag thick with ragged sheets of paper. He produced a small photograph of a girl with an orange Afro cut and freckled white skin. 'This is Melli. Things were going well for her but then she got this job in a bar in Jo'burg. Before I met her. After a few months there, she fell in with a rough crowd. We had some problems, and I decided I'd better put some money together. As it happens, she knew some people who had connections over here.'

Looking at the picture, it wasn't easy to imagine these two as a couple. I asked if she had written. Albert had been four months at Klong Prem.

'No. My sister says she's not working there any more.'

Rick didn't look up from his book, but must have been listening, as he asked, 'So, Albert, how long was it that you'd been going out with your little tiger before you came to Thailand and got arrested?'

Albert did not speak for a minute, and then answered, 'Three weeks.'

So, not much honey in the trap for Albert. Sobriety in KP had done little to clear his vision. For the next few weeks, Albert would slyly confide to everyone that his mercenary soldier pals within South Africa's right-wing extremist Broederbund would soon be staging a commando raid on the prison to free him. That was before a letter arrived from his mother. She had written that the man who had spent afternoons drunk in the kitchen of their small farmhouse was not his true father. A Jewish merchant from Pietermaritzburg had in fact sired Albert on one of his mother's town visits. Immediately, Albert's heritage changed.

'David, I'll be out of here in two – no, two-and-a-half – weeks,' Albert stage-whispered one morning from behind a factory pillar. 'The JDL are coming for me. Probably a chopper. They don't fuck around, those guys!' Words may be the tool selected by nature to help us humans deceive our competitors, but Albert had practised so thoroughly on himself that he now fell under every bus with a cunning smile.

No aircraft arrived for Albert, piloted by young aviators from the Jewish Defense League, only his final court van taking him for sentencing. No one had taken the trouble to translate the court proceedings to Albert, so he arrived back at KP in time for his visit with his sister. She had arrived in Bangkok the previous day with the intention of saying something good of Albert in court. She was a nurse, and a fine woman. Albert's court-appointed lawyer had not wished to spend another minute on the case, so the sister was not called upon, nor told what was going on. Halfway through their visit, a trusty translated the news to the siblings: Albert had been sentenced to death, reduced to 100 years in consideration of his guilty plea.

Eddie had been on his way back from speaking with some Swiss officials when he paused with Albert and his sister. 'You know,' Eddie later told me, 'even with all the crying and madness, Albert still pushed that stupid list through the bars to his sister.' Albert had been adding items to his shopping list for weeks, at the top of which was a deckchair for his place in the umbrella factory.

'As much as Albert's a dork,' Eddie said sympathetically, 'it's terribly inefficient of him to let his case turn to shit like that.'

The Thais were not so inefficient; they had Albert transferred to Bangkwang the following day. Watching him that last night in his chains, I hoped I would soon find someone to take his corner who would have a longer shelf life.

* * *

Escape

Perhaps the greatest luxury of our cell was the light switch. When we had tired of cards, Scrabble and storytelling, the darkness provided an illusion of freedom for some of us. Only the slow turn of the ceiling fan and the low murmur from our secret radio provided any rhythm to mark the hours.

Outside, in the grounds, I had found quiet space for rent. In a small garden behind the art workers' factory, I set chairs, tables, a desk, iceboxes and cupboards. Under a canvas awning, Jet and his friends cooked and kept Thai visitors away. Foreigners were usefully kept beyond the factory gate by the factory guard. The old man cast the most fearsome expression from under hooded eyes as he sat at his desk, bare except for a covered glass of water and a pack of cigarettes. In truth, he was perennially hungover, and quite tame. We rarely spoke to each other beyond a nod each week, as I would carefully place an envelope of money next to his cigarettes. Over the months, we built a mutual respect from those silences. He would post my sealed letters without comment. Since he had no special interest, this seemed safer than asking Pornvid or the chief.

All this was well enough; but now, able to breathe, I had to look beyond relative comfort and find a way out. My trial could not be delayed for ever, many doors remained to be tested and other people tried.

CHAPTER SIX

Corruption in high places may be a phrase that rings with promise and hope, but rarely gives reliable service. That's not because those highly placed are less corrupt, but because they lean towards the safety of corruptly servicing others also in high places. People at the fringes are usually no more significant to these high-ups than gardeners are to movie stars: spoken to with false confidentiality while never invited on set.

Dean Reed arrived, as promised, a couple of months after his release. He'd taken some care preparing for the visit by printing a phoney letter from an embassy and then bribing his way into the lawyers' area. Wearing a white suit and tie with jacket held over a shoulder, Dean appeared alarmingly official now that his beard was gone.

'I gave Eric a couple of thousand for you,' he said, waving at the trusty from Hong Kong. 'Anything I can get you from the shop?'

Sceptics of human nature wouldn't like any of this attention. I tried all the usual gambits: 'I've a friend coming over to help. He'll stay with you, and handle the money. He's a cut-throat by profession, but don't worry, his instincts are sound. And don't forget you'll have to get something out of this – you can't be doing this for nothing. And then there'll be your expenses . . .' But Dean didn't blink.

So I gave Dean a Bangkok telephone number and a note requesting he be given $10,000. There's always a fat slice of vanity in trusting a scoundrel, yet I'd had some success in the past with unlikely people. The name I'd given Dean was one such. Myca was a man I'd known for 15 years, and when we met he was close to poverty. The link to Myca had been one Johnny from Patpong.

In the 1970s, those smugglers who claimed roots in the counterculture tried to maintain a reputation for street cred. This usually meant scoring from strangers in the red-light districts of unknown cities. Bangkok's Patpong Road had red lights and a wide range of touts, most of them tied to local crooks of influence. That could mean trouble, as local crooks normally paid local cops, both hoping to profit from the foolishness of strangers. So, the thing was to avoid street hustlers with those rough connections. The Patpong stroll demanded the rejection of those touts who seemed too enthusiastic.

'Lie show, mister?'

This spoken by Johnny, I remember, who quite reluctantly peeled himself off a wall after I'd rejected two earlier offers. Some confusion at first: I'd taken Johnny to mean light show. That had sounded a bit tame for this part of town.

'No, you know,' Johnny persisted. 'Lie show. Girls.'

Ah, live show.

'Um, not for me.'

'I get you nice girl?' Johnny did his best to demonstrate 'nice'.

'No, not what I'd like.' I was being coy.

'You want boy? I get you boy!'

'No. What do you take me for?'

Some puzzlement then in Johnny, stretching his imagination to grapple with whatever exotic perversion this *farang* might want. Then, eureka.

'You want Thai stick?'

And so, we were in business.

Johnny was a fussy dresser for a man so plug-ugly. Shiny, electric-blue shirts and inflated black hair that might have come as a single plastic shell from a novelty shop. Whenever we drove away to score, there would always be a few minutes spent refining the Johnny-look in the mirrors of his borrowed Toyota.

Escape

On arrival, Johnny would leave me in the car while he disappeared into one of the many rusted, peeling and dimly lit apartment blocks where he claimed his contacts lived. Leaving me in the littered alley was only to keep me from seeing the large massage parlour where Johnny did his business.

One afternoon, Johnny had to call at his digs to respray his hair, and I stuck with him. An acre or two of skewed, muddy planks holding up ill-fitting corrugated roofing; inside, rooms had been partitioned with three-ply veneer, and only a resident could tell one family from another.

While waiting for Johnny, I spent a few minutes with a young man who lived in a room and a half with his wife and baby. He appeared more Hispanic than Thai, and although we exchanged only a few words, he offered a subdued look of sympathy at my having to deal with Johnny. The next day, I returned to this rickety maze behind the old Metro Hotel. I found Myca at home, and we sat on the floor to talk.

Myca was not yet thirty but spoke six languages as though he'd grown up in a yellow taxi plying through five continents. In some ways, he had: only three snapshot memories of his infancy in Waziristan remained, before teenage life in Bangkok. Then to South America working on coastal traders until chance took him to Greece, and then a Mediterranean dockland with the damp-carpet rooms of a dozen boarding houses. Myca's minuscule savings were quickly lost on his return to Thailand a decade later. A chauffeur service he set up went bust, and by then the only evidence was his cherished '69 powder-blue Buick, set fast on the forecourt of the one-pump gas station next to the Metro Hotel.

I returned to Thailand three weeks later, entrusting Myca with most of my life's stealings (I was almost 22) while he bussed north to the Golden Triangle. Not wishing to make any more new friends, I retired to a modest hotel in Silom Road to wait. After a long 11 days looking at wet skies, Myca returned. Pleased but modest still. In Western cities, the heroin I'd known well from small paper folds in cafés, or in sandwich bags in car parks, was ordinary stuff.

Escape

A starchy mix of cream flecks, and sugary if pressed. Myca laid upon my hotel-room quilt a sofa-cushion-sized clear bag of the purest white crystals, rolling under their laboratory's brandmark like Styrofoam pellets.

Later, in another country, as I exchanged the pouch for a suitcase full of money, I felt a fool's sadness, as though selling a fair child into slavery. I didn't want to see such purity leave my hands.

By the early 1980s Myca had bought a fine new house, become a landowner and was watching his children fumbling their way to class distinctions. He had no other customers, however sensible that might have been. With time out, we travelled to his ancestral province near the Khyber Pass in Afghanistan. Super-8mm film records the homecoming, with Myca introducing himself to tearful village ancients. The tribe soon collected a roomful of cloth-bound hashish for Myca and me to scratch our heads over.

Contrasting fortunes and different skies had since kept Myca and me apart for 11 years. We had managed only a brief meeting during the heady three days before my arrest. No warmth had been lost over the years, and we remained old-fashioned friends.

If nothing else, Dean Reed could describe my circumstances accurately. Until some clear vision explained my arrest, I would not send Dean north to those with real influence and power.

Although I'd paid my way out of trouble in the past, I was too superstitious to await one plan's failure before launching the next. Besides, bribery is more a hope than a plan. One of these early schemes required outside help. So, who in KP could best provide secure communication?

I found Charlie Lao at the tailor's shop, being fitted for a new uniform as a blue-shirt trusty. Top-drawer trusties usually paid several thousand baht for their jobs, as they would recoup this fee within a month. Some guards bestowed trustyhood upon ruthless blackmailers for the regular cut they'd receive. Others appointed loathsome grovellers who met their every comfort. A fine example of this grovelling was provided that week when I had been convincing the accommodation guard, Pornvid, that I needed to return each day after breakfast to my room to take a shower after exercise. It was forbidden for all except key boys to enter the cellblocks during the day.

'Why don't you shower at the tank like everyone else?' asked Pornvid, without moving from his deckchair.

'I'm shy,' I suggested, giving Pornvid an envelope.

The guard understood, and throughout the negotiation Pornvid's trusty was servicing his boss with a deep-fingered leg massage, given in utter silence. When I looked down at this toady, he returned with the most theatrical expression of rapture-in-servitude, as though the pleasure were all his. Charlie was different. He bought his rank outright, and attached himself to no guard.

Charlie's new uniform had all the trimmings: the braided lanyard, an engraved nametag, extra flaps and sewn creases, even the aviator's wings and a parachute-regiment badge. For all that, Charlie was not to become an extortionist or sycophant.

'I'm going to work on the visit area.' Charlie dropped a banana into the hip holster, where other trusties kept a baton. 'This will be good for you. I can help you. Any time, you get a good visit.'

As we left the tailor's shop, I explained to Charlie that I needed to make a secret phone call. He then took me to the secret phone booth, a stack of rice bags behind a curtain in the coffee shop.

I dialled a pager number in Adelaide. The pager was one of many kept by Harvey Oldham, and would have been silent for months. Harvey did not keep many friends, so we could each have unique numbers.

Harvey Oldham had been a professional bank robber since quitting his job as a clerk in his 20s. He had been behind the counter of the Commonwealth Bank one afternoon when three men entered the bank with guns. They'd left five long minutes later without the money from the time-locked safe, and had made a mess of the manager. Harvey thought he could do a better job of it.

Fourteen stick-ups later, one conviction had set Harvey back a few years, and he vowed never again to work with anyone other than a driver. He had since been successful, and was living under a carefully constructed identity that included membership of a respected gun club. Such was his fine reputation that the renamed Harvey had been granted a licence for a machine gun to more fully participate in the club's sporting events.

After 15 minutes among the rice sacks, the mobile I'd been given vibrated. Harvey must have found a phone booth. He spoke as soon as I answered.

'I was wondering when you'd call.' Harvey's interest in small talk was limited, but greater than his interest in flamboyant living or intoxicants. Even food, Harvey regarded as mere fuel. It is rare to find someone who enjoys his work for the simple pleasure of a bad deed well done, rather than for the notoriety.

After giving an outline of my position, I asked Harvey to fly to Thailand and make an appearance in the courts of justice.

'I'll have more detail after another court date or two,' I said. 'In a month there'll be a lemon letter for you at your post-box.' We had been using ultraviolet ink for many years now to conceal messages under plain text letters, but the old lemon name had stuck.

'How's the traffic outside those courts?' Harvey often worried about the getaway.

'Shitful. But if all goes well, it won't be an issue.'

'If all goes well—' Harvey paused. 'I'll do a bit of research. Let you know.'

Ten days later, the steel bus taking me to court was packed. I could barely see daylight as each lurching stop jerked my head from someone's pimply ear to another's rancid armpit. The bus stopped at the old city prison to collect more prisoners due for hearings.

A guard shouted, 'Make room. Get back. Plenty of space down the back.' Those at the rear whose faces were pressed into waffles by the mesh might have argued, if they'd been able to speak. With a little nuzzling from the guard's machine gun, half a dozen more prisoners clattered their chains up the steel steps. One of them, a paleface, tripped, but merely fell into the press of bodies.

Escape

Over the next hours of fuming traffic, the tripper introduced himself as Roddy Keyes, an Englishman who was under trial in an airport case concerning just under 100 grams of heroin. He had a case partner. Nothing unlawful had been found on Roddy, but the young woman had been undone during an X-ray of her lower body. Cassie was arrested; Roddy and his girlfriend were allowed to board their plane. Cassie held out for a solid five minutes before implicating Rod, who had barely buckled his seat belt before being hauled from the Tokyo-bound flight.

'So, is Cassie going to stick to her story?' I asked.

'It's not in her interests to say a word in court.' Roddy was trying to sound confident. 'The only thing is that she's had a good moan up, and that's been all over the London papers. The BBC films our every court date. All that can make a person want to stand up and sing.'

'I hear you've got some well-known lawyers.' I wanted to know if using the high-rollers would make any difference. 'How are they calling it?'

'Fifty-fifty. Which is what all lawyers say. I suppose it's all down to how the Thais see the publicity.'

Roddy told me more of the way Thailand's big lawyers operate, and that when it came to foreigners, few of their usual tricks work.

A year later, Roddy would be acquitted. Cassie received thirty years, but was home in England within two years using the prisoner-transfer scheme. In many ways, she found life in British prisons harder, although she did well with a coquettish book of her adventures. Roddy gave up smuggling after that, although I don't think he felt a lot better for it. He had been lucky the cameras had been there, and that there was someone to take the fall.

The evidence presented against me that day was thin. Literally. It was a newspaper cutting taken from a Melbourne tabloid the day after my arrest in Thailand.

'It seems your embassy has decided to assist in your case,' my lawyer Montree said with sarcasm.

Escape

The story quoted two local narcotics policemen giving their idea of the inside story. 'Caught with just a sample,' said one. 'Would have been one of the biggest dealers in this part of the country by now,' pronounced another. To give it authority, a translator from a university read the story into the court record.

Surely a second-hand bite of hearsay from a distant scandal sheet could not be held against me. 'Well, that was a waste of time,' I said to Montree, dusting my hands.

My lawyer looked down at his papers and held his hands over his head, not wanting to say more.

By the time I climbed into the van to return to Klong Prem, I had the best part of a plan in mind. At my next court appearance, I would as usual be escorted to the eighth-floor court by one or two guards. I would be in leg irons, but without handcuffs. The previous afternoon Harvey, by then in Thailand, would have gone to the court wearing one of his banking outfits: suit, wig, briefcase and an identity tag claiming something diplomatic. From the seventh floor – at that time, still vacant – he would've let himself into the emergency stairwell that runs adjacent to the small lift that moves prisoners to and from the courtrooms.

Harvey's large briefcase would hold quite a lot. A mobile phone, a gun, two pairs of handcuffs, large cable ties and duct tape, a set of foldable bolt cutters with extendable handles, another wig and a suit. The suit my size and the wig blond, to contrast with my dark hair. Being thoughtful, Harvey would include some sandwiches and a flask of coffee, for he would be spending a long night camped in that stairwell waiting for my arrival. A dusty stairwell, upon which I'd seen no recent impression of human feet, although more than a few from birds alighting from the open windows.

An accomplice would be needed for Harvey. Someone to note which courtroom I had been taken to – any of nine spread over the upper three floors. That someone should phone Harvey to tell him when I was on my way out, and who would be with me. Nothing more. As soon as the guards closed the single door from the courtroom corridors, Harvey would appear from the stairwell as we waited by the lift. Harvey would have the gun in his hand. A brief conversation would ensue.

Harvey and I would then lug the trussed up and by-then peaceful guards to a stage landing of the unused stairwell. Harvey would sever my chains, and I would try on my new shoes, adjust my tie and straighten my wig. We would then take to the main stairs and walk from the courthouse steps to the roadway. Any accomplice with half a brain would be on his way to Rio, so I supposed Harvey and I would have to catch a cab to the domestic airport. From there, south to Hat Yai, then across to Satun and the short ferry to Langkawi Island, Malaysia.

On my two-inch foam mattress that night, under the condensation of these freshly baked plans, I could see nothing that might deflate this simple recipe.

With the loss of Albert of Johannesburg, there was a gap to fill in our room. Building Six provided many candidates, as all newcomers came there first. The worthy Thais who arrived were usually snapped up, and who could blame them for not wanting to share a room full of crazy foreigners, who either spent the night in a morbid funk or would flop about laughing at absurdities.

Among a new batch of foreigners was Sten from Sweden. While his English was perfect, he was not inclined to speak of family, his youth in Uppsala or lost loves. So, having met these initial conditions for entry to room *ha-sip jet* (room 57), Big Sten was welcome.

However, we were all eager to hear any unsentimental recollections, and Sten had plenty from his last decade bumming around Asia. His first local mischief saw him running gold from Singapore to Bombay in the days when India levelled a weighty tariff on imported bullion. The pay wasn't so golden, but the flights were short and the turnaround quick. Apart from the ability to step on a plane, some skill was needed in moonwalking, for the gold was packed in the soles of large shoes. Airport metal detectors are less perturbed by non-ferrous pure gold, and quite untroubled at the base of the walk-through detectors then in use. So the trick was to glide through without appearing to shuffle.

'How the hell did anyone work that one out?' Rick wanted to know.

'Ah, trial and error, Mr Rick,' replied a polite and wistful voice. 'Trial and error. Too many times.'

That was not Sten, but Bruce the Pakistani speaking. Bruce was also new to No. 57. He knew all the India scams. His room-name had been immediately bestowed after he had voiced his Bollywood ambitions to remake *Die Hard* in the Indian film capital. To be titled *Dying Hardly*, the all-singing, all-dancing action thriller would not star Mr Willis, but a new heart-throb of the subcontinent – at that point in telling the dream, modesty would demand that Bruce the Pakistani lower his head and shyly look away. Bruce was serving seven years in KP for drugging tourists on board Thailand's trains, and had been made a foreigners' trusty.

Sten demonstrated some gold-footed moonwalking before recounting elements of his next job. So impressed were Sten's rich employers with their young Swede, they promoted him to tour manager for packages of illegal emigrants hoping to leave Asia for a new world.

From China, groups of a dozen or less would trek into Laos to quietly cross the Mekong River into northern Thailand. Assembling in Bangkok, their photographs would be laminated into European passports stolen or sold by penniless backpackers. They would be given tickets to fly from Thailand to Japan and onwards to the USA. Although the US embassy kept 25 staffers in the capital to thwart illegal immigrants, the Chinese had moulded a silent army of corrupt officials at Don Muang airport who would be blind to the small exodus of hopefuls.

These Chinese wisely assigned the task of dodgy paperwork to the Indians, and Sten's job was to shepherd the emigrants and safeguard the passports. The documents had to be collected at Tokyo once the passengers had been issued with boarding passes for Honolulu. These passports would be recycled with new faces until their bindings disintegrated.

'I'd take them to Bangkok airport in a minibus,' Sten explained. 'Collect all their little bags of food, which they wouldn't need, and point them at the right counter for check-in. That would go all right. We had half a row of the passport clerks under control. The worst part was at Narita. They'd all wander off shopping and I'd have to round them up or they'd miss the next flight.'

Once found, Sten would redirect a Mr Landsburger to the correct gate, or empty a Mr Stanley's bag of the two dozen free travel guides and airline timetables. There had been the moment when one of Sten's travellers had objected to being asked to abandon a stack of paper cups before boarding. 'But I be businessman,' protested Mr Tarkington. 'Don't worry,' assured Sten, adjusting the gentleman's tie, 'anyone can see that.'

Within minutes of the final call, Sten would move his huddled mass to the boarding gate, collect their passports and wish them well. On arrival at Honolulu, the first-time air travellers could be themselves: lost and confused. They would do what the law asked, fudge their origin, nationality and previous route; request sanctuary and freedom from hardship, persecution and fear. Their unknown status would see them sent to immigration detention prisons for questioning by distrustful officials.

'I'd have to turn around and go straight back to Bangkok,' Sten complained of his boss. 'Not even a night on the town in Tokyo.'

'How did the Chinese get on in the US?' asked Eddie.

'Who knows? In those days, they mostly did all right. They were shitting themselves. But, you know, thrilled to bits.'

CHAPTER SEVEN

Having settled in Building Six, it was then time to do a grand tour of Klong Prem to survey the openings. Eddie and I thought our cell bars in Six were sufficiently narrow, at just over an inch, but the building was deep within the prison, very far from the outer wall.

Calvin and Martyn had lately arrived from the Cure, so we set out with trusty Charlie to roam the grounds. Our pretext was a bogus survey of Easter religious needs. We set out walking along a main road that fanned with others from the central administration block. This square building had a 20-metre concrete post topped with a large glassed watchtower.

'I've never seen anyone in there.' I directed Martyn's gaze to the top.

'Probably never is,' Martyn said. 'Too many stairs.'

While Eddie and Calvin compared vices, I asked Martyn how his case was going.

'Oh, I had another day of hearings last week. All day spent chewing over two photographs.'

Martyn's case was full of holes, now being heavily filled by his trial judge. The claim was that two Canadians had been plotting to export 15 kilos of heroin by some unknown means. One of the Canadians was later revealed as an undercover narcotics policeman. He had long ago returned to Canada, and since died from heart failure. The other Canadian, a well-known villain, had also returned to Canada charged in another case, and was not expected back to resume his trial for 12 years, if at all. This left only Martyn and a driver to face trial in Thailand. The dope, if it ever existed, had disappeared, although a fuzzy Polaroid of a white bag resting on a coffee table had earlier been accepted as evidence. With the undercover agent sadly deceased, only the Thai police captain on the case remained alive for the prosecution. This captain had been transferred to Udon Ratchathani and was fully occupied with a new girlfriend near the Cambodian border.

The photograph at issue during Martyn's last hearing had been a black-and-white picture of four people at a table outside a café. Supposedly taken by the Canadian agent (remotely, perhaps, as he was in the frame), it was made an exhibit through a police sergeant who worked in the office of the missing captain's deputy.

'Well, Martyn,' I said with a flat sarcasm, 'not much to worry about with that.'

Martyn assumed his trial judge's manner, and quoted: 'The photograph as exhibit number 23 clearly shows the suspect Martyn translating for the Canadian drug syndicate as they planned their strong crimes.' Adding, 'If I get less than the lot, I'll have done well.'

Our conversation then turned to old Cure friends, and I told Martyn of American Dean Reed's visits and promises.

Martyn sympathised. 'Well, I don't have to tell you his reputation, although you can't fault his enthusiasm, whatever he really intends. Sometimes the thirst for sweet lies must be quenched before there's strength for bitter truths. Feeling stronger, these days?'

We had walked past Building One, which held Klong Prem's ladyboys and *kathoeys*, their partners, and other oddballs. Thai law has no provisions for altering the sexual status listed at birth, so the prison for men held many transsexuals in various stages of transformation. When illicit supplies of female hormones ran low, Building One could be a hairy old place.

Almost all of the 90 Western foreigners lived in Building Two. The building's small grounds were filled with ramshackle huts grouped by nationality: English, American, French, Dutch, German and Australian. The Scandinavians seemed to mingle.

'I'm told they're not much,' Martyn said of these huts. 'Like deserted trading posts in the old Congo. But I'll move over there when I'm due. Apparently, there's a small electrics workshop.' Then, turning to me, 'And I don't have your ambitions. I know I'll be here for quite some time.'

As Building Two appeared near the outer wall, Martyn promised to give me a detailed report on his new home. We moved on to Building Four, the higher-security building for people considered a risk. Its grounds were cramped, with almost no yard space, as so few were let out for more than an hour or two each day. It had been built mostly as tiny single cells, each with heavy, slab-like, impenetrable bars. Whey-faced prisoners shuffled about in chains.

'It would take only one word, just a little whisper,' Eddie looked about morbidly. 'Any of us could be put in here.'

Most of the foreigners of Building Five were African, more than 200; their days absorbed with food issues. A few years ago, they had spilled into an aimless riot of frustration. It had led nowhere. Few made it beyond the gates of Building Five. When some Thais were pushed to the ground, the afternoon of the short knives began, with 50 yard-cooks supplying twice that many would-be Thai boxers with hatchets, choppers and paring blades. They formed mobile gauntlets and cut the Africans to pieces.

Some buildings were out of bounds. Building Seven, a punishment house, was overgrown with vines and low-hanging trees. Utterly quiet, yet full, we were told. Sweepers, ragpickers and kitchen workers were housed in Building Eight. Buildings Nine and Ten had short-term prisoners and students without a school. Both near the wall, but off-limits to foreigners. Officially, guards volunteered as teachers. Diplomas were advertised on a colourful notice board, priced by grade. The only accommodation with cell bars as thin as those of Building Six was in Buildings Eleven and Three. Building Eleven had 500 prisoners dying from AIDS, and the hospital-recovery wards of Building Three held large dormitories rather than cells. Although any climb from Building Six to the outside wall would require scaling three internal walls, all other available accommodation in KP had fat steel crosshatched over cell windows. Even the most well-equipped mountain climber would never see snow if he could not first open his bedroom door.

Gambling within Thai prisons is forbidden, and so an especially clandestine pleasure. Even the most powerful trusties kept their decks of cards hidden. Possession of a pair of dice carried the risk of a costly punishment. Consequently, daytime betting was often facilitated by those possessing some unpredictable handicap.

One such was a young man who had an advanced parasitic infection in one limb. His right leg was swollen to the size of a tree trunk. He would sit by the toilets most mornings attempting to extract one of the thousands of worms that riddled his leg. These thin parasites under his skin looked like fishing line, and seemed just as long. The only method of removing a worm intact was to pick out a looped segment as it moved into view through one of his weeping pustules. Then, to roll the worm carefully around a pencil until completely extracted. If the worm broke, the two halves would live on to produce large families.

Eddie and I were calling odds one morning as a small crowd of Thais and foreigners bet on the number of worm-inches made visible before a snap. Charlie Lao had joined us, and as he was no gambler I waited for a break to take Charlie aside.

'David, you know the coffee shop is coming up for sale? It would be good for you. I can speak to the chief, if you want,' Charlie offered.

'How much does he want?'

'Maybe $10,000. There's one Thai man bidding, but I can keep the price down.'

'I don't think it's for me,' I said, with thanks.

'You can make your money back in six months, maybe four.' Charlie saw the coffee shop as the ideal investment for any would-be KP Tai Pan.

Escape

'It's not a question of money,' I told Charlie, and went on to explain my hopes to excuse myself from all further KP sports. By the time I'd finished outlining a few escape plans, we were walking through the clotheslines, that morning heavy with drying bed sheets. Charlie's smile had frozen.

Charlie had been in Klong Prem for over seven years. He had seen the few escape attempts fail tragically, and had heard of one attempt from the courts that had become notorious. He hoped the story would teach me a lesson.

'These were Chinese guys, David,' Charlie implored. 'So they had friends, you know. Some money, too.'

Charlie's recollection of the escape plan of the four inmates from their court-bound van mirrored the dreams of almost every prisoner transported through hours of stalled traffic to his courthouse. For eight months, five men had been held on remand at Klong Prem for the same drug case. Before the trial began, the oldest among them had become too ill to attend hearings, and confined to the hospital. The remaining four had planned their escape three months earlier, and had used local – that is, Thailand-based – contacts only for acquiring equipment and finding a safe house. All those who were to use guns had been brought from Hong Kong. They spent several weeks on motorcycles learning routes and techniques for threading through Bangkok's congested streets. Few, if any, Thais were involved. The father of one of the escapers later confided that an earlier version of the plan was to snatch the prisoners from the courthouse as they arrived, or even at the jail upon return. These ideas were rejected because the court police are too heavily armed, and at the prison the guards in the towers had a serious advantage with their rifles. Shooting would have been assured, with inevitable losses.

The four men had left KP one morning on the bus, along with fifty others. They had prepared carefully, with each man knowing the location of the safe house in case any found himself separated. Their confederates had planned well, too.

Underneath the first overpass from the prison, a stolen truck stopped and stalled in front of the court bus. Abandoning the heavy truck, its driver and another man left their cabin, and walked amiably towards the bus driver before pulling down facemasks. They kept the talk to a minimum by unloading a few shots from handguns into the driver's window. At the same time, two others moved up quickly from behind the prisoners' bus, one pointing a shotgun at the rear guard. The rear door, as usual, had been open to give the guard some air. The second man took the guard's keys to unlock the prisoners' cage.

Of the four prisoners who planned to leave that morning, one had second thoughts at the sight of guns and the sound of cold threats. Worse, those inmates not part of the plan noticed his hesitation. With the cage door open, his more willing accomplices quickly picked their way through the pack and slipped to the roadway, catching and tripping over their chains. The masked watcher at the rear door had the sense not to speak to the doubter directly, but shouted encouragement at all the prisoners. A few began to move, but not he who had his doubts. Oddly, the guard was moved to protest at these fresh prisoners attempting to join an escape not of their own making, and had to be put to sleep. The sight of that ended any initiative by the remaining prisoners.

Several motorbikes had arrived. A masked pillion passenger from one went to work snapping the steel ankle rings of the three freed men. As this seemed to take too long there was shouting, and the bolt cutters were abandoned. While the masked gunmen kept their weapons trained on the prison guards, the prisoners were driven away on fast off-road bikes. Less than a minute later, the last of the gunmen backed to a car waiting by the roadside, climbed in, and was driven behind the others through a building site to a far entrance. There, the gunmen took to bikes of their own, and the freed prisoners transferred to another car.

'So, they got away all right.' I turned from Charlie, pleased at last to hear of some success.

'Well, the four main men got to a small place in the middle of town,' Charlie continued. 'Too many police everywhere. Too risky to move outside.'

Escape

And too risky to stay inside. Minutes after the remaining prisoners were hauled back to Klong Prem, these inmates identified the one who had hesitated. He was then questioned. He held out for almost four hours. That night, a special police unit raided the house in Thonburi. Two of the policemen were hospitalised from injuries caused by their own ricocheting bullets. Six of the seven people in the house were killed immediately, the last dying during the night at a police station.

Charlie was using this story to tell me that what hadn't been done couldn't be done.

'It's not destiny,' I protested. 'Destiny is when you stand around looking stupid in a pineapple hat while the bad men are at the door instead of going for the back fence. As soon as that chicken one wouldn't go, the others were crazy to stay in Thonburi. Anyone can see their mistake!'

'Can you see yours?'

Charlie had me there. Even then, I still couldn't understand why the Thai police had been waiting for me at Chinatown.

Around the same time as I heard that dismal tale of the massacred Chinese, I found problems with Swiss Eddie. We had been sitting behind the coffee shop watching Rick cook lunch, something he rarely attempted.

On a bare patch of earth, Rick was cooking a chicken in what he called a Russian-army oven. A ten-gallon oil drum had been taken from the autoshop and then cleaned. A soda-pop bottle was half filled with water and wedged upright in the ground. The chicken was then jammed over the bottle.

'I learned this in Dubai,' Rick explained as he lowered the tin over the be-chickened bottle. 'Now, I seal the tin good with some dirt. And now throw on the rags.'

The rags were three large oil-soaked jute sacks that had cost more than the bird. These were set alight to make Rick's pressure-cooker. Almost engulfed in flames, and to whet our appetites, Rick told a long story about the pet chicken that entertained his customers from the days when he ran a bar in the Persian Gulf states. The chicken was deranged, apparently, and had been named Floppy. Although Rick's feast was ready in 20 minutes, the unfunny chicken story made it seem longer.

As we ate Floppy II, Eddie announced that he was intending to take his sentence in court the following week.

'I thought you were waiting for your uncle to come from Zurich – to say nice things in court?' I'd been expecting Eddie to delay his trial as I had.

'Yeah, well, he's not coming.' Eddie looked around. 'And I'm sick of waiting. I just want to get it over.'

Later that day in our factory, I told Eddie something he already knew: 'You know, if you get more than 35 years, you'll be off to Bangkwang. OK, it's got no moat, but you'll be on your own. Does the court know about your past?'

'It seems so. Well, not about Switzerland. The court knows my Thai record.' Eddie meant the year he had served for stealing a TV set from a hotel.

'You did your bit in the Swiss army, Eddie. Why don't you soldier it out here? Then we can both get away.'

'Look, David. You know I wasn't in the army. Pretended to be crazy – remember? And seriously, you don't think you can really get out of here? I mean, come now!'

That left nothing more to say. Eddie had been the most fitting candidate for an escape partner.

I looked across the factory towards two old guards wearing their ill-fitting uniforms. Happily arguing with each other, like mummified but animated corpses, their chicken necks shrunken within the fabric so carefully pressed by their trusties: a version of Larson's cartoon of the Old West in which vultures pick over the bodies of dead pioneers. Just for fun, one vulture has strapped on a corpse's six-gun and donned a big hat. 'Hey, lookit me!' the vulture says to the other birds, 'I'm a cowboy!'

Within a fortnight, Eddie had been sentenced to 50 years. He was sent to Bangkwang the next morning.

Escape

A day after that, a letter arrived from England containing a small black-and-white photograph of Eddie. It was for Eddie's new, false passport. Copied from a large charcoal portrait. Originally a colour snapshot taken of Eddie in front of a street stall in Phuket. Little Jet had sketched a copy, carefully eliminating the background, and that I had sent to London. Jet, for some reason, had no talent for making portraits from life. I placed Eddie's picture in my drawer along with spare buttons and paper clips.

That afternoon, I was looking for an excuse to get away from the sour atmosphere of Building Six, so when Charlie told me that most of Klong Prem's Australians were at the visit pens, I left Jet in charge of our office and began walking to the gate.

'Embassy people?' I asked Charlie.

'Not yet, but they're coming. Right now, some Christian girl is for the boys.'

The girl was in her 20s. She looked as though she had slept through infancy on one side of her face, but otherwise would have been called pretty. The visit pen was packed and deafening, so the boys were taking turns at the young missionary. A sallow-skinned man in shorts the colour of wet cement was calling through the bars.

'I haven't got any more horror stories for you, luv. I'll see what I can do next time.'

Others were not so unkind, and were pleased to see someone from the real world. Even so, this meeting was more a chance for the Australians from different buildings to get together than to supply the girl from the Christian Brotherhood with material for prayer meetings. Since their grandfathers' survival of the World War Two prisoner-of-war camps in Singapore, Australians had acquired a reputation for resourcefulness and pluck. Unfortunately, this lot looked like they'd never left that Changi camp.

While Sallowface yelled at the girl, I was introduced to Rickets, who also had skin inflammations; Hollowcheeks, whose yellow skin advertised liver damage; Greengills; and Looseskin, who had matted hair and was taking his time dying from AIDS. These were the years before anti-retroviral drugs.

The noise in the pens made talking hard work, the mosquitoes' scouts had signalled a formation attack and I'd seen enough. I walked with Greengills across to the hut reserved for officials. Inside, two consular reps spoke with a Czech-Australian and another Aussie in a wheelchair who had tuberculosis. A woman with a large handbag and short hair was telling a story of her work. As a vice-consul, one of her frequent tasks was to repatriate tourists who had found themselves in Thai nuthouses. Usually, those visitors who had stopped taking their antipsychotic drugs in favour of oriental medicine. Jill would collect them from the asylums, usually meeting them as they stood behind ward bars ranting obscenities.

'That, I don't mind,' Jill told us. 'It means I get to fly back to Sydney at least twice each month. It's when they spit on me, I get upset. They spit a lot, I don't know why.'

By the time the remaining Australians had coughed and limped their way to the official hut, Frank Maugre, another vice-consul, was closing a large file on the Czech. The Czech's file included half a dozen theft convictions from Australia, as well as several minor arrests in Europe involving explosive arguments with strangers. He'd been asking for support for a royal pardon in Thailand. His sentence was 30 years, about the average for foreigners in KP.

'Sorry to say it, mate, but you're fucked!'

Frank then announced that royal amnesties would no longer include those with drug convictions. Royal amnesties occurred almost every year in which the king's birthday contained a zero. Sentences would normally be halved.

'As you know, murderers have never been eligible,' explained Frank. 'Now, it looks like you druggies won't see any change out of a dollar, either. Some of the other embassies have never been too keen on the amnesties as it is.'

By that, Frank meant the US State Department, which saw the amnesties as undermining the attractiveness of its prisoner-exchange programme. American prisoners who were due to be sent home would first be re-sentenced at the Thai jail before departure to US prisons. The sentences could be reduced by a high level of co-operation with the DEA, and long Thai sentences were one way to encourage that.

This news ended the consular visit, so we all wandered from the hut back towards our buildings. Greengills was serving forty years, and had spent the last six in Bangkwang prison before moving to Klong Prem.

'It's better there, really,' he coughed. 'It's more high-security, so they leave you alone. Not so many rules, so you can do what you want.'

'More high-security?' I asked. 'Like, how?'

Greengills stopped for a moment, puzzled. 'I don't know. You know? Real long-termers. They let you just get on with it.'

Stopping at the gate of Building Six, I beheld that group of shrunken, lost people. It seemed that I could have held them all together in my arms as a thatch of rubbery sticks. Given time, I would be like them: an afternoon's diversion for consular staff, a foreign nuisance for Thais; the pathetic madman to whom family and friends would sadly post books and food parcels. A man whose letters would ramble, sapping the strength and resources of those outside who still cared. A creature without the dignity of dogs and dolphins that, when denied their own world, would die quietly and quickly. Worse, given the ruthless adaptability of man, I might somehow survive 20 years in this place and, eventually released, be left with no mind other than that of a once-caged circus bear, able only to take two paces forward, then two steps back.

CHAPTER EIGHT

Once or twice each year, the prison would allow open visits where inmates were permitted to sit in contact with their visitors. These took place in a large walled garden with marquees shading tables. These special visits were limited to prisoners of excellent behaviour and the wealthy, so put little strain on Klong Prem's management. Besides, few prisoners had anyone prepared to visit them.

Charlie Lao was on duty pretending to be a trusty, and had set up a small table with a beach umbrella to shade Sharon and me from the crowd. Sharon wore a light dress, and looked good.

Sharon seemed to imagine my imprisonment in KP was some kind of self-indulgent whim of my own invention. Now, she thought it high time I stopped playing Devil's Island, and that I should simply leave.

'There are one or two difficulties in that, my love.' I waved an arm at the eight-metre walls.

Sharon frowned dismissively. 'Oh, you're not going to let that worry you. I know you'll come out.' She then unpacked the food she'd bought while bouncing around Bangkok playing giddy tourist. 'I believe in you so much, you'll turn into the man I love, even if you don't think you are. You won't be able to help yourself!'

As I tried to figure that out, we became children at a pretend afternoon tea party, pouring imaginary milk, crumbling fictional biscuits and toasting the air, all to disguise kisses. Then I ate a real salmon sandwich, and looked over people we knew in snapshots that Sharon had spread upon the table.

'What can I do for you, David? Tell me.'

I put down the sandwich and looked thoughtful. 'Did you bring your camera?'

She had.

'Have someone take your picture out there near the moat. There's a shop that sells some of the crap they make in here.' I nodded towards the front gate. 'Not too close. It'd be good if the guard towers were in the frame.'

Sharon and I had met at a noisy birthday dinner at a glitzy restaurant. Big, gold-rimmed plates with small, ugly food. The birthday girl was a tall Italian whom my friend Matt hoped to seduce. Matt was trying to go straight, underworking a sooty storefront named Home of Chrome that electroplated chunky car parts for obsessive petrolheads. It hadn't helped to straighten Matt that he kept the shop running with easy loans from his crooked friends. Already, a secretary had intuitively renamed the company Home of Crime. Matt was to have no chance with the tall girl.

'How do you think Matt's doing with your friend tonight?' I'd asked Sharon, as we were seated together. The girls had long been friends.

'Maybe. It's a birthday night. He deserves to succeed. He's been trying long enough.'

'I don't think so,' I said. 'It's her birthday, not Matt's.'

Sharon laughed too loud at that, and squeezed my arm.

Over the following weeks, Sharon and I spent long nights together. At first on neutral ground in bright hotels, later at country weekend retreats. Sharon dumped her part-time boyfriend; awkward because he was her boss and believed himself a big man in the car trade with a reputation for something. Married, too, and grumpy about losing a mistress. He didn't like the idea of me when he heard, and made noises about it when drinking. That stopped after he gave it some thought. Sharon had decided to put together a band, and would find a job teaching in the afternoons. I introduced her to my tastes. She introduced me to two young children previously kept under wraps. There were fewer hotel nights after that, and more nights at Sharon's house in Melbourne's outer suburbs. After three months had passed, and as Christmas approached, I got myself arrested.

Now, under the sky of Thailand, I stopped flipping through Sharon's photographs. These included pictures of Sharon singing with her new band, About Time. Weddings, parties, anything. Sharon picnicking with children. Laughing with girlfriends.

'None in here of Matt.' I stacked the pictures together. 'Are they still together?'

'Nope.'

'Home of Chrome?'

'Gone bust.'

I nodded and moved to put the photographs back in their paper wallet. I'd never introduced Sharon to any of my keystone friends, although she'd met some since my arrest. As I slid the pictures into the wallet, I saw an envelope behind the negatives.

'Oh, that's for you,' Sharon said.

Harvey Oldham, I thought immediately. I hadn't heard from Harvey for a month, and had begun to think he had got cold feet – Thailand being all foreign to him. It would be all right with me if he did no more than slip me a gun in court and leave the briefcase in the stairwell. I'd be happy to work on the rest.

The letter wasn't from Harvey. It was from Chas, a mutual friend who kept our little family in touch when misadventures kept us apart. Chas told Harvey's story, as Harvey was no longer in any condition to communicate.

Ever conservative, Harvey had overestimated the amount of money he might need in Thailand. Proud and fearless, he had not asked Chas or me for funds. Instead, he called at a bank to steal the cash delivery. Whether careless or unlucky, he ran into three armed policemen on his way out. Harvey shot above the officers' shoulders, but one lawman behind his patrol car managed a clear shot at Harvey's chest. The bullet tore through a can of green paint with which Harvey had just finished decorating the lens of the bank's security camera. Picking himself up from the footpath, Harvey chased the policemen away using the remains of his ammunition. He then drove into the South Australian desert, and dug the mangled lead from his sternum before calling friends for help. Harvey was not expected to survive long.

'Bad news?' asked Sharon, for I had become quiet.

'Not good. I think it might be a good idea if you could ask Chas to come and see me when he can.' I'd had enough of phones.

'Your Chas doesn't really trust me, does he?' Sharon was unaccustomed to people who listened more than they talked.

'It's not that, honey. Chas is like an unwilling foreman on a jury who can't argue culpability but won't claim virtue. He doesn't judge.'

Sharon stared at her fizzy drink. I went on, 'Listen, kiddo, I tried to tell you often enough before we got tangled up. I'm rotten to the core. OK, there's some things I won't do. Kidnapping. I hate to haggle and can't stand tearful negotiations. Theft? I'm too bigheaded. Armed robbery? I'd only steal if they thanked me for it somehow. Arson? I don't work nights, and you can never get the stink of kerosene out of your clothes.' I went on like this for some time.

When I'd run dry, Sharon asked, 'So, if you're so rotten, you wouldn't tell me this. And if that's a real warning, then it's sweet but I'm not taking it. Or it's a double bluff, and you're saying that really to make me think you're all right but really to keep me, which is OK because I want to be kept.'

I think there was more but I was already lost.

By the time our afternoon ended, Sharon had agreed to call Dean Reed, and to meet him for a drink somewhere. 'Perhaps the riverside bar of the Oriental,' I suggested. 'Thai royalty sometimes visit, and they don't allow cheap gunzels to sit eyeballing the customers from their pricey sofas.' Not that I was worried for Sharon's safety with

Escape

Dean, and I wanted a female take on the man who had promised to have me released on bail. It was true, though, that any local surveillance would not get past the Oriental's discreet security. Ideally, I would have liked someone to go to Dean's house and poke through his sock drawer. Had that been Sharon, she would have returned with a sock.

That evening, arriving at our cell, No. 57, I saw that Sten had found a replacement for Swiss Eddie. His name was Theo, another Swiss. English Rick was introducing Theo to his new roommates.

'Sten, you know, of course. There's our little helper, Jet, so named as he is the seventh child in a large family. Bruce there from Pakistan likes to travel on his own. Has a job with me in the chief's office, although I still can't tell what it is he does. And now here's Mr Westlake – not his real name, you'll find, and David's found himself in the land of a thousand Westlakes. Little Biplane will unroll your bed next to mine, if that's OK.' Jet took Theo's bedding. 'Now, Theo, we have a new cook. You can meet him tomorrow, and he'll supply our evening meals that the kids will collect and bring up here. The cook's name is Bo-Jai. We call him Blow-Job, but don't let that put you off, it's no reflection on his food. It's just that he's half-Korean and thinks he knows karate. And you'll notice that we never call him that to his face. Actually, he's serving about 8,000 years for passing bogus travellers' cheques, which may be why he frowns a lot. And we have a cat David seems to encourage, but she's not turned up for dinner the past few nights. Perhaps she's been eaten by one of the rats. So, welcome.'

This was a bit much for Theo to take in, so he spent some time unpacking his clothes before joining us at dinner and then telling his story.

While still young, the fair-haired Theo had become a cargo manager for Swissair, and later promoted to Bangkok. He was full of energy, more than his job could consume. Swissair Cargo transports most of Thailand's foreign currency to Zurich for redistribution, as well as tonnes of gold in and out. Theo spent fruitless months trying to predict when these shipments would take place, for the cargo manifest often said no more than 'banking documents'.

'Surely the weights would give you a clue?' I couldn't help myself.

'Sometimes, but they'd break them up into smaller parcels before being listed,' Theo explained. 'And, anyway, I couldn't think of anyone I'd trust to help me grab it all.'

To concentrate his mind on these and other problems, Theo began taking several Ecstasy tablets each day. Unhappy with the quality of the local pills, Theo began importing his own. His trust in people grew along with his daily doses and his thriving E-tab trade. He was arrested at the Swissair office taking a dozen padded courier bags out of his in-tray. Amounting to 35,000 tablets.

'Is that it?' Rick had hoped for more complications.

'Well, yes. But I can't understand why so many Americans were all over my case,' Theo complained. 'I never did any business with the US. What business of the DEA's is this?'

We all agreed that America had made everything its business, although I suspected that the interest was no more than the effect of having 60 drug-enforcement personnel stationed in Bangkok with little to do.

As we picked at the remains of our meal, there came the sound of many bare feet along the corridor outside our cell. Bruce was quick to report with his hand mirror. He was a dedicated watcher. Outside, a trusty was leading a large group of newcomers, and had stopped at the cell next to ours. The cell was empty, as it was to be leased to a group of trusties unwelcome elsewhere. Most trusties' cells were two floors below us, near to ground level. This cell, completely stripped of fittings, would serve to introduce newcomers to Klong Prem. Jet began a count.

The trail seemed endless, a sad parody of phone-booth cramming. Finally, there were no more, and the trusty eased the door shut.

'Thirty-nine, my teacher!' Even Jet was astounded.

The cell next door was the same size as ours, and we were six. By any measure, and even accounting for their smaller Thai frames, those prisoners could not have had the space to do more than squat, knees against back and head against head. That night, our neighbours were eerily silent. After their exhausting day, new fears and several humiliations, these captives must have been fully spent. Perhaps they would spin emptily into sleep, the sleep of concussion where the numberless torn animals of the mind scurry, huddling in doubtful crevices.

Towards midnight, I felt a flop at the foot of my bed and heard a happy meow. Our cell door was made from steel bars but we'd fitted 18 small frames of mosquito screens, the lowest of which was left open for the cat.

Sitting up, I saw the young puss had something in her mouth that explained her unusual absence. It was a kitten; a few days old, and the lone survivor of her first litter. Mother cat deposited her child between my knees, and then curved down onto my bedsheet, rolling on her back and squirming with bright musical yelps. This was not the joy of motherhood. She simply wanted to revel in the splendour of a magic trick astoundingly performed, the production of that little thing. Rick pronounced this as a bad omen.

'You watch, she'll be a rotten mother.' No special knowledge there. Rick saw all of God's creatures damned, but he would be right about that cat. 'Lucky she didn't take it next door, they would've eaten them both.'

Sharon was already at our table when, one day later, I arrived for our next visit. We canoodled for a few minutes before turning to local news.

'So, were you impressed with my American friend?' I was asking of Dean Reed.

'He seemed OK. Nice.' Sharon adjusted her wrist bracelet with one finger.

'Er, is that it? Nice?' So much for a character analysis of he who was to disperse lumps of cash to have me freed.

'Well, we met, had a drink. Chatted, you know. Then Dean left. He had to go somewhere.'

Escape

I began a gentle cross-examination.

'Uh-huh. A lot of people at the Oriental?'

'No. Well, we ended up at a place called the Rembrandt. It was easier for Dean, apparently. Though not much, I guess. He was a bit late.'

'So when you called him yesterday, that was the arrangement?' I had to keep prompting.

'Mm . . . no, we agreed to meet this morning. And Dean called about nine-something, and suggested the Rembrandt at eleven.' Sharon moved food things around our table as though it were time to move on. I would not.

'OK, what was he wearing, by the way?'

'A suit, tie.' Sharon made sham crazy-eyes. 'We met in the lobby, if that helps you. I gave him that bag of your clothes, just like you asked.'

'I don't suppose you remember if he was wearing a watch?'

'Yes. Gold. Looked new.'

'His phone switched on?'

'No!'

'How'd you pick up on that?'

Sharon rocked her head from side to side. 'I wouldn't have, except that when I told Dean I was going to get this man to let me use his phone, because he was late – like I *said* – Dean took out his phone and said the battery was dead anyway. Which is why he had to go early, I suppose, to his next thing.'

'Ah, right. Say, who was the man with the working phone?' I asked casually.

'He was in the lobby, too. Didn't look like a tourist. Tall, fair hair. Waiting for someone who didn't arrive on time, as well. Or at all, because he left before Dean came.'

I took up the narrative. 'And this man got tired of waiting. And you said you were waiting, too. Perfectly natural, and his phone never rang. He made some calls to his late friends. Twice. The second time to say he wouldn't wait any longer – did this man use the bathroom?'

Escape

'No, smarty-pants, he went off to the business centre, and how did you know? What is this – the Spanish Inquisition?'

'No, honeybun.' I held Sharon's hands. 'I'm trying to do something about being here. But it's like playing chess by mail, one long move at a time. I'm just trying to find out if Dean's the genuine article.' I took a drink. 'Well, I know he's *not*, but he is an oddity, and sometimes oddities will do things others won't, or can't.'

Sharon relaxed a little. 'I suppose I should say that the mystery man gave me a lift back to my hotel.'

'Really. And I suppose he had his car and driver panting in the driveway as you walked out of the Rembrandt?'

'He was quite charming,' Sharon said with assurance. 'Not a problem at all.'

'OK. One last thing. Did Dean leave you with a drink or something to keep you seated as he walked away?'

'No. Dean left, and I had to use the loo.'

'Good. And Dean wasn't taking a car because it would be easier to walk, what with the traffic and all?'

'Yes.'

'Fine.' I'd finished.

'That all?'

'All done, sweetheart.' And with that, I leaned back and assumed an expression of thoughtfulness.

'Well?' Sharon wanted the results.

'OK,' I began. 'It's not much. The mystery man – in a suit, too, no doubt – was a stiff, all right. Whoever he is, he wasn't working with Dean, or he wouldn't need to give you a lift to find out the name of your hotel. And he wanted to see who you were meeting. By the way, Dean keeps his watch in his pocket when he visits me. That just means he'd prefer me not to know how he spends his research-and-development money. I'm not worried about him padding his expenses. To be expected. Dean kept his phone off because he talks a lot of shit to a lot of people, and it cramps his style to mix them up if one of them calls. All I can suggest is to keep an eye out for mystery men.'

Escape

Sharon liked the sound of that. After she'd given me a description of her new friend, we dropped the subject of Dean Reed. He had promised to call her soon. I didn't tell her that I thought it likely that the man in the suit had come from Dean's world without Dean knowing it. That was an unhappy thought, and one Sharon need not carry. I would not question her in such depth again. Sharon did not deserve to have the weight of my black creations forced upon her. Besides, she was not made for sleuthing.

These probable intrigues were disheartening, but so far Dean had not proved all mouth and trousers, so when next he visited – as expected, within a week – I gave him a note for another ten thousand dollars.

CHAPTER NINE

The photographs Sharon had taken of the wall revealed a featureless drop without footholds. The upper rim held a metre of barbed wire threaded with electric cable running between insulators.

Sten was visiting fellow Swedes in Building Two the morning these photos arrived, so I asked him to tell Martyn that I'd meet him at church on Sunday. Martyn would know all about Klong Prem's wiring by now.

These thoughts were interrupted by Jet, who had just collected the day's ice from the fish-wagon-ambulance-ice-cart. Next to my desk he had the large ice chest open, with all our plastic bags of chicken, beef, vegetables and blocks of butter stacked on its upturned lid. For some reason, that day Jet was breaking the ice blocks with a pick at a distance from me of less than a foot. I said nothing as my coffee mug and hair filled with shards of flying ice.

'Sorry, my teacher,' said Jet, laughing despite himself, and becoming more frenzied with his ice picking.

'All right, Jet. What is it? What do you want?' I stood up, brushing flecks of ice from my shirt.

Jet explained that he was so busy supervising our laundrymen each day, he would need help with the daily ice grind. He tapped the pick's handle, toed the ice chest and shook his head at the shattered blocks, as if to say: look what I have to work with!

'Got anyone in mind?' I asked with a smile. Not surprisingly, he did.

Escape

'A good man. Nice boy – he has no family, nothing. Not money. He eats shit.' Shit was one of Jet's favourite English words.

'We already have two laundrymen on the payroll, Jet. And a food collector, plus your own servant – whatever *he* does – and that idiot who's supposed to be a carpenter. And an ironing man and those two twits you hired last week. Where are they, and what do they do?'

Jet shrugged, professionally.

'All right, Squirt.' I gave up. 'Bring him over this afternoon. We can always use another orphan.'

Sten returned from Building Two carrying an old video player barely disguised in a sack. Martyn had brought the antique VHS machine back to life.

'Any movies?' I asked.

'Not yet.' Sten slid the sack into a cupboard. 'Only the one Martyn was using to get it working. Some Hong Kong chop-socky movie starring Fuck-me. He says he'll be over at Building Ten by eleven.'

Building Ten was the venue for church services, held each Sunday. There was no actual church, and the service was conducted in the yard under the short-termers' block, attracting mostly Africans. The hymn-singing must have sounded wild and threatening to the Thais, whose meditative chants were directed at a god not so hard of hearing.

Martyn and I moved away from the shoulder-rattling roar of the chorus, taking care not to stare directly at the wire-topped wall.

'What do you think?' I asked Martyn.

'No real hazard.' Martyn swept his eyes across the electric wire. 'Connected to the 240-volt mains. No transformers that I can see, so you'd have to be well-earthed to get any arcing.'

'So, what's all this stuff about people being fried on the wire?'

'Only expectations.' Martyn thought that those few who had climbed near the wire had felt a tickle through their sweat. Fear was enough to make them fall to the ground.

Escape

'Staying in Six?' he asked.

'I have to. Six's got four major walls just to get to where we are now, but I cut off my options if I go anywhere else,' I said, outlining the new plan.

Rather than deal with cell bars and scale five walls, I would take advantage of a friendship formed with some of the Frenchmen I'd met in Klong Prem, allowing me access to the car-repair yard. Although the prison's autoshop in Building Six was more or less off-limits to foreigners, a tiny patch of ground had been allocated to an old Frenchman whose poor health rendered him harmless.

Jean-Claude rarely moved from his chair beneath a tamarind tree, where he spent his days reading books on mysticism. The old man's career with the underground *médicaments sans frontières* had ended with his arrest for keeping a bucketful of amphetamine tablets under his bed. Night-time snacking had made him too talkative, resulting in a morning arrest. Here in Klong Prem, Jean-Claude's needful condition provided an excuse to visit. The old man's meals were brought by his compatriot, Raymond, who was the best cook in KP. Already I'd given Raymond books for Jean-Claude about psychiatric curiosities; they were much in vogue at the time, and, unaccountably, sent in large numbers to us by the British embassy.

The greatest difficulty with the new plan would be the high level of cooperation needed from people outside the prison. It would require a VW combivan to be modified with internal panels to provide at least coffin-space for one person. Raymond was supposed to be on good terms with a guard who arranged the private repair jobs in the Klong Prem area. The doctored Volkswagen would be delivered to the guard for a re-spray. This van would then be brought in to Building Six by the guard, painted during the week and returned for collection on the following Monday. This guard normally drove these vehicles out of the prison before noon. Once inside, I would not be missed until early evening.

'How many people would knowingly be involved?' Martyn, I could tell, saw more ifs in this plan than I.

Escape

'Certainly not the guard. He would believe only that it would be just another repair job. Probably old Jean-Claude. If the van is parked in a bad spot, he might need to pull a heart attack as a distraction. I've got a friend outside who can make up the secret panel.' I was thinking of my former Thai partner, Myca. Then I stopped talking, waiting for comment. None came.

In the pause between psalms, I asked Martyn, 'What do you think are the odds?'

'From that, not knowing who the people are—'

'No,' I interrupted. 'I mean the odds against anyone getting out of here using any scheme.'

'Well, since no one has ever done it, there's no percentage success rate from which to draw a table,' Martyn began in his considered-opinion mode. 'Imagine this. You're sworn to secrecy and led to a ginormous warehouse. Big enough for a Saturn Five rocket. Inside, this warehouse is filled with black marbles. Billions of them. But there's just one red marble. You go inside where it's pitch dark. You've been asked to select only one marble, and you flop around in there being bruised before realising nothing you do is going to make any difference. So, you grab one, and ask to come out.

'In the bright sunlight, you find yourself holding the one red marble. You think you're pretty special but your hosts tell you that everyone in the world comes to this warehouse at least once in his life. All six billion of us. You still think you're special, and damned lucky, too, till you ask what's the prize for the red-marble picker, and they say, "Oh, nothing. We don't give a monkey's who picks what. We just don't give a toss. After all, sooner or later someone had to pick the red ball."

'Look at all those people singing to the heavens, praising a creator.' Martyn gestured to the congregation who had now turned to the real business of the morning, trade. 'They feel pretty special. Around all the stars with all their planets, there had to come a creature who would one day think about the rarity of his existence. We're probably the only creatures in this galaxy who try to build machines like ourselves, but it had to happen some time. We feel special, and we just can't help it. We can more easily tell our hearts to stop beating than prevent ourselves from instantly forming theories based on the feeblest throb from any one of our senses. Add sight and sound, and the thing becomes a fact. Tell another of your experience and a universal truth is born. We're programmed for this. Seeing something special in red marbles used to save our lives. Don't worry about how people judge the odds, David. Let the plan evolve, one thoughtful jump at a time.'

French Raymond was in our office cooking us lunch that afternoon. A new set of coiled elements on our electric stove produced iron-foundry heat that forced him to keep both wooden spoon and spatula constantly scouring deep into the large wok.

'Always, I like to work fast,' Raymond said. 'Outside, I am the same. Fast.'

Raymond was four years into a twenty-five-year sentence for a trifling eighty-five grams he'd been moving too fast to conceal at the airport. He would soon be repatriated to France to itch through a few years more at St Denis prison before release. Raymond was not a career criminal, yet non-judgemental enough to help those who were. Like many in Klong Prem, he was simply careless with his drugs. His one earlier drug arrest had occurred in rare circumstances (bus stop, bomb threat) in Paris, and after Thailand he would end his courtship with heroin.

The food was ready. While standing close to Raymond as he plated five servings, I was advised, 'The man you need to speak to is Luc. The friend of old Jean-Claude, not in the autoshop, he's in the hospital. Sick, dying I'm sure. I told Jean-Claude you'll go there next week. He visits his friend often.'

As a young man, the now-dying Luc had put himself about in Algeria with his friends until no longer welcome. Rejoining some of his group, Luc went to Vietnam, making soldierly trouble before moving on to Thailand. From stories he had heard, Raymond thought that Luc's old mercenary chums were just the team to weld and shape the VW van into the habitable steel vault I would need for the autoshop plan. I was less sure.

After we had done with Raymond's duck, Jet served slices of panettone to go with some pineapple wine aged since August. While playing the butler, Jet chewed the scenery, brandishing his tray to get our attention. He wanted to secure the introduction of the latest stray into our family.

'All right.' Sten took the tray from Jet. 'Let's see your iceman.'

Jet led forward a short young man with Persian features who would have been stocky had there been more flesh on his bones. Jet shoved a chair behind his knees, and he sat perspiring under a permastubble over transparent skin that revealed blue veins.

'So, you're looking for a career in frozen goods, young fellow?' I tried to sound avuncular. My mispronounced Thai was different from the mispronunciations of this newcomer, so he held a frozen smile without comprehending.

Jet took over the interview. 'His Thai is shit, my teacher said.' Jet explained that Arib, as the Thais called him, spoke some Persian, incomprehensibly accented Arabic, gutter Thai and a few words of English. He had no first language to share with anyone else. An only child, he recalled only the cooing of a Kurdish nurse from infancy and had never been to any school.

'So, how old are you, Arib?' He looked 30, I thought.

'Ah, I not know exactly—'

Jet flew in, 'Twenty-four, we think, but no one—'

'Shut the fuck up, Jet,' Sten said kindly. 'Let him speak! He's got the bullshit ice picker-upper's job, OK. We're just asking.'

After some time pooling languages, we found that Arib was probably born in Jordan, but had been moved to an aunt and uncle in Isfahan when aged about five. The couple told Arib that his parents were dead, blaming some warring factions, and they did not burden Arib with any schooling in their large, cold-floored house. Arib did not learn to read, so his memory of place names, and even dates, had been garbled with new accents. At some point the Isfahan house was sold, and Arib was given a little money, a ticket and a passport of some kind ('Red!' claimed Arib, responding to our subsequent question, pointing to a cucumber) as he was taken to the airport. From there, the 16-year-old Arib landed in one of the Gulf states (don't ask), where his new uncle's driver collected him and took him to this uncle's house, where Arib was promptly forgotten. Neglected in the social sense; there is no starvation, physical pain or sexual misuse in this story.

Within 18 months, Arib and his new uncle moved to Thailand. This new uncle was a Jordanian diplomat, Arib thought, although he was unable to recall His Excellency's name, and was too shy to ask the servants, and even less inclined to ask his uncle's frequently changing Thai girlfriends, who left the big house in taxis.

'Is this poor cunt simple, or what?' Sten exasperated, now conceding Jet's authority in such matters of the street. Jet assured us that Arib was simply without communication skills.

After a few months in the new house, the new uncle was called away on affairs of state more and more often; sometimes absent for weeks at a time. Arib, tiring of the maid's food and her Udon Thani nattering, began sorties into Bangkok. Having no money, Arib mostly walked. He apparently made some friends, and would spend nights away from home. Following a week away from his uncle's house, he returned home to find the maid gone. A caretaker, previously unknown to Arib, told him that the master had returned to Jordan. Arib returned to the streets and his new friends, and was soon arrested for what we would call vagrancy.

Arib's one-year sentence for being poor had been completed, and he now found himself in the unfortunate position of being a stateless foreigner.

'How long ago did he finish his sentence?' I asked Jet, who then turned not to Arib but to the circle of bent old men outside our office who hungrily scooped rice at the carpenter's table. '*Meua-rai?*' yelled Jet.

'Five years!' – 'It'd be five, easily.' – 'A *good* five,' agreed the wrinkled KP pundits without pausing in their gumming, or looking up.

A considerate five, according to the prison authorities, for Arib would normally have been sent to the notorious Immigration Detention Center to starve, or to the insane asylum, where by now he would be mad. In losing Arib's file, the prison authorities had performed an act of kindness.

'So, can he stay, my teacher?' asked Jet after sending Arib to the taps with our dishes.

'Of course, Jet,' I replied. 'Let's not give him the ice-pick for a day or two, eh? Start him off with the basics of carrying the blocks, just so he doesn't get lost.'

Old Jean-Claude was not yet at the hospital when I arrived, so I used a few minutes with the doctor complaining of kidney stones. The doctor had no particular experience with renal calculi but gave me what I wanted: an appointment for an X-ray in Building Nine. That was the AIDS hospice, adjacent to Building Six, and on my list for study, as it was one block closer to the wall.

The hospital honoured a Thai-prison architectural tradition of impressive façades, with its reception and administration area appearing newly glassed and brightly gloss-painted. The doctor made a practised speech about the need for constant donations in order to provide the latest equipment. He did not seem a total incompetent, just supremely uninterested in his patients.

Near these consulting rooms was a newly built, air-conditioned suite with an engraved sign in English: INTENSIVE CARE UNIT. Looking through its glass porthole, I saw what could have been a guestroom from any one of Bangkok's four-star hotels. Except that there were heart monitors, respirator pumps and machines with many dials, their connecting tubes neatly looped, and their casings covered by colourless matt plastic. In one corner stood a dialysis machine. None of these devices surrounding the large bed was in use.

The gently breathing lump under the silk bedspread had a face I recognised. That of Police Major General Prompon Phoont'ang, admired for his investigation into the case of the Saudi royal gems robbery.

Escape

Some years earlier, Thai servants had stolen the personal jewellery of some princelings while working at a Saudi palace. The jewels had found their way to Thailand, and an investigation began. The palace worker had sold the gems to Thai dealers, one of whose wife and child had been found dead in a staged car accident. Anything royal is always a serious matter in Thailand, so Major-General Phoont'ang took immediate charge of the case. A combination of brutality and inducement quickly led to a recovery of part of the haul.

Everyone concerned was pleased with the outcome until the gems were examined after their return to the princelings. Over a quarter were fakes. Phoont'ang had somehow arranged for glass copies to be substituted for the rubies, emeralds and diamonds. The Major-General and some of his lieutenants were arrested, and since then witnesses were being systematically killed before any might testify to a link with Phoont'ang. The Saudis later sent a businessman to investigate. He, too, was abducted and killed.

This Major-General was someone with whom I should speak, so I called for the hospital trusty to arrange an appointment. The trusty soon appeared. A wild-eyed marionette, so wired on hospital amphetamines that he rarely stood still.

'Impossible, good sir.' The trusty skipped and bounced at the porthole. 'The general is sleeping now.' He then made stagey hard-guzzling gestures with an imaginary bottle and a long arm, and then winked, 'Two bottles of whisky. Every day,' proudly thumbing his chest to credit the regular supply of Phoont'ang's medicine.

'Anyway, today's show is about to start. Come and see!'

I paid for a seat, and was then shown to the darker of two operating theatres. I sat in a chair near the door so I could watch for Jean-Claude's arrival. A withered Thai patient had been lifted to the dark-green vinyl of the operating table. The small audience gasped as a sheet was removed by a trusty with a magician's flourish to reveal a man whose chronic infections had rendered the flesh of both legs no more than gnarled bark.

'He's alive,' insisted the trusty-nurse. 'Come and feel his pulse!'

Escape

We spectators suspected some ugly surprise in this, and no one moved.

From a curtain, I caught sight of Jean-Claude's matchstick legs walking along a corridor. I stood to leave.

'But wait,' called the trusty. 'See the bones.' He lifted the long-dead husk of thigh muscle and skin whose underside dripped from the pustulations below to reveal a surprisingly clean femur. I left the theatre as the stench of putrefaction reached my nostrils.

Jean-Claude was seated at the bedside of his old soldier friend, his head bowed, and with a long webbed curtain of yellow hair half-covering his face. There was no conversation between the two. I brought a chair from the doorway of the half-empty ward, and sat next to Jean-Claude. The ward's beds were steel-framed relics, only one step up from the sponge mats used everywhere else in the prison. The other patients, perhaps ten, were quiet, although one would sometimes find the strength to cough.

'I've brought that Temple Grandin article for you.' I rolled an old *New Yorker* as a tube, and then had to close Jean-Claude's fingers around it so it would not drop.

Jean-Claude looked up and spoke. 'Thanks. You know, I first met poor Luc in Phnom Penh. That was before Pol Pot ended everything. He was quite something, then. No man could play tricks on him in those days.'

There was to be no talk of secret vans and escapes that day. Luc's eyes were now open only as slits, through which a milky fluid was turning crystalline. I felt his wrist, and lifted it as slightly as possible. Guessing, I thought Luc had been dead for less than 24 hours. Luc – or perhaps some friend – had folded and packed his shirts and two books in a plastic bag placed next to his bed. I spoke with Jean-Claude for some time, and then walked with him back to Building Six. It was no big thing to see the minivan-stowaway scheme die as well. The story of these old men surely must be at an end.

After lunch the following day, Raymond called by with a gift for me from Jean-Claude. It was a hand-made leather belt in good condition. Stitched into a panel on its left side was a bird's feather.

Raymond looked doubtful as he gave it to me. 'It was Luc's, you know.'

'I'm not superstitious,' I said, unrolling the belt. 'And it's just my size. What kind of bird do you suppose this is? Looks like a hawk's feather.'

'I don't think so.' Raymond squinted at the quill. 'Maybe the bumfeather from a dodo.'

The visit pens were crowded when I arrived to see Dean Reed. Crowded with 50 Nigerians who, after a dozen or more years of imprisonment, were finally hearing words of hope. Two Nigerian embassy representatives had that month flown in from Lagos to find some solutions to an old problem. Nigeria kept no diplomatic offices in Bangkok, so it had been impossible for Nigerian convicts to renew their passports. Without that basic facility, these prisoners could not begin to request royal pardons from the Thai government.

Klong Prem's 120 long-serving Nigerian inmates were excited by the prospect of release, but much remained to be done. Photographs taken, forms completed and, most troublesome, money to be found for airfares home. Thailand would be happy to see the Nigerians go, but was not willing to pay for that happiness. The bigger smugglers had started a fund, so far contributing only for themselves and their friends. Debts were being called in, and threats and promises made. Embassy officials scribbling some prisoners' home contacts. It was noisy.

'You're looking sharp,' I called to Dean Reed.

'I shouldn't be. It's been a hard week.'

Eric, the slimiest of the visit trusties, began herding the Nigerians from the visit pens. Someone they had been expecting had failed to arrive. Dean looked towards Eric, but I shook my head. To pay Eric for the use of the lawyers' cage would spark his curiosity. Eric would always want to know who wanted privacy so that he might not miss any opportunity for blackmail.

Escape

'So, Dean. It's been over four months. No one will agree to terms?'

'Well, they agree to terms all right.' Dean held the bars with both hands. 'But not for the kind of money we have.'

Dean detailed the list of people in need of fixing. A judge, a prosecutor, some policemen and all the spongy cement that held them together. A total of a quarter of a million dollars.

'That seems a lot for my small case. Less than 200 grams found – and found not with me, only in the large airport I once used.' I added that this price was about five times the amount Bangkok assassins would charge to kill them all, 'Just by way of a comparison.'

Dean shrugged. 'There are complications. A small case, in some ways. But people are . . . interested in you.'

That would have been a moment to ask about the mysterious suit who'd spoken to Sharon at the Rembrandt. Yet there was no point. If Dean had spotted any surveillance, either he would have told me or he would have done something about it. If he were blind to spooks, telling Dean would not improve his eyesight, and might scare him out of the game. Either way, more money would not help.

I folded my arms, and leaned forward. 'Dean, I think we need to stop being golden geese. Keep things simple. Keep in mind that the single object that would get me out of here is no more than a piece of paper. A piece of paper sent from the court at six any evening. You can manufacture that paper.'

I gave Dean my own list of people: minor functionaries who dealt with court papers, those who carried the documents from court, the jailers who stamped bail orders when received, and those who passed them on to others who unlocked the lucky few after nine each night. 'You've talked your way in here for months using bogus embassy letters. How hard can it be to make bogus court papers?'

'Possible. Yes, possible,' Dean answered too quickly, so I knew he had something else in mind. 'David, I don't want any more money.'

I wasn't expecting that.

Escape

'If you give me a contact, one in Europe, I mean – I'll do the business. Just a kilo or so. That is, I'll make the money we need, come back, and then it will be one, two, three!' Dean snapped his fingers. 'All I really need is someone you know who'd be ready to see me.'

Now, that was something to wonder at. Never before had Dean mentioned going into trade. I returned to Building Six thinking of someone suitable who could be ready to welcome Dean Reed with all the care his efforts deserved.

CHAPTER TEN

April, and the Songkran water festival, when unimprisoned Thais cheekily splash water on one another in a celebration of life. At Klong Prem, the mutual bucketing altered the canvas of the jail in one big wet, with no one truly joyous, just going about the business of survival with the addition of drenched clothes.

Sten and Swiss Theo had built a hut behind the chief's office, and had both taken up hobbies. Sten's included making oil paintings that took longer to explain than to paint. In lighter colours, Theo painted wobbly tables and chairs of his own making to ward off his fear of a long sentence. He then painted the walls of their hut, the outside of the chief's temple and nearby trees, and had begun whitening the kerbstones leading to the gate of Building Six.

Calvin had been sentenced to 25 years, the minimum for attempted export. 'That's OK. I'm pleased with that,' he'd said, looking suicidal.

Dean Reed had submerged into his new mission as a smuggler without asking for any further guidance. He had abandoned his supposed European plans and had asked for friends I might have in Australia. I presumed he had left Thailand. After some time, a huge care package had arrived from Dean postmarked Hat Yai, southern Thailand, containing useless and expensive clothing, carved boxes, delicate Japanese prints, religious ornaments and hand-made stationery. All carefully wrapped in tissue paper under flocked gift-wrap. Everything smelled of incense. No note.

Escape

Charlie Lao had been granted a royal pardon, at last. One night, in a rush, he ran to cell No. 57, and had breathlessly shown me the long-awaited document. Simply worded, but bearing a huge regal seal. 'I have to go to Sydney,' Charlie had said, then promised, 'I'll be back.'

My little cat was growing, although not well. Her mother had lost interest in nursing after less than a week, and then the kitten had been kidnapped. Jet put up reward posters, and Dinger – so named because her mother had been gonged on the head by a guard – was returned. (The posters made the threat that further kidnappings would be costly.) Her captors had fed her spicy food, resulting in long-term intestinal damage. Cats in KP learned to move fast. As soon as they grew beyond cuteness, they would often become subjects of the inmates' surgical experiments. Dinger now required especially bland food to restore her health. Our cook, the middle-aged cheque-kiter Bo-Jai, was kind enough to prepare each day a tiny portion of milk-boiled chicken. Bo-Jai ran his busy evening-meal takeaway service from the boot shop. It was Sten who'd privately renamed him Blow-Job. (Due to his physical similarity to Goldfinger's Odd Job, and his aikido skills – the surly, brusque chef would sooner grill customers than kiss them.) Each evening, Jet would fetch the stack of steel tins from Bo-Jai with the tiny tin for our ailing cat.

Americans Big Bill and Andy had disappeared. Suspicions about the pair's resilience became very strong when they began to have frequent visits from two DEA agents dressed in the matching black suits of Jehovah's doorsteppers. Bill and Andy had agreed to return temporarily to the US to appear as state's witnesses against a Chicago rookery of Nigerian smugglers. After testifying, Bill and Andy would be returned to Klong Prem despite their unwritten contract with the DEA, which included quick transfer back to a US prison followed immediately by parole.

Referring to his former employees, Big Bill said, 'Those idiots, they even paid for one of our tickets using a stolen credit card,' this lapse presumably making Big Bill's role as state's witness a fair response. 'No wonder the Feds knew all about them.' Andy held fears of a hatchet job once back in KP by agents of the Nigerians. Neither would be in any danger. The damage of the testimony would have been done, the fallen quickly forgotten and the Nigerians saw no value in financing an unprofitable revenge for those whose luck had failed. As for DEA policy, clearly its administrators were now demonstrating that there would be no more collusion with the drug traffickers to the point of nominating potential couriers such as those I'd met in Bumbudt. Collusion would now be limited to striking a deal for prosecution testimony, a tradition too useful to sacrifice.

By the time the waters of Songkran had dried, I had surveyed almost every foreigner who'd shown any inclination for escape. After eliminating those who were incapacitated, and those unlikely to keep silent, the list was short. Just Sten from Sweden, Theo and I forming the vanguard of a non-existent counterforce.

'And if I hear anyone suggest an escape committee, I'll quit!' Sten said, although none of us held illusions of team spirit.

The next month's court hearing brought some new faces to the show. As I shuffled along a corridor to the courtroom, I was given a beaming smile from the police major who'd arrested me in Chinatown. He had never appeared at court before this day. With him was a tall, urbane Westerner in an expensive suit, and I intuitively thought of him as the friendly gent Sharon had met at the Rembrandt. After taking my seat at the defence table, I asked Montree who he might be.

'An American. He's with the major.' Montree tapped the desk, indicating that no more information had been given.

This day's witness was a seedy police detective wearing a black leather jacket. He claimed to have found a bag at the airport. A bag containing 200 grams of heroin. He also said that he had seen me at the airport that day.

'Don't ask him anything, Montree. Please,' I said when the time came for cross-examination.

Escape

'I didn't plan to,' Montree whispered to me, at the same time smiling at the judge. Montree knew the policeman would have been well schooled to say bad things if asked any wider questions.

As I returned to the holding cages, a great fuss of guards' shouting broke out near the parking bay. The prisoners' buses had been moved for some important arrival. Then, two new, sparkling police cars arrived at speed, between which a black Lexus with tinted windows and glaring halogens was guided to the cage doors. A bemedalled policeman quickly stepped out to open the rear door of the modest limo.

Police Major-General Prompon Phoont'ang jauntily stepped from the darkness, dressed in inappropriately tight shorts, a golfing T-shirt and top-shelf white trainers. No chains, of course. He was trying to give a carefree impression, smiling at everyone, winking and finger-pointing at the respectful guards as he took a cage alone.

In a short time, the guards left him, having covered their bets by asking politely if all of Phoont'ang's needs had been met. Within a few minutes, I walked to his cage, and then paused, trying to think of a way of introducing myself. This proved unnecessary.

'Come in, Westlake,' laughed the Major-General, as though my name alone was a great source of hilarity. (Perhaps 'Westlake' means shithead in Thai, for this was not the first time a Thai had enjoyed speaking my name.) It was not yet noon, and Phoont'ang was drunk. 'Welcome!'

It would have been impolite to ask immediately about the faked Saudi royal jewels, so I simply complained about the length of our trials.

'That doesn't matter. A long time can be good.' Phoont'ang clapped his hands in slow motion. 'No witnesses.'

Ordinarily, a man of such high rank and power as Phoont'ang would have had no trouble avoiding punishment, but it had been an indirect offence to Thai royalty to filch another royal's personal knick-knacks. I hinted to the Maj-Gen. that he might have to wait for the quiet of the appeal courts to get free. When he didn't respond, I set out my reasoning in a disinterested yet respectful tone.

Finally, Phoont'ang sat up from his bench and gently clapped me on one shoulder.

'Westlake,' he said warmly. 'Very sorry. You're fucked. Everybody knows.'

When a stranger tells you that which everyone seems to know, you might as well believe it. Yet, to understand why my case was hopeless, I would have to think back to the days leading to my capture. As always happens after each life-wrecking arrest, I had shed the memory as a snake sheds a skin that becomes too tight. Now, I must revisit that discarded husk, and pick over its scales for clues.

CHAPTER ELEVEN

In the months before my journey to Thailand, I had been living in a small flat in the renovation of a 1960s motel that had been bypassed by a motorway leading to the airport. There, I kept only my name and clothing, so nothing for which I cared. But the bed was large and comfortable, and I was prepared to check out at any time without notice. Each day, with $5,000 and a passport in my tracksuit pockets, I would take a morning run, skirting the playing fields of parkland, ducking through bracken and ascending over the rubble to the high ridges of an old railway line to stop and view the nearby cityscape of Melbourne. This routine would also allow the first shift of detectives to let themselves into the flat to poke around. More widely, my phones were tapped, I'd found (and left in place) bugs in my office furniture, and this early-morning riffle through my drawers was for them no more than an eye-opener before beginning a day's four-car surveillance.

Most youthful indiscretions are forgivable. Some are not. Unlawfully – or even legally – making a fortune before the age of 20 is unpardonable in any land. It didn't matter that twice since I'd lost and re-made that fortune, there would be no forgiveness. Newer religions might aspire to fundamentalist rigour, but nothing tops Christianity for eternal damnation.

Two previous police groups had exhausted their funding, so these surveillance tasks were now maintained by the Target Identification Branch, a federal agency. Every three months federal and state agencies would exchange these duties until one of them could convince the boss that a dedicated taskforce would be worth the investment.

For me, an impractical amount of each day was taken up merely communicating with friends: burying my car in the concrete of big car parks before taking trains and taxis to meetings, locating un-tapped payphones away from telescopic lenses to make calls. Inevitably, the time came when I needed to speak with distant friends using real names and dates. At the same time, new equipment had been installed in the capital's phone-tapping bunker, making every phone in the country unsafe. I would need to travel, just to talk.

'You could do nothing, and wait for the police to go away.' This was Michael, a friend formed strong within the pressure of our carbon mountain, where lives are lived under heavy condemnation and risk, producing mostly coal dust, but the occasional gem such as he.

'Or I could grow old and die' – although I doubted that Michael was making a serious suggestion. We were standing at the front gate of Michael's suburban house. Parked at the kerbside, 100 metres away, stood a white delivery van with mirrored rear windows.

'Let's move into the garden.' Michael nodded at the van. 'Maybe they have a lip-reader today.'

Michael and I had worked together, on and off, for over 15 years, although we'd met earlier by chance just before dawn at the Electro Doghouse, which sold takeaway hot dogs, and in those days was one of the few places open around the clock. Michael was dressed in a buckskin jacket and wore snakeskin boots. I carried a cane and wore a large felt hat. I was new to the game and foolishly wore the uniform. We had both finished work for the night, having quietly met our last customers at the Doghouse.

Michael's ex-presidential convertible was parked by the pavement rubbish bin, and I spoke as we both dumped our unopened hotdogs in the bin.

'Looks like it'll be a fine morning,' I declared.

Escape

'It sure does, but I won't get to see much of it,' Michael said. 'I work nights. I'm a waiter.'

'Really, now there's a coincidence. So am I.' As I spoke, a police cruiser had eased around a corner. 'But let's not wait here.'

Now, 17 years later, we sat on the cushions of two large cane chairs under a cloud of microscopic summer insects rising from the untended ferns of Michael's back garden.

'No other way?' Michael stared through his rusting incinerator drum, which had burned more evidence than Saigon's embassies. 'You've tried phoning Thailand, I suppose?'

'The usual waste of time. Tommy's wall of voodoo goes up. And, of course, yes is always the answer, even when all the questions are misunderstood. I get yessed to death.'

So that I would not be missed by the watchers, my tour of Bangkok, Brussels, Copenhagen and London needed to be completed within five days, with a return by Friday lunchtime. I explained to Michael that I'd leave a wig and moustache in the bus-station lockers near Sydney airport for the return journey.

'How about passports?' Michael removed his wire-frame sunglasses to give them a needless polish. 'The forces of darkness know all our old names.'

'Indeed. I've left the birth certificate and application for a New Zealand passport lying around the office.' I stood up from my chair. 'The spooks couldn't have missed that. But I have a new one. Very deep, and another crap passport to sacrifice in Thailand.'

'You'll still be missed.' Michael didn't like the idea of the cops running around looking for me.

'Could be, and that's where I need your help.'

One thing on which I could absolutely rely was that my mobile phone was not only tapped, but also routinely traced to the nearest transponder. So, using a dictating machine, Michael and I recorded a phoney, but still guarded, three-minute conversation in which I hinted at an immediate journey to the Murray River marijuana fields. On a recent buying trip to the area, I had spotted a shadow (ultramarine T-shirt, black Nikes, city hair and a bumbag), so felt confident the watchers knew that I frequently visited the Italian countryfolk. As I gave the recorder to Michael, I told him what I thought it best to do.

'Wait until Wednesday next week. That'll be my last day in Bangkok. Go into Melbourne, downtown and on foot. Take my mobile and find a payphone out of sight. Dial my number. Of course, my phone will ring in your pocket, so answer it. Then, I think it's best if you play the recording into my mobile, not the landline in your other hand.'

Michael agreed that this trick should convince the monitors that I was still somewhere in the city, at least, rather than 10,000 miles away. Even so, 'Don't overdo it with the red herrings, David. That can excite them more if things seem too busy.'

I squeezed my hands together. 'I'm breaking the rules, anyway. I suppose, with this much heat, I'd be smarter to leave the country and not come back. Call it year-zero in a new land.'

An evil-eyed crow speared into the tall grass at the end of the garden, and Michael said, 'It's a long way to go to make a few phone calls.' Then, smiling, 'Good luck.'

The portly young man sat in my office waiting for the laser printer to deliver a sheet. I sat at the desk. He had covertly entered the premises by the back door, a task slowed by the fact that there was no back door.

Barry plucked some remaining twigs from his jacket, and we began.

'It's you.' I feigned surprise. 'I didn't recognise you under that beard. And you're all wet! Take off that sou'wester and sit down.'

'Thanks. I could use a drink.'

'Sure.' I rattled the ice in my Coke. 'So, tell me. How'd it go?'

'Well, the third Zodiac sprang a leak, but other than the usual thing with Gomez, it was a breeze.'

'I thought you might've had trouble with the handshake.'

'No, my granddad was a mason,' Barry answered. 'By the way, Maxwell Kenton gave me a message. You're to go to the beach hut in Esperance next Tuesday. He'll call you then from St Kitts.'

'How do I get in?'

'He left the key in a barky bole of a tree at the back. The one that looks like a big W on the grassy knoll.' Barry made a coughing noise. 'What's in this drink?'

'Your usual,' I assured. 'Absinthe with – oh, sorry. I'm fresh out of persimmons. Kumquats OK?'

'Yeah, I guess. Are we all right for New Year's?'

'You bet. Just tell Damien to bring three trucks and park them away from the coast. We'll radio in on 468.75 megs. You want to write that down?'

'That's OK, I'll call if I forget.' Barry lowered his tone. 'Um, have you got any of that whatsit?'

'You mean the, ah, how's-your-father?'

'No, no. The thingummy with the slight, you know, look about it.' Barry made orchestra conductor's gestures.

'Oh, right. The wazzername. Yeah, sure, but put *well* away. It'll have to be tomorrow. I can only get it between two and three in the morning.'

'Well, if it's not too much hassle.' Barry was apologetic.

'A bit, but no problem. We'll make it Monday, say Sunday. No, Monday's fine.'

'S'Monday it is.' Barry understood. 'Where's the boss today? He told me to call some time.'

'Dammit,' I swore. 'Lost the number, but it's room 589. Sydney Hilton, under some cover name. Don't call between eight and eleven tomorrow night. It's all happening then. Wait until the Latvians have gone . . .'

And more of the same nonsense. When we'd finished, I led Barry down into the dark street, gave him tickets to four cities and advised, 'Just keep it up for a week. I'll be back by then. Even if they only follow up a tenth of that crap, they'll be stretched.'

'Dave, you really think the cops will go for any of it?'

'Maybe not. We were talking right on top of the bug. It's built into the drinks cabinet. Anyway, I'll pull it out tomorrow and dump it in the river. The more crap they think that lot is, the more they should believe Michael's call. By the way, did you really want me to get you some stuff?'

'No, not at all. Did you really think that? I was ad-libbing. You know, give it the touch.' Barry was the night porter at an edgy city hotel that I used sometimes for afternoon chemistry. He had ambitions as an actor.

'Don't ad-lib, Barry, I'm confused enough already.'

My travel schedule required a flight from Melbourne at lunchtime on Monday, then a flight to Bangkok arriving late that night. Australian immigration computers log details of all incoming and outgoing passengers, and for this exit I would use the new passport, gained in utter secrecy.

Passports could no longer be acquired safely by the simple mailing of the birth certificate of someone who had died in infancy. All new applicants were now required to appear in person at a local post office, where senior staff would check for their existence against entries in a National Health database. In addition, whoever countersigned the applicant's photograph – usually a doctor or dentist already on record – would be telephoned for confirmation.

The path through these traps lies with encouraging someone who's never had a passport to prepare all his documents, including having his photographs countersigned. Then, as may happen, all those documents are mislaid. A duplicate set, with a new photograph – but otherwise with all the same details – is then presented to Mr Postman. Should he call the doctor, the conversation would never turn to a description of the new applicant. Eye colour and height no longer figure on applications, even for biometric passports.

On arrival at Bangkok, I would not tarnish this pristine passport with the stamp of a 'country of interest', but present another. This second passport was not of such high pedigree, but good enough for moving into and out of Thailand. As this was in a different name, I had bought duplicate tickets. (Under the hard labour of three hours on five trains, and underground pedestrian links to a lunch-hour carnival of Vietnamese travel agents' shoplets beyond my watchers' eyes.)

Tuesday in Bangkok would begin at 7 a.m. with the first of an ambitious three meetings – I'd dreamed of more before considering the city's traffic jams – then a late-night flight with SAS to Belgium via Denmark.

On arrival at Copenhagen on Wednesday, I'd have the opportunity to unburden myself of the second passport I'd been using in Thailand. The Copenhagen transit lounge had a small post office, from where I could post the passport and any other bothersome documents back to Australia. (Sadly, that post office is these days landside, and there exists only one lonely red-and-bomb-proof postbox near the A-gates. Intrepid travellers must now bring their own stamps and apply caution as well.) I'd hoped a fellow traveller who was resident in Copenhagen could join me for the flight to Brussels, although I now doubt that Søren would have managed to get out of bed in time for an 11 o'clock morning flight.

By then in Europe, I would switch to an old British passport, the third in use for this five-day trip. European Union passports are not stamped for travellers anywhere within the continent. This UK passport was necessarily dog-eared. European officials, especially the British, regard new passports as objects to be thoroughly examined. The reverse is true of Australia, where holders of new and rarely used passports are considered good citizens. Perhaps the opposing attitude of customs inspectors is explained by their contrasting views of international travel. The English are expected to seek imperious amusement at the expense of foreigners, while Australians feel they should take foreignness in small doses. Alternatively, it may be that Britons so loathe their local neighbours, they take any opportunity to flee the cold, whereas any Australian daring to leave even temporarily his God-blessed and sun-kissed land cannot be less than a traitor in the eyes of airport officials. A careful smuggler in transit may only meet these prejudices, not dismiss them.

So, arriving in Brussels with Søren on Wednesday, we would taxi into town to meet Hanna at the superb Austrian patisserie in an arcade by the old Metropole Hotel. Straw-haired Hanna, originally from Saarbrücken, had just turned 31 and felt unhappy not having a Danish friend within her business network. Søren would meet Hanna; they would take each other's numbers, and their time at the café, while I would have to tear back to the airport for the afternoon Sabena flight to London, taking only a box of strawberry-custard glazed tarts (the finest in Europe) and Hanna's francs (the fairest).

Keeping to the third, UK, passport, I planned to arrive at Heathrow and sink into an Underground tube to arrive at Hammersmith in time to visit a self-storage locker before a meeting at a hotel in South Kensington. The hours between 7 and 9 p.m. would be set aside for anything spontaneous. Collapsing to the floor, for example.

At nine, with free time done, to the airport again, for a British Airways flight to Sydney, stopping at Singapore to refuel. There, another transit-lounge posting of documents, and a final bit of work on the passport on which I'd left Australia. Although it would already have an exit stamp from Sydney's Kingsford-Smith terminal, it would be otherwise blank. No record of any landing, anywhere.

I'd prepared a UK Immigration stamp using a toner-transfer sheet from Letraset that allows original artwork to be photocopied onto small sheets of plastic. This sheet would be hidden within my hand-luggage lining, and would include extra dates in case I missed any flights. I planned to apply this transfer-stamp to my passport in the aircraft toilet once airborne from Singapore, as many transit-lounge toilets have hidden security cameras. Finally, I'd made ticket stubs for the SYD-LHR-SYD-only travel that I would claim on arrival.

Arriving at Sydney on Friday morning (Thursday would be lost crossing the dateline), I was to retrieve my wig from the left-luggage depot, make a final posting and then board a domestic flight to Melbourne in time to make my one o'clock appointment with Melvin, my probation counsellor at our club for the reformed at Carlton Gardens – by then minus the wig, of course.

Escape

There are those among you who might argue against the ambition of this itinerary, and I shan't argue back – although I'd undertaken such intensity before without failure. That fall at Bangkok cannot be attributed to overreach or fatigue alone. There had to be more.

Monday morning. The Honda in which I'd been waltzing with surveillance police for the past months was now in an underground car park where it could do no harm. Police had earlier installed a tracking device in line with the radio's antenna. From the car park, the signal would not reach ground level. I was on board a flight from Melbourne wearing a grey-flecked wig and an itchy moustache.

After touchdown, I left the light disguise in a locker, then checked in and boarded the flight from Sydney to Bangkok. Not so much as a ripple of interest passed the eyes of the burly immigration officer as my new passport was scanned into his computer. Airborne, I was sure that no one knew of my departure. This much was true. Arriving in Thailand after midnight on Tuesday, I became Mr D. Westlake.

For many years I'd lived under the most severe observation and monitoring. That burden evaporated at altitude. Now, I became cleansed, as though by a transfusion from poisoned blood to pure ichor. Even more years had passed since last I'd stood in the land of the Thai. Finally, I had returned, and was immediately blasted with sense memories as I stepped into the heat outside Bangkok's Don Muang airport. Under a mask of aviation fuel, sweet-scented Arabic jasmine blossoms curled around the terminal from 200 taxis whose mirrors were draped with garlands. Ginger seared by cooking oil added to the mix, along with a confection of cosmetics-and-soap odours propagated by hard-working air-conditioners. The driver who took me into town couldn't understand why I wanted to keep the window open, what with half the smells of the city flowing in from the highway. For all my detailed scheduling for this week, I hadn't factored in the sudden loss of gravity that occurs when freedom mixes with a concentrated elixir of refreshed memories.

Escape

Still, such things are of no substance; only a sentimental milksop allows drops of time to interfere with business.

A polite but otherworldly voice woke me at 6 a.m. after I clawed across the bed into consciousness. I'd signed Westlake at the reception desk of the Oriental hotel just three hours earlier, and had booked a wake-up call before blacking out.

Barely awake, I walked from the hotel along Silom Road after dawn to check for watchers, and there were none. Stacks of newspapers lay unopened, and taxi drivers slept in their cars. The only sound in that near-empty street came from their cars' radios. Despite many years visiting Thailand, I'd never before heard the national anthem at that hour. Of course, I think this now but I'm sure it passed my mind then to keep walking, keep flying and speed to Europe. To unearth the Luxembourg money, and buy a house at the edge of the Mediterranean. Spend afternoons in the sun with the gardener's wine and the English papers, tut-tutting at others' follies. No, that thought never really came till later.

By seven, I was at the Montien hotel eating breakfast and reading *The Post*, waiting for Tommy. He was late.

In his younger days, Tommy had been one of the most well-travelled independent traffickers from Chiang Mai. His world map was studded with pins for all Europe's capitals. When travelling west, ports in the UAE, Morocco, British Columbia and California would welcome him before he went on to the frontiers of Auckland and Melbourne. Among Tommy's holdings sat the guesthouse in Chiang Mai, a safe haven in the north for any scratching hippie or tense foreign adventurer, for Tommy's assessing eye watched his guests' sleep patterns with a professional interest. His lodgers were never troubled by greedy local policemen or even unpaid board if Tommy saw them as potential dope connections. For these travellers were Tommy's, and would form a contact network that kept him in the air for many years. These new sons and daughters were not permitted to leave with the white cargo they sought. Tommy would deliver. At considerably greater cost, but deliver he did. Wantonly.

Escape

When Tommy came of age, I'm sure his respected – and quietly infamous – uncle took him aside on some estate patio, warmly gripped him by the shoulder and said: 'I've got just one word to say to you, my boy – narcotics.'

Tommy's uncle on his mother's side was one of the big four of the Golden Triangle. A man with his own brand, the Flying Horse. Uncle Lou had opium farmers under contract deep into Laos, and agents who protected the most well-equipped laboratories, producing heroin with purity greater than that of Khun Sa's agencies, and a density above General Lee's. Working through Cambodia, Lou had supplied heroin to US troops during the Vietnam conflict, a branch that could not have made him many official American friends, although in later years – just to show that there were no hard feelings – Uncle Lou would send his own children to American universities. At home, Lou kept a firm hand on his subordinates, and grew cautious concerning his nephew's ambitions. Perhaps that was the reason no drugs were dispensed from Tommy's guesthouse. I'd been told Lou had once been arrested. The US DEA had put in a lot of work and money to ensure that Uncle's Volvo was sandwiched on Chiang Mai Road when its trunk was packed with 400 kilos of heroin.

What with so many round-eye foreigners nosing into the case, it was not until the highest Thai Supreme Court appeal that a final judgment was applied. Uncle Lou's acquittal was one of the most expensive court decisions ever bought in Thailand, Tommy had proudly told me – half a million dollars. '*Gosh*,' I'd said, although I rarely use cuss words.

'What does my horoscope say?'

I looked up from my paper at the booth of the Montien coffee shop to see Tommy smiling. Almost an hour late.

'Well, hello.' I stood to embrace Tommy. It had been over ten years, and we'd both survived. 'And happy birthday – you don't look 50.' Tommy's smooth face, more Indian than Thai, concealed all thought.

Escape

'Let's not stay here.' Tommy folded his arms behind his back. 'My wife's got a townhouse across the river. We can talk there.'

'Sure.' But before leaving the Montien, I gave Tommy his birthday gift, a German teddy bear. Tommy was a collector, so it seemed odd that he took the bear from its box and tucked it under one arm.

'I'm just a kid at heart,' Tommy winked, easily demonstrating his colloquial English.

On board the platform ferry crossing the Chao Phraya, I asked Tommy about his phones.

'Absolutely fine,' Tommy assured me. 'I've got one of the best policemen. High up. He'd tell me if there was anything.'

Even so, by the time we were drinking coffee at Tommy's townhouse, I had asked for the telephone number of the shop next to Tommy's Chiang Mai office.

'If I need to call, I'll call the place next door,' I said. 'Then you can just walk through one door. I don't mind waiting on the line.'

We then got down to talking shop. Tommy would not easily accept the changes that had occurred with the 1990s, when the collapse of the Berlin wall had opened the way for a cascade of cut-price smugglers.

'Tommy, there's no way you can make a quarter of a million dollars on a kilo any more.' I wanted to sound reasonable. 'There's Albanians trading women for kilos of brown shit. Standards have gone right down the plughole.'

'How about Iceland? I heard prices are very good there.' Tommy was usually enthusiastic about the few places he knew nothing about.

'Sure, and the Galapagos has quite a little scene, too.' I shook my head. 'Who've you been talking to – the three monkeys?'

The Three Unwise Monkeys were a trio of halfwits who had tried once and failed to sell a kilo of heroin in Britain. Large Raj, a tall chubby Hindu; Tramshed, a gangling, nervy Sikh; and Shemp, an Indian conman from Singapore, had all arrived in England to jointly mismanage an operation any one of them could have capably bungled on his own. Unsatisfied with the price offered by their expatriate countrymen, they had roamed London, approaching strangers.

At the time, police scanners had just come into vogue among techno-villains. Our little crew had accidentally tuned in to the radio chatter of the surveillance police as they shadowed the then unknown incompetents.

'I don't believe it.' I recall overhearing the voice of some under-cover man coming from the scanner. 'The skinny one is sitting in the Water Rat. He's in a cheap suit and tie drinking 7-Up, trying to collar the passing druggies. They're running away from him!'

The skinny one, I would later learn, was Tramshed scouting for talent. He'd thought it wise to dress up for travelling and business meetings, and was a total abstainer. Despite all the radio talk, no clear information was given identifying the three monkeys' hotel, so we were unable to warn them before their arrest. Yet for a week, our afternoons were absorbed by tuning in to this sad soap opera.

These unlucky Magi had survived their consequent years in prison. It was said that Shemp never slept under the covers of his bed, not wanting to be seen – even in his prison cell – without his designer footwear. Tramshed tried to leave the prison upon release with eighty-three unopened tins of sardines that he'd saved during his five years. Large Raj was the clever one, and had later taken over a run-down travel agency in Bangkok, where he and Tramshed now spent their days. Shemp had since been arrested in Singapore for trying to sell phoney contracts for ammunition to the Israeli army.

'I was at their little agency about a year ago.' Tommy brought me up to date. 'They're running a thing where they take money from Pakistanis who want to go to Japan.'

'Is there anything to it?' I was always curious to know about new trade routes.

'Oh, it's for real,' Tommy said. 'Expensive, but for real.'

The emigration scheme relied on two anomalies: first, that one of the few places to which Pakistanis may still travel without a visa is Fiji, the Pacific island nation. Second, that the only flights from

Escape

Bangkok to Fiji were via Tokyo's Narita airport. This airport did not operate after midnight, so when transit passengers arrived too late for their onward connection, they would be issued a 24-hour transit visa for Japan, take the bus into Tokyo and then disappear.

'Large Raj and Tramshed would be happy to see you.' Tommy wrote their agency address on the back of his used boarding card. 'They're always asking about you.'

'Sure, why not. No problems with that lot, is there? No one on their case?' I didn't want to arrive just as the duo were lighting exploding cigars.

Tommy assured me that no officials had any interest in the skulduggery at Large Raj's agency, and we spent the next hour haggling over the merits of shipping a tonne of Thai sticks. Tommy thought anything involving ships was hard work, and he had no patience for sailing times.

'And you know Thai sticks have to be ordered specially,' Tommy added. 'They don't make them any more.'

'No problem. I can wait.'

Tommy and I crossed the river once more, and I left him at a furniture showroom. He was arranging the delivery of a garish, black-wood, three-piece lounge suite with lurid silk cushions. It would be a gift for General Lee's birthday. All the Triangle's competitors insisted on outdoing one another with expensive, ostentatious gifts.

The office of Concorde 999 Gold International Travel Agency wasn't easy to find in the narrow arcade of Bangkok's Chinatown. Two fluorescent tubelights inside the small office had trouble lighting further than its peeling green window plastic. The single door's hinge had broken, so Tramshed had to leap from his couch to let me in. Perhaps that was his job.

'Ahhh, Mr David, come in. Please. Have a seat!'

It was good to see Tramshed had lost none of his enthusiasm. He and Large Raj immediately began an inventory of their disasters, and gave me a Fanta with a rusty top and dusty drinking straw. I recall none of their woes, as I was thinking hard about Tommy.

Escape

He had paused for some time at the furniture store's entrance, in front of its showroom windows. Not looking at carved goblins and brass cauldrons but to check the reflection in the glass for anyone following us. This kind of behaviour was rare for Tommy. He was nervous, and had been all morning, and had strained to avoid telling me why.

After 20 minutes with Tramshed and Large Raj at the C999G agency, I made excuses and left. Visiting Chinatown had been mostly a ruse so that I wouldn't have to tell Tommy that I'd be seeing Myca, my venerable first connection in Thailand. Although I'd spoken to each of the other, they had never met – unfortunately, old friends seldom accept that need to retain even older ones.

CHAPTER TWELVE

Still Tuesday. Just 12 hours in Thailand and already back in the world of spooks and shadows. While waiting at the Nana hotel for Myca, I sipped an orange juice, hoping to wash away the sweetness of Tramshed's Fanta. I concluded that Tommy was being followed over something he thought might put me off my game if I knew. From the agency, I'd taken a three-floor walk through the Siam Center, hoping to spot any watchers before taxiing to the Nana. A foreigner in a strange land cannot easily make tails, yet in Asia, local police don't expect diligence from Europeans, a small advantage. If Tommy was being followed, I could live with that. He had been since the day we'd first met, and I hadn't changed.

Myca had gained some weight over the years, but still held a child's eyes. He'd moved house four times, and in each had built an extra bedroom, always made up in case I should arrive unannounced. As we sat in the Nana coffee shop, Myca described the growth of Bangkok with the pride of a farmer before his lush crop.

'I'll show you. How many days will you stay? Ten, twelve?'

'I'm very sorry, Myca. It's like I said. Just passing through. But I'll be back, I promise.'

Myca's face didn't disguise his disappointment. He then asked, 'You need something? I haven't been doing much for years, just the land business. Oh, a little here, a little there. Just for friends. You know.'

Escape

'No. Nothing thanks. Next time I'll make a proper visit of it.'

Myca leaned back against the bench within our booth. Shyly, from the side pockets of his padded jacket, he withdrew two fat envelopes.

'Here's just a little. It's your Christmas, isn't it?'

'There's no need.' But I took the envelopes, and a quick calculation from their open flaps came to $10,000.

'No, you come to my house tomorrow,' Myca insisted. 'Then, I have a lot more. Relax a while. You should see our new land now, all shops and apartments.'

Had I forgotten how much Thailand held for me? This tight schedule was no way to retrace my steps, not that that was part of the plan. I left Myca and walked to my next appointment, at the nearby Grace Hotel.

The Grace Hotel on Sukhumvit had been a magnet for tarts, double-bent cops, single-trippers, sub-orbital space cadets and those spring-necked noddies who spent their waking hours peering into the dark side of the spoon. In the 1990s the hotel's reputation had barely improved, so one might think it a poor choice of flophouse for Sam Gilburne, an old player and professional courier. Yet he lived by omens and signs, so the Grace must have proved lucky for Sam.

Sam Gilburne would tell people that he had been born and raised in Colorado, but if so, he'd changed his voice. I did know that sleepy-eyed Sam had joined a team of boys and girls from Quebec who would launch mass landings at chosen Canadian airports in the mid-1970s. Six of them would disembark dressed in full hippie colours to attract customs staff. The seventh man, trailing behind, would then pass through unhindered in plain-clothes camouflage.

Sam now lived in Toronto, worked alone and was considered one of the most reliable independent couriers of my acquaintance. Druggists paid Sam $7,500 for any Asia–West haulage. This was more than twice that paid to the Paolos, Saleems and Eddies, and worth the premium, for Sam would always stand his ground. I'd

Escape

phoned at the front desk of the Grace, and Sam came downstairs to greet me, avoiding the lift. Sam wouldn't open his hotel-room door to his mother bearing an apple pie, and had suffered many cold breakfasts.

'Sam, you old ham. Look at you. It's been, well – hasn't it?' I looked at Sam's silk Pacific-island shirt stretched over his now porky torso.

'Yeah, at least. And then some.'

I lightly prodded Sam's colourful shirt. 'About time for the extra large, Sam?' The wiry build of Sam's youth was now well padded.

'Too many hours at the tables.' Sam meant Las Vegas. 'And I'm not losing this shirt. Let's go upstairs. Too many freaks down here.'

The bed in Sam's room was covered by new shirts still in their plastic wraps. He would never wear them. They were part of his elaborate ritual purchases and abandonments that underpinned his faith in luck. As a person who lived perennially in temporary lodgings, Sam would litter his nests to imitate the surroundings of a family man, as though the gods would be kinder to those with a life in full.

'Up to no good, Sam, I hope?' I had some work for Sam, and wanted an outline of his bookings.

'Don't worry, David. Not the Pakistanis, not the Nigerians.' Sam lit his cigarette with a chipped black lighter I'd seen before. 'Remember Wolf from Stockholm?'

A good man. Wanted and on the run, but careful.

'I'm off Thursday,' Sam continued. 'Afternoon Swissair to Zurich. Shouldn't be a problem.' Sam keyed the links of his gold wrist bracelet, a gift from a girl in La Coruña. He'd said that the heavy bracelet's rattling into the metals-tray at airport-security posts always distracted the staff.

'Everything bedded down?' I made a stirring motion with one hand, enquiring as to the quality of packing done for Sam's Zurich run.

'Yup.' But Sam would say no more using sound. He stood, walked to the open wardrobe and crouched next to a pair of long leather boots. Looking at me, Sam slowly guided the back of his hand along the length of a boot. Then stood, moved to a hand-luggage case by the minifridge and stroked a finger across the bag's handle. It was a double-grip leather handle, and I estimated that it could hold around 300 grams.

Sam had revealed more than he usually would, so rapidly moved on. 'Right, where do you want me?'

'It's an island hop.' I unfolded a travel map upon the bed. 'Starting in Margarita.'

'That's Venezuela, isn't it?'

'Yeah, but full of European tourists. You fly to Santo Domingo, and then on to the Caymans.' I could see Sam wrinkling his nose at the thought of the Dominican Republic. 'Well, I'm looking at some way of cutting that out – but the Caymans flight is the important one.'

'Mmm . . . I know it. Air Canada to Toronto.'

'Right. And you're the man for Toronto. You must know that airport like the palm of your hand.'

'No need to sell it to me, Dave. I'm on. Will you be at the other end? I don't want to meet strangers in my own town.'

'This won't be for a month or so. I should be able to fly more easily by then.' I was less sure than I sounded.

Sam bounced around the room tearing scraps of paper into tiny pieces, which meant he was thinking. 'OK. Sounds good. Can I catch up with you later tonight? I've got an early dinner not far from here. Won't take long. Not a friend, really. Might be a gig for me.'

'Anyone I know?'

'Doubt it. Colin Mackenzie?'

I shrugged.

'I met him down at Naklua.' Sam was talking about the beaches near Pattaya. 'He's a Kiwi. I thought you might know him. Lives in Vancouver when he's not here. I was a bit doubtful at first, but he knows his stuff.'

Escape

'Well, be careful,' I said routinely. 'And I'd like to stay but I'll be gone by ten tonight. Just a whistle-stop.'

I walked with Sam to the restaurant of his meeting. We ran through our communications protocols. I gave him a business card for an optician in London's Baker Street.

'My number's on the eye-chart.' I pointed to a graphic on the card that I'd had printed. 'The code-phrase is *frozen days*. Just follow the letters from the top.' Each letter represented a number from zero to nine, corresponding to those letters in the code-phrase, so chosen as no letter is repeated. All good stuff, except that 99 crooks out of 100 will go home and phone immediately from their dodgy landlines or infected mobiles.

As Sam turned into the restaurant, I walked on to a jewellery store. I'd already selected a gift for Sharon before I realised the choice of a charm bracelet had been influenced by Sam's company. Reversing to the corner, I paused to look through the windows of La Grande Bouffe. And there he was, at a table towards the back, sitting opposite a man with a beard. The beard did most of the talking, Sam looking down to rearrange his unused cutlery. I suppose there is a particular order for knives and forks with Sam.

Returning to the Oriental just before seven, I half-packed my bag and broke the cellophane of a fruit basket to eat some hairy rambutans. As with most hotels in Bangkok, the Oriental would not include durian fruit in its baskets, or even allow any in the building, despite its rich confectionary taste. If a durian's alligator skin were peeled in a confined space, the pungent bile stench would have guests complaining.

At that moment, staring at the fruit basket, I remembered the real identity behind the beard of Sam's dinner companion. He was Keith Kellaway.

Twelve years earlier, and without that beard, Kellaway was flipping burgers at a greasy café in Port Moody, not so very far from where Sam now lived in Canada. Third-rate burglars and street girls would sit in the booths until their dealers would slide by to tuck matchboxes behind the serviette racks. This was Kellaway's first experience of the lowest trading floor. When he finished calculating the money he'd seen changing hands, Kellaway decided to go into the drug trade. And as an importer from the outset. For Kellaway, even buying his minced beef from the butcher next door seemed an imposition when there were cows roaming the countryside unchaperoned. Within a year, he'd financed a couple of awkward runs from Thailand after grilling junkie-backpacker customers for contacts. Needy street people had been hired to swallow 30 or 40 condoms filled with heroin, and Kellaway never let them out of his sight until their last meal was back in his hands. The dope would be ground and cut on Kellaway's steel benches, then sold straight to the consumers from his café. The night I'd called in for a thick shake and to watch the show, he'd turned ugly at someone who couldn't pay. Only the smell of burning egg and onion rings drove him back behind the counter. I guess the value of the debt was less than a burnt burger. Kellaway's frustration was that his couriers could not swallow enough, but he was too stingy to pay for professional couriers whose luggage would not be picked over by customs.

The next I heard of Kellaway was from a mercurial smuggler who'd lost a couple of large wooden elephants in the post. He and Kellaway had once shared a Bangkok connection. Kellaway would never risk posting his kilos, and often spent weeks seeking gullible Canadian tourists to whom he could entrust his cargo. 'I know just the shop where you can buy fine carvings cheap,' Kellaway would tell the elderly couples he'd befriend in hotels. The plan was to drop by one evening sometime, once they were all back home, and take the pensioners out for dinner while an accomplice elbowed the couple's back door to retrieve the elephant. However, that would mean Keith trusting a friend. That would mean Keith having a friend.

'Keith never had the patience for that,' recounted my elephant-posting acquaintance. 'I don't think he did that trick more than once or twice. He'd go around for evening drinks, then lose his rag with the oldies if he couldn't immediately spot the pachyderm, and start yelling – "Stick your sherry up your ass, where's my fucking elephant, you old stinkbags!" Then, Keith would get nasty. That was his way, no patience for the last mile.'

Over the years, I'd hoped to hear of Keith's timely death, but there had been no news until Myca told me about a Canadian who had been looking for a particular Burmese doctor who had a reputation for silent treatments. This medic would sew up gunshot wounds or provide suitable poisons as a solution to business disputes. This doctor was not quite so silent when he drank.

Keith Kellaway had persuaded a young man to travel with him to Thailand. (I'd elsewhere heard of Kellaway organising charity raffles at a services club where lucky young singletons could win trips to Thailand, although there may be no connection here.) The young man was chubby, nearing obesity.

In Bangkok, Kellaway and Chubby spent a few evenings together paying bar fines to take out girls. Kellaway wouldn't have kept that up for long. One night, after drinking too much, Chubby and Kellaway stumbled out into the street to a confrontation with alley-boys. There was a fight. The alley-boys had knives.

Chubby woke up the following morning in a strange guesthouse, bruised and sore, to see a foot of fresh stitches curving along his gut. Some swelling. Kellaway told him that the fight was touch-and-go. He wore some mascara for a black eye. He must have also invented some dangers in going to local hospitals, perhaps spoken of months awaiting the courts if the fight were to be reported to the police. Chubby was grateful, he had found a true friend at last. *'T'weren't nuthin'.'* I imagined Kellaway affecting modesty.

Through some mix-up with the flight reservations, Chubby had to return to Canada via Seattle. At the last minute, ticketing difficulties were in part resolved. Kellaway got the direct flight, but promised to collect Chubby at Seattle rather than have him wait for a transit connection. He made Chubby promise to keep taking the penicillin.

Kellaway was waiting in a rented car at Seattle when Chubby limped out to the kerbside.

Escape

Another two years would pass before I heard the conclusion to this elaborate bit of staging, although I knew that Kellaway was dealing again within a week of his return. More quietly, that time.

I telephoned the Grace Hotel, but Sam had told the desk not to put through any calls. His Canadian mobile was only taking messages, and Sam did not keep a local mobile number. Unlucky, he had said. Even so, I reasoned that Sam was no fool. A scoundrel such as Kellaway would have no easy job talking Sam down a blind alley. Besides, in two hours I would be leaving Bangkok to get some desperately needed sleep aboard an SAS flight to Copenhagen. On the other hand, Sam *had* put on a lot of weight.

I finished packing after seven, so went downstairs to the Riverside Café for some alcohol to clear my head. With bags packed and only 20 minutes to spare before leaving for the airport, I ordered a fruit salad and a Cointreau with ice and lemon, and began reading an *International Herald Tribune* taken from the lobby. Frank Zappa's death had allowed rock historians a few columns, and Boris Yeltsin was in trouble. Our universe would be spared never-ending expansion by a mysterious dark matter, and Europe's internal borders were to be unmanned. A small box in the paper reprinted an angry letter from 1922 complaining of the continued requirement for passports at international borders. The Great War was over, wrote Angry, so the need for such intrusive documents had gone. *Groundhog Day* was playing everywhere, opening to more screens due to word-of-mouth recommendations. I raised my snifter, swirled its crushed ice and drank to Sam. I made a decision.

At that moment, looking through the glass, a girl had appeared in the diamond lights of the hotel entrance some 30 feet away. She descended the timber steps to the torch-lit garden. Softer than the night, and dressed in wind-drifted layers of yellow and sunset-orange organdie, the tall blonde floated in an arc around me to the water's edge, quietly taking a corner seat at a large table. I thought it unusual to find such a woman unattended, for she was beautiful. She lifted her eyes from her hands, spread flat upon her table, and spoke.

'Would you care to join me for a drink while I wait for my girlfriend?' Her voice, kept low, easily carried across the three-metre gap as if the sounds of Bangkok had suddenly stilled. She spoke with a New York City accent a touch harder than her features.

'Of course. That would be nice.' I abandoned my newspaper to take a seat at her table.

Her name was Jacinta, mine was Daniel. I wondered if hers had been adopted between boyfriends, or, as mine had, between terminals, for unchivalrous suspicions were beginning to form.

'I've been drinking brandy but I'm ready for a change.' I signalled a waiter.

'I feel like champagne.' Jacinta then spoke to the waiter, though keeping her eyes on me, 'Do you have Dom Pérignon?'

As the waiter left, I began to defend the wine from the prevailing view that it was the choice of nouveau-riche but Jacinta broke in, saying, 'The first bottle's on me. My treat!'

'I wouldn't do that,' I said, lifting my key tag to the bar staff to indicate billing to my account (and taking the opportunity to replace it facedown from Jacinta). 'The hotel mark-up here is 300 per cent.'

'I never worry about that,' she replied before sending the waiter away with a Platinum Visa card she'd produced from a golden hand-purse. 'So, what is it that you do, Daniel?'

'I'm a goatherd, heading for the Osaka convention.' I emptied my glass. 'And, yes – before you ask – the pay is everything you've heard, but I think we make a difference.'

'Really?'

'Indeed. Jacinta, you're not staying at the hotel, I guess?'

'Oh, no.' Faintly troubled. 'We just decided to come here for a drink.'

In these moments, I knew my schedule was collapsing. I knew it, yet refused to consider the consequences.

Escape

Before I could ask who Jacinta meant by 'we', a small, somewhat mousey girl – also in her late 20s – arrived at our table. She was introduced as Linny, Jacinta's travelling companion. Jacinta eye-signalled the waiter before saying, 'Linny, Daniel has invited us to dinner. What do you think?'

'Why not? But let me have a drink first.' Linny's voice was from the New Hampshire class that tries not to speak of money. Never college roommates, these two.

As a child, I'd seen a cabaret act with Zoltan the Great and his sequinned assistant. The assistant would sparkle at a customer's table while her blindfolded master on stage would intone, 'Does the young man at table five have a scar on his wrist from a skiing accident?' That act, too, required fine coordination between two performers.

Jacinta announced an excursion to the toilets, allowing me to question Linny. The girls were on vacation, she said. They'd just arrived from Vietnam, and were due to travel to northern Thailand the next day. Jacinta had hinted earlier at being employed as a travel consultant, but Linny sidestepped work talk to reveal her companion's well-masked sadness.

'Jay has just broken up after a long relationship with an older man. They shared a house on Fire Island.'

'Fire Island? That was once some kind of artists' colony, wasn't it?' However, my time questioning Linny was over. Jacinta had returned, absent not long enough to find the toilets, much less use them.

My suggestion to eat at If It Swims We Cook It, the open-air Thai family restaurant in Phetburi Road, was dismissed without negotiation. The girls had chosen the Joss Stick, a multi-storey tourist venue with execrable food. Jacinta and Linny asked our driver to stop at their hotel for repairs. I left them at the Rembrandt, after promising to return within 20 minutes. The Grace was not far away.

Sam Gilburne broke his rule and allowed me to come directly to his room after I'd called him from a house phone in the lobby. The door was open when I arrived, and Sam was at the balcony railing, letting warm, damp air pour in.

Escape

'Don't jump, Sam,' I said by way of a greeting. 'It's only two floors.'

Sam smiled and said, 'Come in. I didn't expect to see you until whenever.'

'Yeah, well. You know how it is.' I closed the room door. 'Plans change. How was The Big Pouffe?'

'La Grande Bouffe,' Sam corrected. 'Not so good. Too much sugar in – were you watching me?'

'And just as well, I think.' I poured myself some water from his jug. 'Do you mind?'

'Just as well about what?' Sam slid the balcony door shut.

'Sam, have you ever heard the phrase, "A Night on the Town"? In smuggling terms, that is.'

He hadn't, so I took my time telling him the Keith Kellaway story. Sam didn't interrupt, and I assumed nothing that Sam knew contradicted my description. When I got to the part where Kellaway leads Chubby into an alley where the knife-wielding locals attack, Sam objected.

'Didn't the fat guy put up a fight?'

'Maybe, but less effective when you've just gulped down five Halcion in your last drink. He wakes up the next morning in Dr Rangoon's spare room looking at a hedgerow of catgut stitches.'

'And having put on weight.' Sam had caught on.

I ended this account with Kellaway and Chubby driving through the Seattle checkpoint to Canada in a rented car.

'All right,' nodded Sam, thinking these events through. 'But one thing I can't see. How did Colin – or Keith Kella-whatever-the-fuck – how did he find a doctor in Vancouver to operate on Lardass? I mean, I just don't see it happening.'

'Kellaway is not a man who'd pay for anything he didn't have to.' I stood from the suitcase rack and folded my arms. 'Kellaway arrived back in Port Moody alone. Chubby was never seen again. I can only assume Kellaway played doctor at the roadside somewhere. Only without closing him up.'

Sam raised himself from the bed and moved to a writing desk.

Escape

Staring vacantly at a large mirror, he opened an empty drawer, and then closed it, all without purpose.

I sat at a bedside chair, and to give the silent room some sound, added, 'Only a few people know the story. It got around a bit a few years ago. Not enough for anything to stick to Kellaway. I thought you might have heard someone say this or that guy deserves *a night on the town*, or whatever.'

'So you know this scumbag?' Sam was turning on the messenger, but he spoke to my chair rather than to my face.

'I don't suppose he'd recognise me. I only saw him once or twice. It's a face I made a point of remembering, and maybe not such a bad thing that I'm a collector of little histories. Sam, never work for a man with bad teeth or a beard. Were you planning on working for Kellaway? Before, I mean.'

'No.' Sam had nothing more to say. He had begun to pack.

'OK, Sam. I've got to go. I've got to go eat an awful dinner. I was chatted up for no good reason by some doll, and I have to find out if she's been sent by someone.' Sam wasn't listening. 'Sam, where'll you be staying?'

'Anna's Café,' Sam answered, which was sensible.

Attempting conversation at the Joss Stick required hand signals, as every surface was hard and reflective. As a consultant, Jacinta must have been compiling a traveller's advisory on the worst nightspots of Bangkok, for she then became insistent on worse: the dank nightclub of the Dusit Thani hotel, a low-ceilinged purple mistranslation with pudgy, just-sponged vinyl chairs squishing into beer-foam-and-ash-scented carpets. Strung out with maybe ten customers, all ugly professionals; men and women with everything to lose.

'I'm starting to believe your story,' I shouted. 'These places must be on your list!'

'What?'

'Never mind, finish your whisky essence, and let's get out of here.'

Escape

I had wanted to walk through the streets to wherever next we were going, but Jacinta refused. She had contrived to avoid any place that allowed conversation. We hunched inside a taxi for two minutes. Linny in the front seat, staring at the lights, next to the driver, his open mouth far enough forward to bite the steering wheel. Jacinta, in the back seat kneading my fingers, whispering: 'Do you think you're gonna get lucky tonight?'

However reasonable it might have been to defer to the girls' supposed fear of being led around a foreign city by a near stranger, their final venue – the Hard Rock Café – was somehow sadder even than those industrial-scale brothels, the bedrock of the tourist's Thailand.

At the Hard Rock, I left the girls with watery drinks that gave alcohol a bad name, and walked outside to get some air. On my way, I passed the platform where a local jazz-funk band was struggling with a drunken, cretinous audience interrupting each song. The singer, a Thai girl who fronted the band, was fending off a tanked and wired imbecile with wet, curly, streak-bleached hair, howling requests while grabbing at her elbows between turning to his blotto mates for applause at his spit-spraying wit. I stopped, about to make a bad day worse, but then the front door opened and the night air pulled me outside. Through the haze of the city sky, a jet climbed into the clouds. Possibly the plane on which I should have been slumbering.

Jacinta appeared at my side.

'What's the matter, Daniel?'

'Don't tell me you like places like this.' I looked at the ground. 'OK, there's no reason why every night out must be an evening of authentic Thai culture, but there is nothing at all of Thailand in these places. I won't go on.' It wasn't clear if Jacinta was with me on this, but she could tell I was about to walk.

'OK, Daniel. We'll go.'

I had to restrain myself from yelling, 'And stop calling me Daniel!'

Another taxi. The Rembrandt; its lobby; the lift.

Escape

Jacinta had pressed the button for the Rembrandt's rooftop as soon as the three of us had stepped into the lift. Once in motion, Jacinta held my arm and Linny punched the button marked 11. No words were exchanged.

The eleventh floor. Linny: 'I guess I'll see you guys later. Nice to meet you, Daniel. Goodnight.'

I find that Jacinta has no suite on the roof of the hotel. She shares her room on the eleventh with Linny. The rooftop floor has a swimming pool, and it is deserted. It's one-thirty in the morning.

Jacinta leads me to the pool, then drops my hand and walks to the rooftop railing to admire the view. There is no suggestion of swimming.

After a minute, Jacinta returns to me, talking about how girls and boys court, despite all my efforts to shift the conversation, and we sit at the edge of the water. Earlier we had been talking relationships. I'd rather have been discussing dentistry. To bring this to a close, I suggest: 'You could take on a temp when you get back home.'

'A temp?'

'Yeah. An intermediate boyfriend that you can dump when you find someone you really want. The trick is to grab someone who gets lots of invitations to galleries, restaurant openings, first nights, weddings – that sort of thing. Wherever the pickings are good. Remember now—' I looked down, the good counsellor '—not someone obviously gay. That would give the game away.'

'You think that would be best?' Jacinta spoke softly and crinkled a smile. Then she leaned back and with two fingers lifted a squashed marijuana spliff from between her breasts.

'Well, no one would think of looking there,' I said, before asking with precise spontaneity, 'Get that locally?'

'Hell, no. I brought this from LA. I'd never risk buying in a foreign country.' Jacinta lit the joint. 'Anyway, I must be choking you with my cigarette taste.' I'd been kissed. 'This way, we both taste the same.'

The grass was too weakly mixed to identify as either Californian or Thai. Not strong enough to make either of us do anything we might normally not. A hotel security man in a neat suit leaned out briefly from the terrace entrance before quickly retreating.

Even with the entirely planned and controlled night that Jacinta had thus far managed, it suddenly seemed hugely improbable that she could be some agent provocateur. Even so, since I'd come this far, the feeble spliff allowed me to move forward.

'You might want to be careful with this stuff, Jay.' I returned her the lion's share of the joint. 'Thai cops in the southern resorts make a fair living from busting tourists.' And, continuing, 'The airports carry a premium for some reason. Penalty-wise.'

'Oh, I'd never take anything out. Myself.'

Uh-huh.

However, I was wrong about her motives. Jacinta went on to tell me of some card she carried. A pass that when swiped through machines at US airports would allow her ingress without being questioned by customs authorities. (She was referring to INSPASS, which does not bypass customs, however it might have seemed when used.) Jacinta then stressed she would never be a carrier: 'If anything, I'd be organising it.'

By then, I'd stopped listening carefully. Jacinta was only saying things she thought I'd like to hear, and was certainly not seeking information. No agency would use such obviousness. I began swatting mosquitoes.

'They're a nuisance, aren't they?' She stood close, and drew me closer by taking my hands behind her back. 'Sorry, I share the room with Linny. We'll be fine here. There's no one around.'

In response, I spoke the words best used for initially declining an offer of intimacy. Helpless words about fidelity to a distant lover. Spoken with compliments and consideration. There's no reason to cite them here: in no circumstances are they ever accepted by women with the grace gentlemen are compelled to pretend.

Jacinta rested her arms upon my shoulders, and spoke low across my cheek as ribbons of her hair veiled my eyes.

'That doesn't matter, Daniel. I never come on a first date, anyway.

Escape

You just tell me what you like. I'll do anything you want.'

Like many people undertaking dark missions, I too carry superstitions when in the field, but there are few rewards in continual restraint and I soon saw Jacinta was not seeking some secret intelligence. She was merely testing her sorcery.

Some little time later, Jacinta and I stood before the indicator lights of the lifts. At some moment, I can't say when, Jacinta had taken a black velvet scrunchy from her hair and encircled it around my left wrist.

'When did you manage this?' I asked, removing the black band. 'Are you in mourning? Am I?'

Of course, she did not answer. One of the lift doors opened, and just before stepping inside, she said, 'I'm going to my room. And you're going down,' just as her door closed and the second lift door opened. To this day, I still toast Jacinta's timing.

By 2.30 I'd returned to the Oriental, and 20 minutes later, folded into bed. Finally, one full day spent in Bangkok.

CHAPTER THIRTEEN

The phone at my bedside woke me at 11 the following morning. I assumed, from the slight accent, that a reception clerk wanted to know how long I'd be staying.

'. . . if you could tell me what your plans are?'

I made some meaningless noises and looked with dismay at the large breakfast trolley, untouched, by the window. I'd let a waiter wheel it in at a ludicrously ambitious 7 a.m., before falling back to bed.

'. . . David, wake up. I didn't think you'd still be here.' It was Tommy. He'd made me promise to call him from the transit lounge in Copenhagen. When I hadn't, he used the details I'd given him to call the Oriental. Not good.

'Where are you calling from?' I asked, as if this would help.

'Home. Chiang Mai.'

Enough. I claimed stupefaction from lack of sleep and promised to call back. Over a slice of oatmeal and a splash of fruit, I convinced myself that Tommy had called from his office. Given his jumpiness when I'd met him, there was a possibility his phone was tapped. If by Thai police, any information would eventually go to Australian FedPol, as they called themselves then. Tommy had once made a spectacular showing in Australia. These inter-agency mechanisms are slow in Thailand, but not slow enough to risk staying put just to test their responses.

By early afternoon I'd checked out and was on my way to meet

Escape

Myca at his new house. In Melbourne, Michael would be using my mobile to put our recorded conversation into the air, confusing any listeners. On the road to Myca's I stopped at the Four Seasons business centre to re-jig my flight reservations. In the process, I realised what a mess I'd made of my schedule by staying overnight. To return to Melbourne by Friday, I'd have to forgo Europe. I would blame Sam for this deserved punishment. Now, I was booked for a Thursday exit, this time via Singapore.

Still in the business centre, I called Tommy to tell him that I was convinced he was under surveillance.

'Not a chance,' he said, then made a familiar speech. 'I have friends in high places, their names would astound you; friends in low places . . .' Tommy said there was no need to go to the shop next door to talk. I had no hard evidence Tommy was drawing heat. Nor from the Oriental, or from Jacinta despite all her poolside tomfoolery, and certainly not from the street.

No evidence of anything but the friendship of Myca, in whose house at Prakhanong I stayed that night. The house had been built as an outgrowth of interconnecting treehouses that allowed us to take our evening on one of the tower balconies away from the insects. Wearing a sarong, Myca reclined and cooled his belly with a beer bottle. As he saw that I was becoming sleepy, Myca ended the night by fetching a remote control for a TV visible from the balcony.

'Take a look at this.' Myca played a tape he must have set in the machine before I arrived. 'I had it transferred from the old eight-millimetre Kodachrome.'

On the screen appeared a young Myca leaning on his old Buick. In the film, he was talking about the land, and waving his arms at the trees. 'In a year this will be all different, Mikey. We'll have a fish farm over there, and here I will make a house for you. Away, we'll go there now. We'll make shops, apartments.' I had been behind the camera in those days. And I was Mike, the shiny, happy example of the West's glittering bounty.

'Ah, we were in so much of a hurry then.' Myca buttoned off

the tape. 'Wanting to do everything at once. But you're tired. Sleep now. Tomorrow, I'll take you to something new.'

'Myca, I told you. I have to go.'

'Sure, sure. Sleep now. Tomorrow.' Myca left, leaving the remote near my hand.

Naturally, I didn't take any of this good advice. After lunch the following day, Myca drove me halfway to the airport in his Lexus. I'd told Myca that I was spooked and would appreciate the sharp eye of a local. We drove around Seacon Shopping Square, and then north to Bang Kapi.

'Nothing,' judged Myca.

'Thanks. I'll take a taxi from here.' This mid-point drop was a tradition with Myca.

Although I'd thought Sam Gilburne might be at Don Muang airport that afternoon if he'd kept to his schedule, it was unnerving to see him checking in at the counter two rows from mine for his Swissair flight.

More unnerving were the airport people around us whose stance and movements identified them as watchers: a white-suited technician talking to an X-ray machine operator, a spiky woman shouldering authority at the business-class check-in zone at Qantas, two men standing between check-in and immigration who were furtively side-valving each other – talking without moving their heads. Also, a pair of older men, one European, the other Thai, leaning at the rail of an overhead balcony, a few feet apart, yet unmistakably linked.

At first, I attributed all this bad company to Sam, for he would be carrying. At a distance, he and I communicated with head-tilt and eye-slide semaphore, through which he said, 'Yes, I see them but they're not mine!'

Time to see if Sam was right. I placed my Westlake passport on the counter. Immediately, a ripple passed along those people I had seen. I suppose Sam had shivered, too, for by the time I'd turned around he had stepped from his queue and was abandoning a bag that was too big to carry discreetly, and perhaps not worth so very much.

Turning back to the counter, I caught the clerk flicking her eyes back from the man near the immigration counters.

'Mr Westlake?' She held my passport as though it had been lifted from a dead man floating in the Chao Phraya. 'Do you mind if I check your reservation on the office computer? We are having just a little trouble today. I won't take a minute.'

Nor would I.

It was possible that the people at the airport meant me no harm; that I could've been allowed to board and fly so that others might enjoy the harm-doing. I did not want to stay to find out. Although there were taxis within sight arriving at the Departures hall, I moved quickly downstairs to Arrivals and took a taxi from the middle of the pack.

My first stop was the Dusit Thani hotel, as it was right on a major intersection. There I bought some envelopes and stamps before posting some notes and the remaining Westlake documents to London. Then, another taxi to the Sheraton, where I sat in the corner of a bar for 15 minutes, carefully removing a fresh passport from the lining of my bag. I had plenty of money, and at least one passport whose name was surely unknown. It bore no entry stamp for Thailand, but Myca could fix that. Yet, before going to Myca's house, I had to be certain that I would not be leading a posse to my friend.

Even at the Sheraton, I felt sure the trace had been through Tommy. Not with his knowledge, but through his phone call to the Oriental. Too much time had passed between his call yesterday and the airport that afternoon. Time enough to find the name Westlake, and to match that against airline reservations. Quite some effort, and had it been the Thais alone, Tommy should have known. So, perhaps Australian police working with the Thais.

At the Sheraton, I had to accept something else: that in an instant, this latest in a series of lives had evaporated. There would be no more mornings in the Collingwood office, nights with Sharon in her

Escape

warm house. The trivial things that thread together a life – clothes worn, chairs whose comfort is known, familiar voices learned, a dwelling's odours absorbed, faces seen daily – were now gone for ever, and the exhausting work of re-creation had to begin.

In less than a day, it would be impossible to call family, Sharon or friends without risking a trace. It was then five days before Christmas, so if there were farewells to be made, it might be safe to do so only till nightfall. From the Sheraton, I rode by tuk-tuk to the Silom Center, and then moved from floor to floor, looking for followers. There was one call that I had to make first. Knowing Tommy's phone was tapped, I hoped to lead my pursuers south. At a payphone, I called Chiang Mai.

'Tommy. Trouble at the airport.'

'Are you sure?' Tommy usually doubted eyewitness reports.

'Absolutely. I'm going underground. I'm just calling to let you know.'

'Where are you going to go?' Tommy could be relied upon to feed lines.

'I'll take the train south and cross over the border to Khota Bharu. From Malaysia, well, I don't know,' I said.

'How can I keep in touch?'

'Forget about that. It'll be like the three monkeys. Hear nothing, see nothing, know nothing.' Perhaps Tommy would read that clue.

I rang off early, not wanting to stay on Tommy's poisoned line any longer. I planned a path to Large Raj and Tramshed's Chinatown travel agency that would be sure to ditch anyone following me. There, I'd take an hour on the phones making my last safe calls to the life I was leaving.

Again on the street, and still swollen with failure, I stalked towards a sun whose rays slipped from the edges of high-rise buildings with occasional flares. My flesh felt overrun with blind fire ants, and my brain was lowering implacable doors to deny the inevitable changes ahead.

A spluttering tuk-tuk drove me through narrow streets of

tinware shops, hardware shacks dripping with G-clamps, shopfronts barricaded with leaning stacks of plastic buckets, unfinished cane furniture spilling from footpath to gutters, street-food barrows with oily glass shades, old men hammering ruined metals on their anvils and cobblers dredging stubby fingers through biscuit tins of bent tacks. These weathered craftsmen looked at my boots as the tuk-tuk inched through this late-hour traffic. The boots I wore had been made in London 14 years earlier. A shoemaker's cellar in that city held pine lasts of my feet. As I walked, those very boots actually began to disintegrate – an event I hesitate to include here, for such coincidences seem so unlikely when told. Yet, so it was.

Lights in the shops of the jewellery district took over as darkness fell, and I began to feel lighter, having survived sunset. On foot, I cut through the textile-market mazes, slipped through dank one-bulb corridors and arrived at the arcade in Chinatown. I stopped to observe the travel agency. Large Raj sat behind his desk. The office was otherwise empty. Two Thai men in black leather jackets stood nearby. Their cigarettes had been smoked almost to the filters, so they could not have been followers.

I stepped into the travel agency to be greeted by Raj.

'Hi, David. Come in. Tommy called 20 minutes ago. He said you might come by.'

Now, that's something it's taken me a long time to remember. Possibly because at that moment four men moved swiftly into the shop. Of course, at first I thought they were thieves. The $50,000 I had in my shoulder bag must have produced that assumption. Very often it isn't easy to distinguish thieves from policemen, as both use similar body language during operations. However, their exposed hip holsters rapidly identified them.

There was no way out. No rear exit, and in the arcade there would be more police nearby. I had nothing to say, and if they wanted to say something, an Indian travel agency in Chinatown was not where they wanted to say it.

They moved me in a close pack to a nearly full underground car park. As I waited while some other policemen unlocked car

Escape

doors, I leant on the radiator grille. It was almost cool. However they came to know that I would be heading for Chinatown, they'd had time to drive and park. Neither the Thais nor the Australians could operate a live phone tap quickly enough to provide that information from Tommy's call. By the time I was taken to the Narcotics Bureau, an Australian from the embassy was waiting. He looked like a policeman, sent no doubt to have a first gloat. He didn't speak to me. There must have been some other group – obsessed and technical – and I couldn't understand their interest in me, an independent C-list druggist. Who would care?

I was not astonished later to be prosecuted for Sam Gilburne's abandoned grams. As often as not, the drugs luckless pedestrians are charged with carrying belong to friends or fellow travellers.

While in Klong Prem, I could become as obsessed if not as technical as that unknown third force that had directed my arrest. Thailand held the data, and maybe I could not move on until all was revealed. Maybe information has a life of its own, holding everything in its grip until it takes a recognisable form, even if we are too distracted to admit its shape.

CHAPTER FOURTEEN

'The train had just left Bolzano – that's Italy, you know – and then she became very friendly, smiling all the time, and she was wearing many white things, and we were alone, you know, and the train was moving very fast. She was kissing – I don't know how that started. I can speak to you, David, of those things because I see you have your own everything, everything under control. You understand? So of course I'm thinking this is all very good with this girl, you know, and she is giving me pleasure with her mouth, but suddenly in this fast train – it is moving and the lights are moving – and I know then she is putting something into me, and I'm not the one giving to her.'

'Was it painful?' I ask.

'No, no. I mean she is taking my spirit, and putting something bad from her into my mind. Like she is a witch, you know. This was too bad. I wanted to throw her off the train. I did not. She got off at Innsbruck – there was something wrong with this girl. Some reason she was there. Now, there's this magazine,' he trumped, proof upon proof.

'Magazine?' I was talking to the Czech, Karel Stendak, serving 30 years for the usual 2.7 kilos. Stendak sometimes arrived at my desk when Jet was not around to warn me.

'Yes. The magazine,' Stendak began, confident in his evidence. 'I was not in my chair in the factory. I think somebody called me away. So I come back and on my chair is this magazine. Catalogue,

169

really. For some clothes. And of course I see her picture there – the same girl. So. It's no accident, eh? And on my chair. You know who put this magazine, maybe you saw someone?'

'I don't suppose you still have it?' I saw Jet carrying something he'd found back to our office, so began signalling for help.

'No. Of course somebody took it after they made me see it.' Stendak lowered his eyes, rather disappointed I hadn't guessed. 'Because anyway, I don't realise it is the same girl until later. Too late by then, they know. But, you see?'

'My teacher.' Jet had arrived. 'The chief wants to talk to you about your cat. He says your cat's shit!'

'Really, Jet. We'll have to see about that!' I stood, turning to Stendak. 'You'll have to excuse me. The chief. The cat, you know. The shit.'

'OK, my friend.' Stendak rose from the ice-chest seat but didn't move, so I began poking through cupboards as though searching for a weapon to deal with the troublesome chief. 'You are very quiet here, David. It must be good. Can I move into your room? We can talk at night?'

'We'll talk about that some time,' I said, escorting him to the gate.

Once Stendak was out of sight, I doubled back to the office and stared at Jet, who was laughing.

'Jet – *the chief says my cat is shit*? Was that the best you could think of?'

Karel Stendak had alerted me to the conspiracies against him before. Gleefully for them, unhappily for me, schizophrenics can spot me from a great distance, and they see a friend. Karel told me of the card players secretly plotting against him on board a ferry from Caligari, and the little boy on a rollercoaster in Plzeň who had transferred his toddler's fear to Karel by some dark magic. Most of these revelations came during travel in large machines. The key to these mysteries had been inserted during an emergency operation he'd had under general anaesthetic following a motorcycle accident. 1000cc. He was sure the doctors had placed a microchip in his ankle, which had since been transmitting voices into his brain. Stendak's imprisonment was, of course, all part of the conspiracy.

I had been discouraging visitors to the office that month, as I was working on the latest escape plan.

Sten, Swiss Theo and I were to let ourselves out of our cell late at night, and then head for the wall. The challenge would be to walk along the corridors without the trusties and other informers forming a chorus of alarms as we passed. Our armour would be in our appearance, for we would be dressed as United Nations medics: Sten and I wearing blue caps, white tunics and UN insignia. We would carry Theo on a stretcher. Theo would be mostly covered by a blanket decorated with red crosses. We would wear surgical facemasks to protect us from a mystery virus.

The likelihood of such an apparition in the Building Six corridors might not seem feasible at first – or even second – thought, but it would play to our audience and keep those watchers silent as we moved towards Six's sleeping guard. In addition, with each stop at any wakeful guard, the option of taking an alternative uniform would present itself. However, none of us saw any value in trying to appear as a Thai guard. Sten and Theo were too big to squeeze into most of the uniforms, and that illusion would work only at a great distance.

The stretcher upon which Theo would lie could conceal the spars for a ladder that we would assemble at the wall near the hospital building.

'What about an assault through the main gate?' Theo had suggested after we'd calculated the time it would take to tape together an eight-metre ladder.

'A few more there than you might think,' Sten had found after questioning his friends about late-night releases for deportations. 'Sure, there's only four, maybe five guards on front-gate duty after midnight, but half the guards in the prison get down there to play cards and drink. Plus, the local cops call in at all hours to join the party. We'd have our hands full.'

Escape

'And what about the key to our cell?' Theo rightly saw the cell door as the main barrier. 'Are you sure that's going to work, Dave?'

I was not, especially as the key would be made from old clock parts and epoxy resin. Moreover, access to the cell door's keyhole was blocked by a large steel plate on our side of the bars. I was making a device of wooden gears and levers that could be operated by hand from within the cell. Operated blind, and adding stress to the key held in its grip. For all that, I had yet to manage a few minutes alone with the real key to take an impression.

'UN doctors making house calls?' Sten shook his head but was still smiling. 'What if the elephant man sticks his leg out for treatment?'

'It wouldn't fit.' I had to defend the plan. 'I'm talking about a glimpse, and even then just by a few prisoners as we pass. The uniform, the symbols, the stretcher, the sight of high authority, international stuff, the outbreak of disease. Just flash and filigree. They'll be excited but respectfully quiet. And Theo, you won't have to do a thing until we get to the wall. Just lie there.'

That sounded good to Theo until, 'What if a guard stops us?'

'Exactly,' I pronounced as if it were all simple. 'You spring from under the blanket and throttle him!'

That week, I had an unpleasant visit from an Australian federal policeman, Jonathan Snapes. We sat opposite each other in the executive-visits hut. Like all police from Western embassies, he carried a blue diplomatic passport as immunity from arrest. Snapes placed his business card on the table for me to take. I took it, as the FedPol logo was not yet in my collection.

'There are just one or two things we would like to clear up.' Snapes was slightly flabby, and sweated within his suit. 'For the sake of completeness, you understand.'

'Completeness?'

'Yes. Of course, we know pretty much everything already. And you'll be here for some time. Twenty years, most of us agree. Over that time, well, your memory may fail.'

Escape

'Fail?' I would ask him to explain everything.

'Yes. Now look, the heroin from Tommy Marchandat. Only 200 grams. Not much use to you?'

'No use at all.' As Snapes was alone, I presumed he was wired for sound.

'I mean, packed properly, you could take more. In some stuffed toy, for example.' Snapes must have been told about the Steiff bear I gave Tommy.

'A bit old-fashioned, don't you think?' I frowned in disapproval.

The policeman leaned onto his interlocked fingers. 'What's it like in here? Pretty tough – so they say.' Snapes had had enough of my being coy. 'No chains, I see.' He looked to my file, as though searching for an explanation of this oversight.

'Don't worry.' I had to lead him away from that. 'They'll go back on once I'm sentenced.'

'Good to see you're being realistic. Ah, now – one last thing,' Snapes clarifying a trifle. 'Your mobile phone. The one you use in Melbourne. Who has that now?'

'Gosh, I couldn't possibly say. They seem to have a life of their own, don't they?' Evidently, Michael had made the red-herring call, not that it had done any good. 'I say, Snapes, on your way out, I don't suppose you could stop at the prison shop and buy me a jar of instant coffee?'

I told myself that I wanted to give the impression that in Klong Prem I had few resources, although I knew the image of Jonathan Snapes battling with the ornery prison guards' wives who ran the shop would make for an easier night. Snapes would not refuse; such time-honoured courtesies to the defeated were universal. He might resent the act of kindness, but would tell everyone at his embassy of his magnanimity.

I was a few minutes late arriving at room No. 57 that night, as I'd found some excuse to talk to the key boy. He'd been making up the bed used by the night-duty guard. The guard slept in a room with an oblique view of our cell door. Crouching to where the guard's head would rest, I could see that his view of No. 57 would be just blocked by a low dividing wall.

When I walked into our cell, Bruce the Pakistani was finishing his account of the latest from the Nigerian front.

'No passports, no tickets, nothing.' Bruce propped pillows against his wall and leaned back, hands behind his head. 'So, they are very angry, very upset.'

'What have I missed?' I undraped Dinger the kitten from my shoulder and placed her at the foot of my bed. She was still limp from some encephalitic cat flu, and had stopped eating the previous week.

Bruce then detailed the misfortunes of those Nigerian prisoners who'd thought their time had finally come. After many visits with the special delegation of Nigerian consular officials from Lagos, the funds had been raised for airfares home. All the passport photos had been taken, the forms completed. To earn their release money, some had convinced girlfriends and family members to run brown dope to Morocco. Others had traded, fought and clawed together the funds from within the prison. Then the silence.

The consular officials had disappeared. Checked out of their hotels. Emptied the bank accounts. Flown. Today, news had been delivered by one of the local dealers that these officials had no connection with the Lagos foreign office. Or any office, for they were conmen who had spent the past months fleecing the Nigerian inmates and their supporters. They had used a phoney letterhead to contact the prison, and fake diplomatic passports to gain entry.

'I must say I'm not surprised. This is not a new idea,' observed Bruce, a historian of frauds. 'Some years ago – during the civil war in Lebanon, Mr David – officials arrived at Manila to set up for the first time an embassy. They rented villas, an office. Hired secretaries, leased limousine automobiles. With those little flags of the cedar tree, you understand?' The fake ambassadors lived in the Philippines for two months, collecting bribes for promised visas for Lebanon, issuing bogus passports, which in turn gained bogus visas for Europe. The legation collected relief funds for those dispossessed by war. 'They were the toast of the Lebanese expat community, but you know, when they disappeared, they hadn't paid for the house lease, or the cars, or anything.'

Bruce later felt he'd revealed perhaps too much expertise in such matters. After we had dined on Blow-Job's Singapore noodles, he crept over to speak to me in confidence as I force-fed Dinger liquids.

'You know, Mr David, I am not like those people. Not at all.' Bruce rocked his head from side to side. 'As soon as I am out next month, I shall begin work on your matter. I will not rest.'

Gesturing with the glass eyedropper in my hand, I dismissed Bruce's kind offer. 'That's good of you, but that position is already taken', I said, pointing at English Rick in his corner, carelessly allowing a few drops of milk to fall on Bruce's knee. Perhaps those two would talk the next day.

The night guard was unbooted and in his vest by ten that night, but kept wandering about talking to his favourite crooks.

'Do you think he's a drinker?' Theo asked Sten quietly.

Sten shook his head. 'We'd never get rid of him if we started buying him bottles of Blue Eagle every night. Anyway, the fucker might start singing.'

'And he doesn't look like the type to drink alone,' I added.

Rick and I were playing Scrabble near the door so that I could watch. Rick, with his English love of dissembling, had devised new rules for the board game. In addition to the two real blank tiles in Scrabble, Rick's version allowed any number of blanks to be played by placing one's dud letters face down. The opposing player could then challenge the veracity of the blank, but if wrong, would lose a turn. Side bets were made on the issue of whether the phoney blank might in fact be the letter it represented. These bets would follow poker-betting rules, and would be multiples of our respective word scores.

'Rick, old bean,' I frowned at the board. 'What might that word be?' Although I was down by 68,507 points, the board was already a coma-ward of blanks.

'Why, that's *crypt*, of course.' Rick greedily added his new score. 'Unless you doubt my word?' Unchallenged blanks carried a triple-letter value.

'Never entered my mind,' I conceded, even though the board showed only □R□P□. 'As long as you give me your word as a gentleman.'

Beyond the gangway, the night guard removed his trousers, climbed into bed and closed his faded mosquito net. It was just after 11.30. I leaned towards Theo next to me and tapped his watch. Theo nodded, but then twisted his hand questioningly. He was asking about the key.

'Friday,' I answered, not wanting to say more.

'I believe in fate,' Theo began as he returned to his bed mat. 'I'll tell you why. Things happen to me. Unusual things, special things. You know what I was just thinking, remembering?'

No one knew.

'Years ago I was on a train from Silvaplana. I'd been in Italy, and was going home to St Gallen. This was a small train, nothing special, and the carriage I was in was empty except for one man who sat at the other end. He was a country fellow – I could see from the way he dressed. An old farmer type, but dressed well, as they do when they travel to town.

'Now, before I tell you about this old farmer, I have to tell you about my uncle. Or really, the uncle I never had. He died long before I was born, as a child.'

Theo stood and turned down the control dial of the ceiling fan so that he could light a cigarette.

'My mother and her brother – my uncle – lived in a small town when they were children. My grandfather was the manager of the town's bank, and the family all lived in the house attached to the bank. The kids had to stay away from the front banking part, but they used to play in the back yard and on the stone stairs inside. I suppose my mother would have been about six, or something like that.

Escape

'Anyway, in those days banks kept a gun around the place. I don't really know why – I suppose they expected bank managers to shoot at robbers. I can't see my granddad ever doing that. My uncle was eight years old at the time, and of course he liked to sneak out with the house gun and play with it whenever he got the chance. One day he and my mother were playing in the stairway. Little Theo – he had the same name as me – had the gun. It went off. Funny thing is that the bullet never hit him direct. It bounced off the wall – two times, they said. He was dead straightaway.'

'That must have been tough on your mum,' Rick said. I gave him a dark look.

'Yes. She never talks about it much,' Theo continued. 'But that's not the point. Like I say, I'm on this train. This is a few years ago now, and I suppose 50 years since my kid uncle died. Now, I don't know this farmer guy, but we get talking. Why that was, who can say, we weren't sitting near each other.' Theo held up a finger to underscore that point.

'Anyway, he tells me he comes from a town nearby. An even smaller town than my family lived in before they went to the bank. And this old guy remembers my uncle from when the kids were young. He tells me this story – just some little thing, nothing really – a story about when my uncle was six or something. The old man's dad was the mechanic in the town. He fixed the cars and gave the petrol. So the doctor's car comes into the gas station one day. The doctor has been out to see my grandmother, you understand, just finished seeing her for some fever, and now he's stopped at the gas station. There's some noise at the back of the car and they open the trunk, and there he is. My uncle, six years old and he's stowed away in the trunk of the doctor's car. No big deal, they all laugh and take him home. But it was the only time this old guy now on the train ever saw him. He said my uncle was a little tearaway, always getting into trouble.'

There was no third finger to this story, so Theo ended by saying, 'I would never know that except for the man on the train. And he wouldn't remember it, if something hadn't happened with little Theo getting stuck in the doctor's car. The chance of me ever knowing about my uncle was very small – but it happened. You see. Fate!'

No one had anything to say. Theo looked around the cell for some response. Rick emptied out the last Scrabble tile from the green bag. It landed face down. Sten had fallen asleep. Bruce, in the far corner, had been reading a magazine, not listening, perhaps thinking of his forthcoming release. Bruce spoke.

'The life of a woman is easy, really. Easier than for a man. I could even cope with motherhood, if necessary. In every way, easier.' Bruce folded his magazine. 'It's just that I couldn't stand the idea of being fucked by a man, that's all.'

I turned off the light and took a final look at the guard to see if he'd moved. No change.

CHAPTER FIFTEEN

Friday. Key day.

The key to the cells of third-floor-north hung with a bunch on a neck-sized ring kept hooked to the wall of the guard's restroom, an empty cell sometimes made up with a bed at night for dozy guards.

During the day, the building was empty of prisoners other than the principal key boy and three other trusties who mopped floors. Inside the accommodation blocks, guards rarely touched keys. Mornings and evenings, key boys would race along in front of or behind guards, locking and unlocking. Between times, the building was off-limits to the other seven hundred prisoners, with two exceptions.

The first was a small, shiny nut-headed prisoner called Dr Rotkhendek, whose gift for languages supported his claim to having been a diplomat with the Thai foreign service. He insisted his imprisonment was the result of encouraging students within the democracy movement. This was unsupported by his jail file, which credited him with the axe-murder of his wife. His money had bought him a cell in which he lived with two servants. Dr Rotkhendek's habit was to move in and out of Building Six several times each morning, never moving far from the gatekeeper Pornvid's lounge at the top of the steps.

The other exception was Westlake, who had lately taken to mid-morning runs around the compound wearing a tennis outfit. I had convinced Pornvid that these runs left me in need of a shower – with the usual economical argument – and that it ill behoved a guard of Pornvid's status to have a prized tenant showering with the common herd. Well, he took the money anyway.

The large dining hall was being cleared for a special event that morning, the Klong Prem annual beauty contest and talent show. The benches had been removed at one end, and others stacked to make a stage platform. As I completed my laps of the compound, the blind man within the hall was packing up his candy and hand-made cigarette stall behind the chicken-wire windows. At each pass, I heard the old man hacking and spitting out the previous night's phlegm accumulation. Careful in his nest, he would locate a gap in the wire with his gnarled fingers before releasing a massive gob onto the bitumen path. His projected sputum made an increasingly hazardous minefield each time I passed. After my run, I would arrange distractions for Pornvid and his trusties so that I might take an impression of the cell key undisturbed.

On my final lap alongside the smelly old geezer's kiosk, my attention was divided between the sight of foreigner-trusty Tanveer talking to Pornvid and high-stepping through the medallions of mucus on the ground. Too late, I turned in mid-stride to see the grizzled Chinaman standing at the chicken wire as I approached. His twisted fingers were tangled in the mesh, his cloudy eyes staring beyond the infinite and his rubbery lips working through the gap, tongue coiling like a vinegar-splashed worm.

Projectiles often travel faster than the sound of their explosion, and the gurgling clap reached my ears just as my eyes focused on the salvo that had left his stretched mouth. Two sensations remain in memory: one, a monstrous glob shooting through the wire, a yellow-green spoonful of putrid tracheal slime with three flailing arms and several embryonic eyes, spinning through the air in full-throated attack. The other, the sickeningly warm thump of the bow-legged trader's bacteria-laden viscid petard slamming into my white Lacoste single-knit. I fell sideways into a crumbling plaster lion at the entrance to the accommodation block, cursing the old bastard and trying to tear the condemned T-shirt from my chest before the alien snot ate through the fabric.

'You old prick! You've been waiting for me at every turn, haven't you?' I shouted, quite convinced that a suggestion of a smile flickered under the cigarette seller's lips.

Soon afterwards in our office, I found a new T-shirt and tried to make Jet stop laughing long enough to deliver messages on this important day.

'Jet, run over and take Dr Rotkhendek over to Theo.'

I had arranged for the diplomatic axe-murderer to translate a court document in Theo's playroom at the rear of the chief's office.

When Jet had left, I took from a locked cupboard three small pencil tins. Each had a layer of Plasticine within, ready to receive the key impression. Pocketing the tins, I moved quickly to the army boot factory to find Viet Tan.

Tan was a Vietnamese American who had grown up in San Bernardino spoiled by his hard-working parents. When he turned 24, Tan was asked to help at the family bakery. In retribution for this outrage, he signed on as a courier for a Bangkok–Chicago run. He'd reasoned that if he got through, this would prove he didn't need his parents' support, and if he was arrested, then that would show his folks they'd pushed him too far. On the day of his flight from Bangkok, Tan connived with himself to miss his plane, and so leave later in the evening for Honolulu. He had heard of high dope prices on the islands and convinced himself that the Chicago criminals would overlook the theft of their drugs. This plan was ruined when he was arrested by suspicious airport police. He had been at the check-in zone for six hours, alternately sitting upon his suitcase (for fear that it and its precious contents might be stolen), or watching it from a distance while drinking slurpees, building a cunning defence that any drugs must have been planted in his absence. Tan never developed this defence in court. He pleaded guilty, received 25 years and now lived on his parents' wire transfers to the US embassy.

Escape

Tan was in his factory corner training his two Burmese servants to iron his T-shirts. These hardworking Burmese had spent enough time in Vietnamese camps to learn the language, and were unthinkingly attached to Tan. Their master looked worried when he saw me.

'Dave, come over here. Out of the way. If the guard sees you, he'll be ragging me for money in a minute.' Tan drew me further into the factory.

Nodding towards the factory workers spreading heavy glue over army-boot soles, I sniffed, 'Can't see how you pay much for this place. You must be dizzy from the smell.'

After a further exchange of unpleasantries, I told Tan a version of the morning's needs.

'Tan, I'd like your slaves to get over to the trusty outside the building. He's messing with the foreigners' food again.'

'Dave – don't use that word!' Tan looked to his staff from Burma. 'They know that word – *slaves*.'

Once calmed, Tan agreed to send his boys over to speak with the Burmese trusty. Foreigners' food amounted to white rice, an egg and a scoop of chicken-foot soup issued daily to each non-Thai inmate. Rumoured to be paid for by some United Nations fund, this nourishment would be collected by poor foreigners who then bartered with it. Wealthier foreigners exchanged the food for clothes-washing services. The trusty-in-charge this day was trying to take an unreasonable cut of the bartering, and settling that dispute would keep Tanveer and the food trusty away from the accommodation block. To Tan, I provided a different cause.

'The thing is, Tan, all this is right outside my office. When they start arguing about food, they all start shouting, and you know the Africans can out-shout anyone else. The noise is too much. It upsets everyone. Wakes up my guard. You get my point?'

The crazy Czech Karel Stendak was standing at the edge of the smoking charcoal fires where the homeless cooked their meals. He was frowning at a group of Thais performing surgery on each other. The heavily tattooed chief surgeon was inserting the last of a dozen polished beads of mollusc shell into the penis of his patient. These operations resulted in the cauliflower dick-heads so admired among those motherless city tribes who impress each other with body decoration.

'David, have you seen this?' Stendak pointed to the deformed wanger. 'They think girls like it like that. They say it gives them pleasure.'

'Not if you believe the newspapers.' I was talking of a recent story in which a prostitute in Khorat had refused to service a customer whose dork she'd described as a praying mantis. The customer had complained to the authorities. The girl had been freed by a sympathetic judge. 'Karel, have you been over to the chief's office today?'

Stendak shook his head.

'Funny thing,' I said. 'Rick was telling me the chief has you down as a former airline pilot. You dark horse, you! You never told me you were a top flyboy. *Boeing, Boeing!*'

That was enough to send Stendak off to the chief's office. The confusion would – I hoped – take quite some time to be resolved. Especially as I hadn't warned Rick of this subterfuge. Rick should instinctively play along.

Pornvid, reclining at his station guarding the accommodation block, waved me through as I picked at my unsticky T-shirt and wiped no sweat from my brow. The building was deserted, and a band in the food hall was tuning its instruments.

As I sped along the jail's clear corridors and passed the locked and empty rooms, the cells' barred doors seemed open-mouthed and hungry in their silence. I lifted the keys from their hook in the guards' room, gripping the bunch tight to lessen the noise. I already knew the key to No. 57 by sight, so I kept the others clear when turning the old mortise lock in the cell door. The turn was tight, requiring a twist similar to that for a pickle jar left too long on the shelf. The key boys had found trouble with this tight lock before, I'd noticed. However, to change cells now could take months.

Inside the cell I hung the keys on a nail, took off my T-shirt, draped a towel over one shoulder and picked up Dinger, who was sitting on my bed. I took the cat to the corridor and placed her on a sheet of paper she might find interesting for a few minutes. Returning to No. 57, I hoped Dinger would respond in her usual timid manner to the first sight of strangers, and jump back into the cell.

Within two minutes, I had Plasticine impressions of both sides and the tip of the cell key. I pocketed the pencil tins. A minute later the keys were again hanging from the guards' room wall and Dinger was watching me take a shower, wondering why her breakfast was late.

By the time I was at my desk, the Klong Prem all-stoned band was meeting popular demand by playing Boney M's 'Rasputin', and the more adventurous Thai boys were dancing a free-form jitterbug with each other in the hall.

Taking the key impressions to a small table I kept at my first office (a narrow space behind the factory alongside an inner wall), I set the three tins next to one another. From a cupboard, I mixed resin and catalyst to pour into the moulds. This I added quickly, then I placed the tins in the cupboard before locking its door and moving to join the other spectators in the dining hall. I would have to wait until every prisoner was out of sight before inspecting my work.

The band was playing the final chords of 'Yes, Sir, I Can Boogie' when I arrived for the beauty contest. Two dozen ladyboys from Building One were in the finals for Miss Klong Prem. Curiously, most of these transvestites were dressed in a modest and old-fashioned style: long dresses of heavy silk with imitation pearls and fulgent rouge highlights on their cheeks. Those few among them dressed as tarts in leather miniskirts were quickly eliminated. It seems prisons hold the custodians of conservative and prudish views.

Escape

At the edge of the stage I found an Australian, Brian Wittol, who had accompanied his Thai wife to the contest. Brian was disappointed that his Butterfly had been struck from the ranks.

'I knew I shouldn't have let her enter.' Brian shook his head as tearful Butterfly McQueen fled the stage. 'But what can you do? A fellah has to let his woman have a day out.'

Brian's compatriot, Martin Sallowface, was also visiting Building Six for the show, and had never before seen the cream of KP's ladyboys. He seemed disappointed.

'Can't see what all the fuss is about. Pretty fugly bunch. Lucky if they can earn a crust over there.' Martin was referring to the tent city within Building One where the *kathoeys* and the near-enoughs entertained their gentleman callers.

Brian's grip tightened on Butterfly's make-up bag as he whispered to me, 'He's just jealous 'coz me wife's had the full cut.' Brian then jerked his head towards the remaining contestants. 'They're jealous, too, the nobheads. That's why they wouldn't let her win.' Despite what some saw as a risky leisure pursuit, Brian was the healthiest of the other Australians at the time, perhaps because he was at least enthusiastic about something.

I left the hall just as the winner was announced. This particularly tall girl cried as she held her flowers. Her Adam's apple trembled, and badly sewn sequins rained at her feet. 'I never expected – I'm so proud of my friends.' She threw her bouquet to her supporters with such heartfelt force, they ducked instinctively.

My old office and factory was completely deserted when I brought my new key into the daylight. I glued the two halves of the glass-like key together with fast-setting epoxy resin, using the tip impression as a guide to width. There was still time with the festive distractions to compare this resin master with the original upstairs in the block. I did, and I saw that it was good. With that done, I made three copies, two of which were embedded with metal strips for strength.

* * *

Escape

The following week, Pornvid returned from lunch with a packet of expensive X-ray film. He sent the film to my office to avoid any discussion of change from the money I'd given him that morning.

'Photos of family?' Arib asked as he carefully lowered the yellow box to my desk.

'I hope not,' I said, wondering if I could save some of the film for the forthcoming solar eclipse. 'Arib, go get me a blue-shirt, please.' I meant a trusty, as I would need an escort beyond Building Six.

I was taken through the inner wall to the AIDS hospice for my X-ray in search of kidney stones. Beyond the hospice, another wall separated Building Ten, and yet another before the outer western wall. My escort had stopped to speak with another trusty at Building Five, where he collected half an ounce of heroin for the AIDS-ward trusty. There were not many patients there who could afford pain relief, or oblivion, as the dope prices at the hospice were beyond the means of most families. Morphine was never officially prescribed due to concerns about addiction. Over 400 inmates were dying in this building, yet the wards and corridors were quiet. Moans and sighs subdued or repressed. To Western eyes, Thais approached death with great decorum.

As I'd expected, the X-ray room had no other patients, and little space for any, as the ancient machine took up the space of a cold-war computer. The trusty-operator threw monstrous switches, twisted plate-sized dials and then hid behind a narrow, useless screen as the behemoth sucked power from tangled cables knotted through the window bars.

'You're the radiographer?' I asked.

'Yes, sir. Ten years, sir.'

'Ten years' training?'

'No, sir. Ten years Klong Prem.'

When the radiographer disappeared to develop the film, I took in the view from the X-ray room. A direct path from Building Six would mean crossing a field and garden with two watch posts.

Escape

I could not imagine those huts being occupied at night. A trusty manned the AIDS-hospice gate, and since the moment my escort trusty had left to take tea with his fellow blue-shirt, I'd heard no sound other than the footsteps of my radiographer.

When the operator returned with the large sheets of developed film, I quizzed him on the use of heroin in his ward.

'I suppose it makes it easier for them,' I suggested.

The trusty paused in thought, and then answered: 'I understand, but I don't like it. It makes them live longer.'

As I sat at my desk, frowning at tiny abdominal ghosts on the X-ray plates, Jet delivered a letter from English Martyn. It was, in part, his report on the state of the foreigners in Building Two:

> . . . *somehow, the fact that they have separate huts built by nationality has made them more resigned to their fate. Even within these groups of expatriates, there is no cohesion. I don't think that it's the tropical heat or mere apathy, but the drain of continual self-regard.*
>
> *You'll find no serious recruits here; embassies hold out hope, you see. Honestly, I think most of us are better off in this madness than in our Western prisons. At home, even drug crime is seen as pathological. There would be demands for behaviour-modifying therapies, educational courses to address one's offending behaviour. Everyone would hate it, and especially so for being locked up by our own people . . .*

Some visitors had arrived at the office. I folded Martyn's letter on, 'I have something for you. Try to visit when you can.'

Before me stood the two new Chinese-Thai owners of the coffee shop, friends of Charlie Lao. Between them stood a small Chinese boy who appeared not more than 12 years old. The boy had wide eyes and a face of immaculate skin, as if painted in ivory emulsion with the brush dipped too deep. Spotless except for a freshly blackened eye with a yellow highlight on his cheekbone.

Escape

After Arib and Jet found chairs for my guests, I sent the servants away – which peeved them – and began making tea.

'I have a fine wedding cake from Sri Lanka,' I offered. 'I've been waiting for a good moment. You might find it too rich, and the rosewater scent can be a bit overpowering.'

We three then made polite enquiries about the state of our respective affairs. Not before I'd served the tea and cake were the problems of the boy introduced.

'He comes from a good family, but they are not rich,' began the elder. 'We didn't know he was in Building Six until this morning. But Qing only spent one night with the others. We think they – the superintendent and his people – did not want to tell us.'

'Did the blue-shirts keep him in their cell?' I was wondering whose interests were in play.

'No, they found a place for him with one of their friends. Some big men.'

'I see. How can I help?'

My visitors relaxed. 'We will certainly take the boy to our room, but that will not be possible for one or two days.' The older man looked at his cake cubes. 'We are too full. But we will fix that. One or two days.'

This meant that the chief was asking for biggish money for the room change, and that the coffee-shop owners were stalling. Rightly so, for they already paid the chief 200,000 baht each month. Also, my all-seeing Chinese friends knew that Bruce the Pakistani would be released from our cell that night. I put down my cup and wiped my hands with a paper napkin.

'Qing is welcome in my cell. For as long as necessary. No harm will come to him.'

A sorrowful tone of enquiry formed around the elder's next words. 'You may have some difficulty with the ledger keepers.'

I waved such concerns away. 'Pornvid is the accommodation guard. The chief leaves every day at three to beat the traffic. Send Qing to Jet at four.'

My guests soon left, after paying compliments to Dinger the

cat, who sat on my desk like a furry blotter. I was pleased to help these influential friends, and flattered that they'd never hinted at money.

'Well, how about that, Ding?' I spoke to the cat. 'We'll not allow them varmints to get to the kid. Raise that paw of yourn and I'll swear you in as deputy.'

However, I meant it.

That night, Rick, Theo, Bruce and I were already in No. 57 when Sten arrived with Jet and tiny Qing. The little ones were carrying extra containers of food and an icebox of drinks.

'Blow-Job's made us some kind of feast tonight.' Sten threw some towels on his bed. 'I didn't ask him to.' Sten then gave Bruce a lightly disguised sarcastic grin. 'Maybe it's a send-off for you.'

'Is that so, Jet?' I asked. 'A surprise for Mr Bruce?'

Jet burst into derisory laughter. 'Absolutely, my teacher.' He then ushered Qing into our room.

Sten directed traffic. 'Jet, you take Bruce's place when he goes later. Qing can go next to you.'

Jet put down his tins and whispered to me excitedly, 'He's beautiful. Like a little girl!'

Sten overheard. 'And Jet, you can keep your filthy paws off him, you damned giggling little pervert!'

So we settled and ate, and toasted Bruce's good fortune in an evil world, and Bruce gave thanks. Although Bruce provided explanations – earlier promises, cultural loyalties – as to why he could not bequeath us his prison riches (radio, bedding), we had doubts. Bruce was freed after eight. His sentence of seven years was comparatively light, since drugging and robbing people on trains was something done to poor people.

With Bruce gone, Jet turned to making Qing comfortable, and Rick and Theo turned to arguing about drug law. In this I had no interest, but had heard much over the long nights. The opinions of lawbreakers about drugs usually followed the chemical composition of their most recent convictions.

Escape

English Rick was a cannabis man, and so felt a moral superiority to those whose chemicals had passed through a laboratory. As most of us do, Rick believed that everything produced on a farm is good. 'It's natural,' he'd insist. 'Grows wild. Doesn't make people do bad things.'

Sten argued that the drug problem didn't really amount to much. 'If the addictions caused any problem – I mean real problems like influenza or madness – then legalising it would have been tried. It's all a con. They do what they do because they can.'

Martyn had once said that the drug war was the New Puritanism: 'the fear that someone, somewhere is not only happy but can switch it on and off'. Martyn also noted that no new drugs were developed simply for pleasure; that any drug that had no other purpose than recreational pleasure would be outlawed, regardless of its safety. He would go further to say that nature encourages a level of misery and physical discomfort – 'perhaps this unhappy normal state provides the ruthlessness needed for survival' – and so underscores self-denial.

Theo made the usual comparisons with alcohol. 'Would you condemn champagne just because you see some disgusting wino vomiting at a railway station?' As for the law, Theo saw a paradox in sentences. Many countries applied the same sentences to drug traffickers as to murderers. 'But there is now serious talk of legalising drugs, which is good. No one would compare that to legalising murder. And here, the sentences are saying just that!'

None of these ideas mattered in law, according to Sten that night. 'Whether the law's right or wrong, we know what it is. It's no use moaning.' He took another plug of his *snus*, a tobacco snuff. 'A lot of people realise that blasphemy laws are an old joke but if you burn a stack of Korans on a Tehran street corner, you can't say the reaction was unexpected. When the rag-heads chop your head off, the issue of the law being right or wrong doesn't matter any more over there than it does here.'

I had to agree with Sten, and said something about practicalities: that no-nonsense scofflaws cannot waste time arguing the rationality of laws. Rick, wanting to separate himself from the criminals, asked of me, 'Surely you see a difference between selling weed and smack?'

After 20 years in the trade, sitting around chewing over the merits of drug law had become too heavy a meal. To Rick, I replied: 'I like the drug business because I'm a lazy slob. Anything that interferes with eating or sleeping is hard work. With dope, the talk is kept to a minimum and the meetings brief in case the enemy is watching. The health regulations form just one line. No industry watchdog. Industry standards are nicely reviewed at each meeting. So if I buy the best stuff, I can't go wrong. While governments keep it illegal, they keep the prices high. No matter how mindless or self-serving the policy, it suits me. What's more, as soon as possible, my customers eat the evidence. And if I work more than an hour a day, it means I must be stuck in traffic.'

Rick wasn't satisfied. 'Don't tell me you don't think any more of it than that? You use drugs, you've used heroin.'

'Sure, and so what? I'm still looking for something wonderfully chemical. Your garden puff hardly deserves the name toxic. It's a great disappointment that we're stuck with the shabby intoxicants of today. I'm envious of future generations who'll get the good stuff.'

Rick sniffed, snorted and then gave up. It was not easy to make him indignant, and doing so could often lead to further speechmaking.

The next day, after my morning run, I tested one of the cell-door keys. It was a good fit and began to lift the internal springs. Unfortunately, it also began to crack. A second key, again formed from epoxy resin and metal strips, was too rubbery for the torque required. The Goldilocks key would have to be steel. Sten was waiting in our office as I returned.

'Everything OK?' he asked.

'No.' I sat on the ice-chest sofa. 'The keys are a perfect match for the original. Just not strong enough for the old lock. Maybe six or seven kilos' lifting strength is needed.'

Escape

'So, what next then? File one up from scratch?' Sten did not seem as frustrated with this delay as I was.

'Yeah, we'll do that, but it's a slow job. Meantime, I'll send out a plastic copy and try to get a steel one made. Not in Bangkok, of course.' I was irritated, so turned on Sten. 'How's the photo coming?' I was asking about Sten's passport photo, now late arriving.

'It's coming.' Mild annoyance. 'I've written to a girlfriend in Norway. She's got my pictures. By the way, the chief wants us to take in another foreigner.'

'Not if we can help it, Sten. It's just as well Bruce's gone.' With Qing now under the care of the Chinese, we were only five in No. 57. 'Can you imagine what Bruce's reaction would have been if we'd let ourselves out one dark night?'

Sten nodded, saying in sham-Italian: 'Caccaria la pantaloni! Bruce would fill both trouser legs.'

'Right. And anyone the chief would give us is bound to be worse.'

Sten was untroubled. 'Nothing we can't manage.'

In our own ways, it had been just such assumed confidence that had brought Sten and me to the gates of Klong Prem.

CHAPTER SIXTEEN

Rick had returned from court not long after five, and had been bouncing off the walls of No. 57 since.

'She did it! I knew she would. Good girl!'

Rick was applauding his Thai wife, who had befriended the woman prosecuting his case for possessing 15 kilos of grass. Rick that day had been sentenced to a year's probation, a provision in Thai law I'd seen applied only once before to a foreigner in Klong Prem – a year earlier to a hippified Australian with one joint and a pocketful of Thai friends. Now Rick seemed ten years younger than his thirty-five. Between outbursts of self-congratulatory joy, he struggled to show sympathy for those of us remaining with sentences amounting to hundreds of years if combined.

Rick was already shedding the everyman personality he had adopted upon landing at Klong Prem. The convicts around him seemed more scruffy and amoral now. He would no longer have to hide his education with an egalitarian coat. Some rehydrated sentiment towards his upper-middle-class family was now welling beneath his features. No more than sentiment, for he'd had no contact with his parents in Southport for years, and had abandoned those youthful pretensions for the personality formed with his expat chums in Pattaya. I couldn't see the value in class distinctions. In my early years, under the cold rules of business, I'd tried to wring some useful work from such artificial differences, but none paid. It's risky to divide humans from our animal nature, and race has even less significance – no more than a passing fashion, often making traders blind to potential profits. As for class, it rarely earns the stamp of convincing illusion.

Rick could barely concentrate on cheating at Scrabble, but managed a game to present me with a wrinkle in his imminent freedom.

'David, you know I've spent all my money on getting this far.' Rick spoke softly. 'Trouble is, the lawyer said they might kick me out of the country tonight anyway.'

I read from the court order. 'This says you have to report to some office in Damrong Rak at ten tomorrow morning.'

'Yes, but it's the immigration police, you see. They don't know anything but deporting all foreigners released from jail. That would mean tonight. I'd have to fly somewhere and then come back.'

'OK, so you've got a passport?' I wondered where this was leading.

'Yes. But the thing is, although I've got enough cash for a flight to, say, Singapore and back, I don't know if my wife will be able to see me in time before I go to give me more. For expenses and so on, you know.'

Yes, I knew. I returned Rick's release paper and then resumed quartering a worming tablet (for humans) with a nail file. Dinger's worms were eating her from the inside out.

'The thing is, David, I was hoping, maybe, you could lend me one of your credit cards for a day or two?'

Rick had one convincing argument to support his request. A week earlier he had promised to ask one of his oilrig diver friends to make a steel copy of my plastic cell-door key. Now, Rick could do this himself. One part of this new proposal was without flaw: Rick, having worked in the chief's office for so long, could send me the finished steel key undetected, in some kind of gift.

'OK, Rick. You'll only be able to get a thousand dollars from ATMs. Try not to run amok. And let me know what's going on – whatever happens.'

'Absolutely.' Rick then whispered in confidence, 'You're not like the others here. You know, losers.'

Escape

That was enough to make me give him the card that I usually kept for my factory boss, a card with a shallow draw.

At a quarter to midnight, we losers bade Rick farewell as a front-office guard dragged a nearby key boy from his mat to unlock our door. Jet stood by the door like a bellhop to receive the tip for months of disloyal service; a tip that never came. Sten grunted goodbye from behind the shower curtain while taking a pee, and Theo sprayed Rick with an unexpected sneeze.

'Thorry, Lick.' Theo made to wipe Rick's shirtfront. 'Fuggin' bad cold. All the betht.'

Rick's advice about his probation order was correct. Local police took him from the Klong Prem gate and held him for three hours until immigration cops called by to take him to the airport. Rick then flew to Singapore. At Changi airport, officials were impressed by the large red stamp in Rick's passport declaring: DEPORTED FROM THAILAND FOR NARCOTICS. As there would be no narcotics in Singapore, Rick was denied entry. He then flew to Hong Kong, a more welcoming territory. I came to know most of this from a records clerk at KP, and from my Visa card record. Soon, as the card ceased automatically telling, the Rick trail went cold and I knew no more.

A visitor that week told me of a party I had missed, as visitors do. Klaus had been in London, and had stopped at Bangkok on his way to see old friends in Macau.

'Sharon was there. Your mother, too.' Klaus was calling through the double bars of the standard visit zone. He'd arrived unannounced. 'Everyone sort of came together by chance. It wasn't planned. It was just funny that all these, well, friends of David happened to be in London. We were all going to get tickets for *Sweeney Todd*, but there wasn't time.'

'So you held a wake instead.' I wondered what the food had been like. 'And I couldn't even attend my own funeral.'

'Not a wake, exactly. More like a friends-of-David dinner. Though, to tell the truth, everyone was saying this time that we wouldn't be seeing you again. Sorry, not like that.' Klaus paused to find kinder words. 'It's just that some of us are getting old, you know. I brought you some crusty bread.'

'From London?'

'No, that'd be mad. From a Vietnamese-French bakery I found here.' Klaus had owned a large restaurant in London before selling up and retiring to the Algarve. He knew which foods would be rare in a Thai prison. Klaus had more to give.

'I've got some photos for you. Not the ones you want – not passport photos – but all we could find. Copied from your radio operator's certificate, I'm told. Colour, anyway.'

Klaus sealed the pictures of my younger self in an envelope, and then told me that Chas would be visiting next month. Chas had also been at my wake.

'And did Chas share the consensus that I'm finished?' I sounded defensive.

'I can never tell what Chas thinks, but he certainly wasn't nailing down the coffin lid.'

Before he left, I sent Eric the trusty around to bring the photos I would later have delivered to Charlie Lao. There was also a note from Michael. It read, 'Dean Reed never arrived for his appointment. No word since.'

Chess by mail.

Sten was alone in his and Theo's hut when I returned from my visit with Klaus. Sten had almost finished another oil painting. We had found a solution to the problem of making and storing a ladder for scaling the walls: Sten had built ten stout picture frames, each eighteen inches by twenty-four. While two lighter frames had been stretched with canvas, the others would form the rungs of our ladders when bound between bamboo poles from the paper factory.

I tapped the edge of Sten's new painting. 'Has anyone noticed that these new picture frames are less than half the weight of the eight stashed in the office cupboard?'

Escape

'Who'd notice?' Sten frowned my way, although I wasn't being sarcastic about his use of heavy colours.

'That one got a name?' I asked. It could have been called 'Chocolate Bars on Mud Flats'.

'Nope. No names.' Sten closed one eye to make a fine adjustment. 'No names for paintings.'

I placed one of my photos on Sten's easel.

'That's mine done. Theo's, we have – where is he anyway?'

'Upstairs in the room. Sick. Headache. The flu. Said he wanted to lie down.' Sten lifted my passport photo, then regarded it briefly before returning it to me. 'I squared it with Pornvid. About Theo staying in the room for the day, I mean.' Sten peered carefully into the background of his artwork, and then with a broad-tipped brush scraped a knob of eternal brown from his palette. 'You think Rick will come back with a key?'

'Who knows?' I said. 'He's got to get back to Thailand first. Anyway, I'm filing our own copy, slowly. You know, Sten, it isn't safe to run around Thailand without a passport. Not safe to stay, really.'

'I know. I've got some friends up north, if it comes to that.'

'OK. But let me know if I can help. We can retouch old holiday snaps.' I leaned with one knee resting on a chair. 'Is there anything troubling you, Sten?'

'This key business. I mean, fuck the UN thing. What about straight out the window – through the bars?'

I'd thought about that. 'Well, we're three floors up. And two floors below us there's a tiled awning sticking out five feet. Remember when we had to fix the toilet pipes? The lightest touch on those crumbling tiles and they were falling to the ground. If you can think of a way around that?'

We had none, so I went to my old vacant office and continued filing.

That night Theo didn't eat Blow-Job's spaghetti. He took a handful of aspirin and retired early to sleep off his flu.

Escape

I noticed a pack of sulphonamide tablets by Theo's bed and, curious, asked Sten: 'Was he taking these for his cold? I don't think they'd work.'

'It's not that.' Sten pointed to the pack of antibacterial pills. 'They're for his ear infection. He's had them since he was a kid, and regular antibiotics don't work. Can't get through to the ear, or something. The only things that do the job when he gets blocked up. Theo's been blowing his nose today like he's doing it for the Olympics. Says he can't stand the stuff in his ears.'

'So he gets these headaches often?'

'Not that he's mentioned.'

Sten and I ate quietly on the far side of the room, trying to figure out a way to avoid taking a roommate of the chief's selection now that Rick had been released.

'Know who he's got in mind?' Sten asked.

I nodded. 'Another paying guest.'

I told Sten of Miraj, a new arrival in Building Six. Miraj was a Hindu Indian who'd been in the travel business, supplying passports, visas and special routes to Indians and Pakistanis hoping to work in Western countries. He hadn't bothered the Thais much, but he had excited those in the US embassy's immigration-fraud taskforce. There had been little of substance in the case against Miraj – a single Thai visa wrongly identified as fraudulently obtained in Penang – but as a courtesy to the Americans, the Thai court had awarded Miraj 20 years' imprisonment.

'He's made the chief a lot of promises to get a good room,' I warned Sten. 'We'll have to let him in. There's no one else, we can't hold out, just the three of us plus Jet.'

'So what's so bad about this Miraj?'

'Nothing, really. Seems tame enough. Of course, if he sees us packing up one night to take our leave, he'd scream his head off.'

Sten stroked his chin and offered a thoughtful look that suggested he might enjoy taking care of such a problem.

* * *

Escape

Around ten, I offered Theo some tea. He declined. That is, he wouldn't speak, although he was conscious but not asleep. In fact, he couldn't speak. That's the way it is here, I saw then. A moment ago, the room was quiet, and now it is still quiet. A moment ago, Theo was sleeping off a cold, and now he's in real trouble, needing immediate medical intervention. I saw again: this is a prison, the room is sealed. Our Klong Prem island of 12,000 is one of decay and death. Our custodians – village bullies, tyrants, shamans – are not here to help, only to watch us die.

When I returned to my side of the room, I thought aloud to Sten.

'What do you think is happening in our excellent Lardyao hospital tonight?' I lowered my voice, realising that while Theo might not be able to move or talk, he might easily hear. Sten frowned a new question, and I nodded towards Theo before continuing.

'Let's assume we get him there – there would be no doctor of course – and even if one called by, nothing would be done. How do you suppose the Swiss embassy would react if someone called the after-hours emergency number?'

Sten rubbed the back of his neck. 'Whatever's wrong, no one will send for an ambulance.'

We ate some pancakes with maple syrup. Sten finally showed Jet where Sweden is on a map. It occurred to me that Jet could use some better company in our room. We listened to music on the radio.

Shortly before midnight, Dinger uncharacteristically began sniffing around Theo's foam mattress. Theo had peed himself. Sten and I then rolled him from his side to find one of Theo's eyes was turning milky, the lid no longer active. The other eye seemed frantic, although Theo made no sound. Even his breathing was creepily regular.

'Can you speak, Theo?' one of us asked.

Theo could not. Nor could he move one arm, which had begun to curl into a rigid spiral, the fingers of his hand gnarled. Using what control remained of his good arm, Theo swung it over his head, slapping his hand against his ear in a desperate flutter. His one eye blinked furiously.

After fifteen minutes making a lot of noise, we managed to wake a guard. He was not happy, even after we gave him two cartons of cigarettes. Reluctantly, though 1000 baht richer, this night guard woke a key boy to keep watch, and then shuffled to the KP hospital.

'Don't worry, Theo, we'll get a doctor,' I lied.

Sten added, 'We'll get onto the embassy tomorrow if they don't do anything.'

Jet made coffee. We ate biscuits and then Sten pretended to read his book while I read a mail-order catalogue from Alamogordo, New Mexico. Jet stared at the ceiling. A long hour passed. Sten wondered, 'Can we give him anything?' I shook my head.

The guard from Building Six returned with another from the hospital. Perhaps an orderly. They did not want to take Theo from the cell. Too much trouble. We said we could help. I provided the overtime payments, but only one of us would be allowed to help the key boy carry Theo. The orderly guard called the front-gate staff on his radio; told them he had one for the hospital.

The door to No. 57 was unlocked. Sten and the key boy carried Theo to the corridor on his mattress. The guard assisted the key boy only by turning the key to secure Jet and me inside the cell. My last sight of Theo was of his bare feet as he was carried along the corridor, and then his thin mattress being squeezed a little at each end by Sten and the key boy so he would not fall as he was angled down the stairway.

Jet cleaned Theo's corner while we waited for Sten to return. When he did, Sten waited for the key boy to leave before speaking.

'You know, even if he lives, he'll be a vegetable.'

Theo died from the unhurried internal bleeding of his brain in a KP hospital corridor seven hours later. Miraj, the Indian people smuggler, moved in the following day.

* * *

Escape

I found Martyn at a table littered with the skeletons of a dozen VHS video recorders. He had been scavenging for parts to create a working machine. I was visiting Building Two and Martyn to collect some gizmo he'd made for me. We spoke first of the changes to the KP social register.

'I heard you had a suicide,' I opened. 'Someone from this hut?'

'Yes. Well, Maurice was British, but it wasn't suicide.' Martyn dropped a small screwdriver into a plastic cup. 'Not unless he was some kind of Houdini. Tied head to toe.'

'Business?' I'd heard that there were many disputes over food, drugs and space in Building Two.

Martyn shrugged. 'Everyone's content to blame trusties working for guards. And drugs, of course. Makes me suspicious of my countrymen, but I'd rather not think about that. And in your building, Theo? A fellow here says his mother came over.'

The Swiss embassy had made a very small fuss for a few days after Theo's death. A consul visited some of us at the prison. Theo's mother flew from St Gallen to collect the body, and took the trouble to thank those who had helped at the end, not that any of us had. She'd heard bad things of Thai prisons, and had said, 'At least they won't be able to hurt him any more.'

I'd finished my recollections, and was boiling water for some tea I'd brought when Martyn asked, 'You really thought they'd do something for Theo in that hospital, David?'

I lowered the purple tin and looked at Martyn. 'You're a hard man, you know that? Why is it that scientists are so charming when they strip away someone's convenient delusions? Like, holding a martini and smiling over some suburban fence as his neighbour pointlessly digs another foot of bomb shelter.'

Martyn pretended to be mystified, so I got to the point.

'Sure, I wanted Theo out of the cell that night. I knew he was a dead man and didn't want to explain a stiff in my cell come morning. What would you have done? Started tapping a blood vessel?'

'Sorry, David. I didn't for one minute mean to imply—' Martyn stood to attend to the boiling kettle. Few foreigners in Building

Two had servants. 'Now take a look at this. I've a pen for you. You'll see it has some LEDs.'

I picked up the black pen with three tiny lenses set in its shaft. 'Do I have to turn it on?'

'No, just touch it on the wire, holding the top insulated part. That wire around the wall – I'm betting the middle light there will glow yellow. That's two-fifty volts, so use caution – especially so high up – and the white one just means ten volts from some three-phase source.'

'I suppose the top one's red. And if so?'

'Uh, be careful. Or take some marshmallows. How's it going anyway?'

'Not good. Just Sten and me. No real plan. Are you sure there's no one here in Two who's up to no good? I mean, 150 Westerners, I'd have thought this place would be a hotbed of intrigue.'

'There's talk of things but they're no threat to the prison. A hotbed? Building Two is fraught with *no danger*.' Martyn was quoting the broadcast from Radio Moscow's English language service a year after the Chernobyl meltdown in which officials claimed the area safe. Improbably, it was. For some reason, almost a decade after the phrase was first transmitted, it had become popular just that month among the foreigners of Klong Prem.

Martyn and I then batted around and finally dropped another plan in which I'd be called as a witness in someone's case in Songkla. The idea was that I would get lost in transit. I had no faith in the friends of inmates, and wanted no talk of escapes beyond the few. I returned to Building Six with my new toy, alarmed that I seemed to be running on ten volts.

Miraj the Indian travel facilitator might have been an admirer of the great Gandhi, for he brought to No. 57 no more than two thin blankets and three shalwar kameez cotton suits, all of which he wore at once. Perhaps the chief had drained Miraj of all funds, although that seemed unlikely. It was more probable that Miraj had paid his rent with promises, for he was said to be very rich.

Escape

Miraj operated what may be a faultless profession, depending on the level of service. He guided freemen and slaves alike; he mocked our imposing crested and marbled passports, erasing our arrogant borderlines from our bogus charts. He rendered our visas blind. Public-spirited work indeed, and at no more than market prices. Despite his worthy endeavours, every moment in Miraj's company demanded the strength to resist strangling him for no clear cause. Unfair, really. Yet everyone felt the same.

When I advised him that our chief would not easily be put off without cost, old Miraj produced a borrowed smile that suggested he could outwait the devil's eternity without raising a sweat.

'I've met many chiefs.' Miraj set out his tins of food for his evening meal. 'And they are all hungry.'

Sten peered down as Miraj opened his tins. One tin held a lettuce leaf. Inside the other, seventeen beans, sliced lengthwise, it seemed. I sensed that Sten had taken an immediate shine to our new roommate.

'Miraj, you old trooper! What have you got there?' Sten suddenly dropped to his haunches, his knees inches from the polished nut of Miraj's head. 'No need to spend all day over a hot stove. We've got a top cook serving up for us. Our Blow-Job will fix you up with something to get your gums around. You can eat with us.'

'Thank you, but I'm a vegetarian.' Miraj half shielded his meal, as though it might be vaporised into the pores of this massive Viking.

Sten stood upright just as suddenly as he'd dropped. 'Won't cost you much, Miraj.'

'Most kind, but I don't eat more than I need.'

Sten turned, and to me nodded assent. We had earlier agreed to accept Miraj into our room. Others could be worse; they might have friends, have ideas – and for now, the chief would leave us alone as he tugged hopefully at Miraj's steel purse strings.

Monsoonal rains had continued into October with no cleansing effect, just hastening the decay. Under the downpour, thatched roofs disintegrated above our huts, vegetables soured quickly and the filth surfed rather than flowed.

An old friend would soon visit, and it was unlikely he'd be stopped by rain.

CHAPTER SEVENTEEN

harles Stanford had elected to put himself among the wounded. Not in the relative safety after each battle had moved on, but while the dogs of war still tore at the bodies of the fallen. Western law encourages the arrest of its quarry's family, supporters and even well-wishers. So when Chas arrives to help, he takes a risk.

With my vocation in mid-level druggery, I'd brought enough trouble upon myself to scare away many friends, stun family into paralysis and cause once-firm lawyers to stumble and retreat. Through this immobility, Chas would walk. The feature of his interest that most infuriated authorities was that he wasn't a crook, received no financial rewards and could not be persuaded that he was aiding the wrong side. Few things more enrage those who believe themselves to be on the side of God and rightness than the sight of one who should be a knight in their chosen colours giving aid and comfort to an enemy. Even a small enemy, quite vanquished.

A modest businessman, Chas has a wife and grown children who respect his valour enough that their sensible protests become subdued as he again answers the call. I'm sure he would take this praise as nonsense, for Chas no more hesitates to respond to the distress of friends than he might delay answering a doorbell.

The visit pens were quiet that Monday morning when I stood at the empty benches waiting for Chas to appear. Beyond the wire, far away by a guard post, I could see his tall figure as he talked to the guard. He was not alone. Some civilian helper was at his side, settling something with a guard. Chas turned, as though instructed, and set off looking for me. Soon, he was plainly lost, as I was invisible in the gloom of the barred pens. I intercepted him after 50 metres of backtracking.

'Chas. Here!'

'Ah, there you are. Hiding as usual.' Chas peered through his substantial glasses to see that I was upright – walking, breathing, alive. 'Well, very fashionable, I see.'

'Everyone wears shorts here, Chas. It's their way of distinguishing the Ins from the Outs. Well, you found the place. And got through. Good to see you.'

'I had some professional help.' Chas turned to see his helper approaching fast. It was Charlie Lao. 'We met up in Sydney and Charlie flew ahead by a day.'

I hadn't heard from Charlie since he'd returned to Australia, yet here he stood.

Charlie skipped the formalities. 'David, I tried to get the embassy room but the guard today is the wrong one.' Charlie was animated and flustered that he had not done better. 'Is this OK? We can go to the lawyers' section.'

'No, Charlie, this is fine. Thank you. There's no one here today, anyway. It's not the foreigners' day.' I wanted Charlie to calm down.

'OK. Good, good. I'll go and fix everything. You talk to your friend. I'll make sure you get your clothes and food. I'll come back soon.' Charlie scooted away to do more business.

Chas smiled. 'He's been worried since I got here that I'm paying too much for everything.'

I then gave Chas an account of my time in Klong Prem, ending with the uncertainties of my arrest and the certainty of a bleak future. Chas knew some of that, having kept in contact with my lawyer, Montree.

'What do you think of him?' I asked. 'I think it helps that Montree is a little bit mad.'

Escape

'Well, eccentric perhaps,' Chas corrected. 'He means no harm, and we're to have lunch tomorrow.'

'I don't suppose you've heard from Tommy? I haven't.' I'd written to Tommy-of-the-Triangle, yet had received no reply.

'Yes, we keep in touch.' Chas had helped during Tommy's troubles in Australia during the 1980s. 'I'm flying up to Chiang Mai tomorrow night.'

There would be some official interest in that, I thought. 'Any signs of the forces of darkness?'

Chas shrugged. 'They know I'm here. I flew with hand luggage. Clothes only in a collapsible canvas bag. If I need another shirt, I'll buy one as I move along.'

Chas told me of one development in Tommy's world. Tommy's Uncle Lou, number four in the Triangle, was dead. Not so long ago, during a quiet Saturday morning, Tommy's uncle had set out on a country journey in his Mercedes. The car had then stopped on the highway from Chiang Mai because of tyre trouble. The driver climbed out by the side of the road to fit the spare. Uncle Lou got out to observe. A massive truck flew over the rise and ploughed into Lou. He was dead before the truck stopped. An accident, everyone in the north agreed.

'Is that what Tommy thinks?' I asked.

'The driver was questioned. Uncle's second-in-command made his own enquiries after the police had finished.' Chas assumed the deadpan tone of an old-fashioned reporter. 'That part of the road is notorious for accidents. The investigation is closed.'

'I'd like to see Tommy,' I said.

'He'd like to see you. Really.'

Charlie then returned and told me of his arrangements for Chas's further visits and some for himself.

'How long will you be staying in Bangkok?' I asked Charlie.

He seemed surprised. 'I've got a small apartment not far from the prison. Only 15, 20 minutes away. I'll stay as long as you want. I'm here to help you.'

This was too embarrassing for modest Charlie, and he strode off to make sure the guards had done whatever they'd been paid to do. Chas outlined his own fortnight in Thailand.

'I'm spending a few days here and there. Seeing some friends of my jeweller mate who's always over here. A couple of days in Trat, walking on Ko Chang. Then over to Kanchanaburi, and more trails up to Nam Tok. I expect to do a lot of walking. Even in Bangkok.' Chas's preferred response to being followed was to set out on foot early, dressed as though for the corner shop, and then to walk for hours over difficult terrain.

Without urgency, I detailed the pathetic history so far, of Dean Reed who'd set out to make his mark as a smuggler, the promises of Rick who'd absconded with my credit card and the appearance of Sharon's mystery gent at a Bangkok hotel.

'I think the man was there to see what Sharon was up to. American, I think. Took some interest in Dean. Not part of any operation – but I'm guessing there – maybe just some curious official. One thing's for sure, I'm going to get hammered.'

Chas was ever reluctant to talk in certainties, yet conceded, 'I don't think you should have any good expectations for the courts.'

'I can't stay, of course.'

'No. I expect not.' And with that, Chas moved on to the subject of absent friends.

Dinger had been taking care of the office while I was away, and had expressed her disapproval of unfocused management, as Jet reported immediately.

'She shit on your desk, again. Big shit.' Jet accused me of being a bad parent.

Perhaps I had been too quick with the interventions to keep the sick kitten alive, and clearly she blamed me for not curing her chronic enteritis. One morning when I'd squawked at her over another desk mess, she seemed to squawk back, 'Well, do something! What have I got to do – shit on your head?' Dinger had no appreciation that not all events were under my control.

Miraj didn't take to Ding in No. 57, notwithstanding his Hindu wrap. That night, the cat wandered too close to Miraj's mat in his corner as he feasted on a chapatti the size of an eyepatch and a nubbin of tacky dhal. Miraj unleashed a blow with the force of a loosened shoelace that perceptibly tickled Dinger's ear.

Sten looked up and frowned at Miraj. Miraj gaped at Sten's knees and suggested: 'The cat's got to learn?'

Sten, never much interested in Dinger, flicked two fingers at Miraj's head, sending the Indian deep into his corner. 'No. You've got to learn,' Sten rebuked casually. 'The cat was here first.'

To be persecuted by both outlaws and the law is a rare achievement. I suspected Miraj had realised this was his inevitable lot early in life, and so became accommodating yet miserly without delay.

To end the silence that followed, I asked Jet about this day's little mystery. Seven trusties occupied cell No. 58, and were usually gleeful and talkative. Yet for the past two days they had been creeping about. Moving in pairs to their cell and making only subdued noises at night. It seemed unthinkable that they might be planning an exit.

'So, Jet. What's going on next door?' I passed Bo-Jai's rice pudding to Sten. 'And why don't you want to tell me about it?'

Jet didn't want to tell me about next door for perfectly good reasons. None of which he could express. Stupidly, I steamed on, and was told that three of the trusties belonged to the Chinese box factory and its insufferably mean boss, a guard unhinged by the frustration of not being able to extract money as fast as he could drink it. This guard and his trusties served up a little heroin in Building Six, and in protecting their reputations as law-abiding men would pounce on a careless junkie every new moon. The hophead would be beaten and sent to the *soi* for a week or two.

This week, the box-factory guard had gone too far with his specially made lead-weighted truncheon after the dopester had talked back. By the time accounts were settled, the boy was in poor shape. The trusties took him to the back of the factory to recover. When he did not, they took him to their room for the night. There, they administered first aid by injecting an amount of heroin they hoped would beget a fatal overdose. The plan was to put the body behind the toilets in the yard early the next morning. However, the boy had a strong resistance to a drug the trusties were too stingy to mix effectively, and was still breathing at sunrise. Change of plan. The blue-shirts jumped up and down on the boy to hasten his death and then left him in their room for the day.

'So he's alive now?' I asked Jet. 'Next door?'

Jet looked down. 'I don't know, my teacher.'

We in No. 57 could have slept more easily without knowing of this, and I would have spared the gentle reader that knowledge, too, were it not for the change that this caused in the events of the following day.

This was a day for parole decisions for Simple Offenders. An annual event when short-term prisoners would be interviewed, assessed and – possibly for those serving less than five years – released. Such a celebration was too good a spectacle not to be used for the education of young Thai citizens, so several busloads of schoolchildren were brought to Klong Prem. The children were escorted through the streets of Building Six to see the rehabilitation in action.

In preparation for this, the usual rejects were locked in their cells, the foreigners confined to the dark channels of factories, and the cripples, the deformed and all others considered alarmingly ugly were swept from the streets. Kerbstones were whitewashed and the bare earth raked. The coffee shop's bank was shuttered and its displays transformed with royal portraits. Uniforms were unpacked from dank storage and issued on loan to those inmates due to go on show. Some of these prisoners then presented as bowed and penitent sitting at benches in the food hall as they awaited assessors who ruled from five tables, centre stage. Other prisoners were set to marching gaily – and endlessly – around the compound, singing national songs of praise. Sten and I were exempt from the round-up of undesirables, as we were KP landowners and effortlessly lived the lie of cooperation.

Escape

At lunchtime, a colourful saffron-rice-and-chicken meal was provided for the visible prisoners in the mess hall.

'Do they usually eat this well?' some of the schoolgirls would ask the trusties.

'A bit special today,' a trusty might confide. 'They don't always get dessert at lunchtimes.'

Jet listlessly brought plates of the special food to our office.

'I wouldn't eat this if it were mine.' Jet slid the plates for Sten and me on a table. 'It's shit.' Jet was serving 12 years, and so was dejected at the sight of so much freedom on offer but denied to him.

Sten sniffed at and then dismissed the food before speaking impassively. 'The main door to the building's locked. Even Pornvid's making himself scarce. No one wants to be around when the junkie gives up smoking.'

The boy in No. 58 was still thoughtlessly refusing to die on this special day, and the trusties had left the side door to the cellblock open and unattended as all cells were locked. Perhaps they thought they might blame the boy's death on passers-by. Anyone using this side-entrance would be invisible to trusties, guards and the schoolchildren.

'This might be just the time to grab our new bookshelf,' I said to Sten. 'The plank was still there this morning.'

Sten and I walked from our factory office to a secluded miniature garden where a compound guard slept at night. A two-and-a-half-metre scaffolding plank had been abandoned within the garden. Work had just finished on an open gazebo built in the classical style, a gift from the portrait workers to their guard. We lifted the plank and then trotted around to the side of the accommodation block. Sten paused to set two pot plants on the plank, as though the long board were merely transportation.

This plank would make a bookshelf almost as long as our cell. Usually, we would buy our furnishings rather than steal them, but this piece would cause too much talk, need too much explaining. Unfamiliar Western amusements often bothered our keepers. Only a month earlier, I had to make a financial fuss to retrieve a model plane kit that had arrived by parcel. 'It's powered by a rubber band,' I'd assured the chief. And Sten explained, 'Made of balsa wood. We want to play with it on the sports field, *basta*, that's it!'

The corridors of Building Six were empty as Sten and I padded through its side door. We stopped once inside the entrance, and Sten smiled a *why-not?* Certainly, everyone else was locked in or distracted by schoolgirls, but there were so many walls within KP that even dominance of Building Six allowed no real freedom. I returned Sten's look with a grin of rueful hopelessness. We would not get far making a mad dash, and with a plank for a ladder.

'The keys?' Sten suggested as we reached No. 57.

'Not today, not now.' I lowered my end of the plank, and offloaded the potted palms. 'I don't feel lucky today.'

We slid the plank through the cell door's bars, letting it flop to the floor, and then deposited the plants in the empty guard room. Moving back to the stairs, Sten paused at No. 58.

'Wanna look?'

As far as I knew, the battered narcomane was still inside. 'No. If we're not going to do anything, what's the point?'

Sten looked anyway, and didn't say anything until he grew tired of me not asking.

'A lump under a blanket. Not moving.'

Our quiet neighbour died before nightfall. His body was taken to the hospital where medical staff declared he had died from a self-administered overdose.

Our new bookshelf appeared dangerously heavy once mounted on the brackets nailed into the decaying concrete wall. For safety, we positioned it above Miraj so that any noise would be muffled if it fell during the night.

A hospital trusty arrived at my desk the following day. The blue-shirt told me that I had an appointment with a specialist. For my kidney stone, I presumed. I'd almost forgotten about that complaint, since it had been part of Dean Reed's schemes to provide a judge with a reason to grant bail.

Escape

While waiting on the benches at the hospital, I tuned in to a conversation between one of the doctors and the box-factory guard from Building Six.

'You should have brought the boy here earlier,' confided the doctor. 'I could have done something.'

The guard looked uncharacteristically troubled. 'We had the special day. All those schoolchildren – nosy visitors.'

'We have a driver, you know. Many times we take them to the hospital.' The doctor was talking of the practice of loading the dead onto an ambulance and taking the corpse to the military hospital. Officially, the dead would always be alive when they left Klong Prem.

'Mr Westlay?' A doctor new to me stood at a doorway with a thin file cover. 'This way, please.'

The doctor sat at his chair in the small consulting room and folded his hands. He looked past me to the door and gestured with his hand. 'Please see the specialist in the side room.'

The side room looked like a place where staff ate their lunch. At a table with a plastic cover and two bottles of fish sauce sat Tommy Marchandat, last seen by me on his day trip from Chiang Mai before I left him for Chinatown.

Tommy stood and smiled – 'David' – and held his arms open in offhand astonishment at the mess he believed I'd made for myself, while seeming to take a bow for his skill in appearing before me.

I had trouble stifling a smile in return. 'You could at least have worn a white coat.'

Tommy was too cautious to be seen visiting a foreigner – well, this foreigner – and had leased this practice for the afternoon.

'I don't suppose you could take me with you?' I had to ask.

'If only it was that easy,' Tommy had to say. 'Chas came to see me a couple of days ago. Sorry I haven't been down before this, I've been waiting for things to go quiet.'

'When they shoot me – things will be quiet after that.' I was being childish.

'Don't be like that. This is Thailand. My country. You'll see.'

Escape

I nodded. 'You were seen arriving back in Chiang Mai with your Teddy bear.' I wanted to dig the past. 'You know you were being followed? That your phone was tapped? Still is, maybe.'

Tommy wasn't having any of that. 'I'd know if that was true. I even checked with the police. It's very unusual to tap phones in Thailand.'

'It's unusual for Thais to be told, more often.' Then I turned to family matters. 'Who's running the store for your uncle?'

I went on to suggest Tommy's uncle was executed by his deputies. They were all Chinese. Uncle Lou was not. Tommy countered that after Uncle was hit by the truck all diligence was shown with investigations. However, I could see that Tommy didn't much like the sound of his own explanation.

'Tommy, there's so much heat around you, I'm catching fire. A few more Americans in our lives than there should be, too. You know they can listen to any phone in Thailand without telling anyone. Now you tell me, what's going on?'

Tommy did not answer as we were joined by the subordinate doctor, and lunch was served.

Eventually, and later in the day than I'd hoped, I heard the story that mattered. It was bracketed within other laudatory Uncle Lou tales. Many years earlier, in the 1970s, when Tommy and I were still independently looking for trouble, Uncle Lou had wider, grassroots control of his narcotics fiefdom. He would personally visit farmlands, laboratories and town shippers. At that time, the US DEA ran a four-man office in Chiang Mai. Its agents were told not to venture further afield than the office water-cooler.

One ambitious agent wanted more. Using the office maps, he drove to an opium-growing village within Lou's realm. The agent offered inducements and promises to the village headman. Left his card, as crusading spooks might.

The village headman thought about living in America for a month or two before calling Uncle. Unfortunately, the American scout's visit had already been reported to Chiang Mai, where Lou was troubled by this mutinous hesitation. For peace of mind, he had

Escape

the headman beheaded. News of the decapitation soon reached the DEA office, as intended. The chief of DEA operations, CHM, was angry with his inferior officer, and ordered him to stay close and keep quiet. Perhaps misunderstanding his superior's tirade, the agent then began making open threats and public allegations about Uncle Lou.

Uncle Lou was in his late 50s at that time, and experience had taught him not to go about killing Americans promiscuously. Instead, Lou arranged an object lesson.

The wife and two children of the DEA man were also living in Chiang Mai for the term of his posting. The children were taken each day to a private school by their mother and a driver. One morning, as the family were on the way to school, their car was intercepted by two gunmen who put aside the driver and then took the American family to their own minivan. The plan was to hold them for a few hours and then release them as a warning against snooping. We should remember that in the 1970s, events in the Middle East gave thoroughly misleading recommendations as to the value of kidnapping Westerners.

The snatch was on schedule until the gunmen's minivan broke down at a busy Chiang Mai intersection. A traffic policeman soon asked the driver why he had three terrified *farangs* in his van. The traffic cop was answered by two bullets to his chest, but did not die before returning the compliment to the assistant gunman. These exchanges did not help the flow of traffic, and within an hour the scene was transformed. Many police, reporters, even a TV crew from Channel 3 – the military-owned channel.

By lunchtime, a locally famous and respected Buddhist abbot had grandly negotiated the release of the children. This left the lone gunman in the minivan with the American wife. To ensure that there could be no further misunderstandings, the gunman had bound the trigger of his revolver with copper wire so that only his thumb kept the gun's hammer from discharging a round into his hostage's head.

News of the bungled kidnapping displeased Uncle Lou, who

immediately made fresh arrangements. The abbot would now substitute himself as hostage, and the woman would be released. Then, using another vehicle, the abbot and the gunman would travel to Chiang Mai airport. I suppose any plan would appeal to the gunman after seven hours stuck at a set of traffic lights with a dead accomplice and a lethal hostage. Uncle then commissioned an army commander to surround the area with a special unit. Unfortunately, the Americans had earlier reacted by insisting that the army make every effort to have the gunman taken alive. Accounting for this, Uncle Lou ordered in a sniper team attached to the Chiang Mai police, with its seconded rifleman bearing special instructions.

All this had taken time, and the afternoon heat in the minivan was extreme. Just as the abbot approached to offer himself, the sweat upon the thumb of the gunman allowed the hammer to trip. The wife of the American DEA agent was killed immediately by that unplanned shot. Less than a second later, the gunman too was killed by a single shot, fired from the rifle of the man from Uncle.

'So no one knew who was behind it.' Tommy was now emphatic. 'The gunman dead – just like when Kennedy was killed.'

'Or nothing *like*, Tommy.' I felt sure of a connection with his Uncle's death. 'Don't you know the Americans will never forget that? They can't let it go.'

'What do you mean?'

I tried to bridge an East–West divide. 'Why do you think you've had so much trouble over the years? Your uncle was arrested in a big way in a Thai–DEA operation. When that wouldn't stick, he was killed by agreement with his underlings – I don't suppose they wanted the curse extended to them. This killing of the wife of an agent. It's unforgivable, as they see it. You put a foot wrong and you'll be buried, too. And everyone close to you will get hammered.'

Tommy was shaking his head but he was taking this in.

'Tommy. Something you must understand about Westerners, this tribe from the North. We never forgive, even if it kills us.'

CHAPTER EIGHTEEN

So, there was no grand conspiracy with me at its centre. A dark deed had been done many years ago, and still we descendants felt the vengeance of inherited ritual instructions. Uncle Lou eventually paid for the deaths he'd ordered, Tommy would soon be immobilised by drip-fed terror, and I – well, I was fixed to be swatted with the casual brutality by which any marksman might strike a gadfly that obscures his sights.

Some faces became clearer: the guest Australian policeman at Chinatown as I was taken in; his look of mild wonder. Not at me, but at the speed and accuracy of the technology. That in a land still wire-tangled, the DEA could call him within minutes to say that Tommy had just phoned Large Raj at his travel agency to warn that I would be there within the hour. The restrained delight as this foreign liaison officer called his Thai counterpart to announce the future: 'We have information that . . . ' And then bask in the magic by withholding the source of knowledge.

Another face: Abe Sousel's drunken ecstasy of revenge when telling his new clients, *'You'll meet that Westlake out there. He didn't listen. He's for the drop!'*

Before Dr Tommy left, he offered this prescription for hope: that at a decent interval after my trial and subsequent higher court appeal (and commutation of death to life imprisonment), he would make sure that the Supreme Court of Thailand reversed the earlier conviction. Five, six years at the most, he said. I did not take this medicine well. I told him that if he wanted to be one of us, a friend among friends of our tiny smugglers' company, then this feeble assurance was not good enough. That we did not treat each other this way. It was not for me to listen to his words, I said, only to see him act. Tommy and I argued. I might have been harsh in the way a person can be when there is nothing left to ask. It's not worth recollecting the details.

Chas was waiting for me with lawyer Montree on the tenth floor of the courthouse a week later as I clinked across the foyer in chains with my bored guard.

'This is unexpected,' I said to Chas as I stopped at the benches. 'I thought courthouses were on your list along with zoos and funerals as places never to visit?'

'I almost never made it.' Chas watched Montree obligingly distract my guard with gossip. 'I went out to the prison by mistake.'

I sat on the bench while Chas told me how he'd arrived at Klong Prem on foot. That he'd found himself by the south wall, taken a wrong turn and walked 600 metres, only to find himself behind the prison.

'Completely lost, as usual,' Chas said as though it happened often. 'The moat on all sides, I suppose 25 yards across in places. Reminds me of when I took a swimming certificate sponsored by some newspaper when I was a kid. That was a 25-yard swim.'

Blundering on, Chas had to walk along a narrow path some 700 paces before the next turn east. 'Stupid, really. Charlie had told me the guards live in houses along that side. Damned if I could see them, what with all the tall reeds growing along my side of the moat.'

Chas had not long finished his detailed account of his morning's errors when we were separated. My day's hearing was about to start.

'I think you'll find you have another visitor this afternoon,' Chas called as I was taken to the courtroom. 'So, I'll see you at the jail tomorrow.'

The visitor of the afternoon was Rick. The prison was closing its main gates as I returned from court, so I had no time to have my chains removed, and only a few minutes to hear Rick's tales of misfortune.

He had flown to Singapore on the night of his release. Singapore immigration officers refused him entry, and so Rick then flew to Hong Kong. This much I knew. What I did not know was that Rick had been issued with a new passport by the British High Commission within 48 hours, and had returned to Thailand that same week. That was six weeks ago.

'I've been trying to get out to see you ever since I got back. I'd even arranged it with the chief. Didn't he tell you?' Rick held up two bags of groceries. 'I got you some stuff. Clothes, cigs, food.'

'Don't suppose there's a key in the cake?' I joggled the string holding my chains aloft.

Rick pushed a finger into one of the shopping bags, as though making sure he hadn't been robbed in the queue. 'I put some Cheerios in here. The thinking man's Frootloop, you know.'

'Great.'

'Well, sorry – all right! I lost the damn key thing. All that flying about. It was touch-and-go even getting back here.'

'You get to meet Chas?' I had less than a minute to talk, as loathsome Eric the visit trusty was making faces.

'Only for a few seconds, I was on my way somewhere. Seems like a good man.' Rick put the packages before me and searched for his car keys. 'I'll be out again soon. I gave the credit card to your friend. Anything you need?'

To that, I chuckled, 'You'd better go, Rick. They're closing the gate. Don't want to get stuck in here again.'

Chas was puzzled about Rick. We'd been accounting for all the bit-players in conversation the following day at Klong Prem.

'I understand the Dean Reed thing, I think – but I can't figure this

Rick. Why give him a credit card? Did you really expect anything from him?' Chas moved closer to the bars to avoid the noonday sun.

'Not much, I suppose.'

I signalled Eric, who was 30 feet away, grinning at a Thai woman visitor. 'Rick is no informer, and he has a good ear. You should hear him talk about the British liaison officer when he was arrested. The story's not important, but the thing is, Rick recalled every word, every look. He's a good barometer. More than that, Rick has that house at Naklua. Stable, always there. If the day ever came— ' I broke off as Eric was nearing.

Chas nodded towards Eric, asking in a low voice, 'Who's that woman he's talking to? She's sobbing now.'

'She's the sister of some poor doper kid the trusties sat on last week. She came to visit this morning before you arrived. Now she's been told the brother's dead— '

Eric had arrived.

'Everything all right over here?'

'Not really, Eric. We need to move over to the other side. Somewhere out of the sun.'

As I walked along the pen from my side, and Eric escorted Chas, the visit trusty tried to amuse us with the story of the sister. She had arrived for the visit as usual, waited, bought her brother two bags of food from the prison shop, waited, and then after two hours had been told that her brother was in the morgue. Eric had added something imaginative about her brother's drug use, and she had begun to cry.

'Silly woman.' Eric guided Chas to a quiet corner in the shade. 'I told her, "Don't worry, madame, the prison shop will refund the money for the food you bought. Don't upset yourself." Ha-ha!' Eric found his own wit incomparable.

After Eric had lurched away snickering, I told Chas about my consultation with Tommy, and my belief that the intense heat had its origin in the vengeance demanded by the Americans upon all connected to the man who shot the DEA agent's wife.

Escape

'No disrespect, David.' Chas thought nevertheless. 'You're pretty far down the line from Uncle Lou.'

I couldn't see anything else. 'When you salt the earth, nothing should grow.'

'Yes, I suppose there's the point that the DEA is after all a volunteer force – and normally not even front line – and governments have to be seen as loyal to their volunteers. Then again, you might simply have been the only game in town when the moment came to test some new toys. The secret phone gear, in this case. Who can resist testing the latest equipment when it arrives? You know, on that basis, they've smart-bombed the power grids of at least two countries I can think of back to the age of steam. No reason to think that they'd hesitate to blow a small fuse in your case to test a new system – if you'll forgive the analogy.'

Chas then went on to tell of Dean Reed's failed attempts to get started in a new career. 'He tried to get a visa for Australia in Kuala Lumpur. Bowled out in the first over. I don't think he had more than six months left on his passport. Went on to Singapore where the US embassy took his old passport and gave him a one-year temporary. Apparently, Dean didn't like the idea of going back to the US, which will be the only place he'll be issued with a full passport.'

'Is that normal?' I wondered.

'There's something in the closet there, but I don't think it changes things. If you wanted the opposition to think all your hopes are down to Dean Reed, then he's the man to keep them bamboozled, all right.'

'Not for long. I can't keep my case dragging on for much longer – it's been over a year now.'

Chas began rolling up 1,000-baht notes and threading them through the wire. He said, 'I'm heading home for Christmas at the end of the week. Next year, I'll be flying through on my way to Sri Lanka. I'll have a few days here.' Chas paused to check that no one was watching. 'I think Michael is sending you a Christmas parcel.'

'Yes, I'd sent him a Dear Santa.' I unrolled and pocketed the

Escape

18,000 baht. 'No sense giving Eric a commission on this lot. Although some of this might be spent arranging a Chrissy present for my favourite trusty.' I narrowed my eyes, hinting at making life unpleasant for Eric.

'With my blessings,' said Chas.

Charlie Lao had left for Vientiane to visit old family, and Chas had returned to Australia to see new family, for he'd been told of the birth of another grandchild. Sten and I did our best to ignore Christmas while worrying about who to elect to room No. 57.

'What about Steve, the new English kid?' I suggested.

'The disco-biscuit king of Khao San Road?' Sten groaned.

Young Steve was facing trial for selling Ecstasy tablets. His last days free came as he moved upmarket into the clubs patronised by Bangkok's *dèk Hi So* (high-society offspring), especially the glossy daughters of the newly rich Thais. The Thai papas didn't immediately thank this knobbly-kneed foreign git for corrupting their children. In fact, they had him arrested.

'No, not him in the room,' Sten pleaded. 'Talks too much. Anyway, he's only here for a shit and a shave – not more than 12, 15 years. We don't want some flibbertigibbet like that.'

'Maybe your friend Eric wants to move to the room.' Jet was at his easel, contentedly pencilling chubby babies on commission, although he still had spare attention for sarcasm. Eric the visit trusty had fallen from favour, stripped of his profitable job and sent to Building Five, where he held a thin line between 100 Nigerians and ranks of angry Thais. In a related incident, some *farang* troublemaker beyond Klong Prem's walls had aided the sister of the dead junkie with a newspaper contact. A private autopsy had been funded, and a prison doctor and the box-factory guard had taken leave. (Before anyone should become misty-eyed over this, be assured that messing with Eric was only a diversion on my part as I had extra funds that month. However, I shall not speak for Chas.)

I made a suggestion for our room space. 'How about Calvin? He's been asking to come back from Two.'

Escape

'He's the short one,' said Sten. 'Sleeps a lot?'

So we agreed on Calvin, our American friend. Calvin had found the heroin overpowering while living among the many Westerners of Building Two. More than a temptation, a quite affordable vice, for the dope was just cheap enough and Calvin just rich enough to balance an eternal addiction. 'Nineteen shillings and sixpence per annum,' as Martyn had said. He would transfer to Building Six as soon as he could pay the fee. The addition of Calvin would make only four foreigners and Jet in No. 57.

Calvin would never join an escape, as he saw his salvation in a transfer home to an American prison, still three years away. Besides, he couldn't trust his government not to send him back to Thailand if he fled and was then caught. More likely, he feared the prospect of being on the run – and probable recapture – in Thailand more than he valued his freedom. Without asking, I was certain Calvin would have no confidence at all in an escape plan from a Thai prison. Such things didn't happen to him. He had worn the uniform of authority – even if it was that of a male nurse in a drug rehabilitation clinic; he had fallen from grace, he had sinned. This embarrassment he could live with – a self-flagellation he wanted public. Yet to be caught flailing at the wall would be an embarrassment too heretical. Whatever the case, I would not tell him of Sten's and my plans. What sort of force were Sten and I by then, anyway? A lost platoon's disheartened conscripts as a forlorn hope against the wall. Calvin was not the man for the third hand we had long sought.

I'd had some hopes of recruiting a former Rhodesian lately refused citizenship in the new Zimbabwe. White, stateless and unwanted, the former soldier had strong hands and broad feet when I'd seen him during a visit to Building Two. Unfortunately, he'd since become quite mad, and had been transferred to the Bangkok asylum where he was reported as being on all fours and barking like a dog. I'd thought this might have been his cunning plan until news came that he'd begun eating his own shit.

'And not just for when people were watching,' reported Sten, as we were listing the brave-but-fallen.

Escape

'I guess that rules him out.' I reluctantly scratched his name. 'What about that big Swede in Four?'

Sten drove a hand over his scalp and shook his head. 'Won't leave his drugs.'

'Hell – he can bring them with him!' I was willing to be flexible.

'I wouldn't want him along.'

Sten didn't want a fellow countryman and wouldn't say why, so he rapidly moved on to greater concerns. 'Any ideas for the cutters? I saw someone using a saw in the auto workshop last week.' The autoshop sometimes used hacksaws.

'Yeah, I've seen them – but can you imagine the quality? I mean, even new, let alone after six months cutting up Hyundais. We haven't got much work to do on the night, but I don't want us still scraping away at sun-up.' However, I had deeper fears.

We had two bars to remove, meaning four cuts of one-inch steel. With the finest tungsten blades, this could take between ninety minutes and three hours, depending on how much noise we might be prepared to make. Using oil from the umbrella factory would dampen the sound but slow the cutting.

These estimates were not based on watching the family plumber make a mess of the lawn sprinklers but from the seasoned advice of Harvey Oldham, my bank-robbing friend. Harvey, by nature, took exception to imprisonment and had escaped five times. Following his earliest arrest, he broke through the skylight at the police station. Later, left alone during his trial in a holding cell, he cut his way through the steel mesh to leave via the lawyers' rooms. Once sentenced, he ground his way out from the first prison he found with mortar between bricks. Harvey's advice had been strongest on one point: the best blades are also the most brittle; held without a saw-handle, they will break as the hand wavers with fatigue. Two blades would be enough for two bars even allowing for a break in each. I would make sure we had four.

One thing stood in the way of this plan. To buy the blades from anyone connected with the prison – foreigner or Thai – would

Escape

almost certainly result in detection or betrayal. We would need to look outside the prison. We might need to look beyond Bangkok – beyond Thailand.

The New Year had opened with a modest social season for foreigners. A few post-Christmas contact visits and the embassy parties. Consular staff from the missions of Italy, Switzerland, Portugal and Poland each visited their imprisoned citizens, bringing seasonal food. The Nordic alliance of Denmark, Sweden and Norway sent an emissary with less time but more expensive gifts, which had underlined the high value of Christmas in those countries. In earlier years, the richest foreign mission – that of the United States – had mounted full Thanksgiving lunches within the walled garden of Klong Prem. This had stopped when conflicting DEA arrangements for cooperation and testimony resulted in jagged rifts throughout the American bloc. When they were all gathered in one place, there had been ugly scenes.

The British would never throw a party for their countrymen captured by foreigners, and this entirely for reasons of history and class. England had invented prisons as we know them, where bad food is an esteemed tradition. As well, diplomats had once been selected from the nobility, and convicts were very much below the salt, so could never share a table. Perhaps beneath all that lies the myth of empire's conquest and glory: those who choose to fight on foreign soil under their own banners take their chances. If they allow themselves to be taken alive, they should expect no aid from the Crown. By contrast, former British colonies aimed to put on quite a spread – perhaps in part because the British did not.

'Lay out my Sunday-go-to-meeting clothes,' I commanded Jet on the mid-January Monday of the Australian embassy party. Jet sniffed a contemptuous do-it-yourself at my office cupboard and returned to his artwork. He was drawing a poster for Sharon's jazz band, each member a face on a giant watch. I turned to Sten, who had moved to our office after Theo's death.

Escape

'What about if I wore a safari suit?' I asked. 'Would that be amusing?'

Sten didn't care. 'You were French last week. Leastways, you were French enough to eat your way through their embassy food.'

'I sit there and don't say much. Eat a little. Nod from time to time and say "Sure, fine" with an accent. Call me a tramp if you want.'

The French bash had been disappointing, apart from the food and the smuggled wine. After six years in Klong Prem, Raymond had been transferred to a Paris jail, and the remaining French were broken men. None with any skills or resolve. This week, I'd been told I'd meet three new faces at the Australian party, although Sten and I were slowly accepting that we might be on our own.

'So, where do you come from really? Are you Australian?' Sten had never asked before.

I tucked some plastic bags into my pockets. 'I've bought or revised maybe two dozen Australian passports over the years. I think that entitles me to a free meal, wouldn't you say?'

'They might not see it that way.'

I'd spent many years in Australia and had come to respect the land more and the cities less. The outback is an alien landscape of dry, ancient skins suggesting some lost primordial richness. Signposted with resolute trees gnarled and weathered as were the forearms of pioneering country folk, even in the east. Rocks and stones not immovably set in the earth – ready to move on hidden legs if no one was watching. The bush headily perfumed yet chaste; most life camouflaged against some extinct universal predator; its fresh morning sounds all avian bells and reptile whistles that spear warnings and defy location. Above the land, it's easier to apply character to people already several generations dead. The living are not so easy to define.

Lunch had been set upon several large tin tables under a bright plastic canopy on the grass plain between the main gate and an empty warehouse. At first sight, it seemed that half the Australian

Escape

mission had fled Bangkok to set up a field embassy in Klong Prem.

'This is our Christmas-cum-Easter party for you all,' announced consul Campbell Broun with subdued pride. 'I thought I might have trouble making up the numbers but it turned out just about everybody wanted to come.'

The diplomatic squadron numbered sixteen to our nine, without including four children from the South Sathorn Road embassy. Visitors included two clerks from the visa-assessment section, a man from Trade and Development, and some untitled officials with their wives or partners.

'We've tried to bring you a little slice of Australia today,' beamed a woman of middle age still holding her cubist handbag as she stood behind the bowls and plastic cutlery on a red-checked tablecloth.

Square-cut ham, potato and corn salad with diced bell peppers in mayo; more potato salad but spiked with chives, chickens both dismembered and sliced from a fatty roll; bite-sized frankfurters with toothpicks, and jars of black, salty yeast extract that needed rationing.

'There's not enough Vegemite for everyone to take a jar,' warned a plump woman wearing a 1960s-style Japanese silk dress as she tore at wrinkled foil covering a collapsed sponge cake.

A third secretary held a jar weightily and winked some expertise. 'We weren't allowed to bring you guys any beer, but can't stop any of this getting into the fruit juice when you go back.'

The nervous fingers of a woman from accounts picked at cling film covering a large plastic bowl. 'This trifle's home-made with an extra splash of brandy.'

The uneasiness of some consular staff was not due to our position as prisoners, but from the decay apparent in most of us. My earlier acquaintances, Garth Greengills, Ray Looseskin, Dale Hollowcheeks and Martin Sallowface had been joined that day by Tubercular Ted in his wheelchair, Ving, who'd been damaged boating from Vietnam to Perth as a child and damaged flying back as an adult, Brian, who lived with his *kathoey* Thai wife in

227

Escape

Building One, and two AIDS invalids who were held upright only by the interlocking molecules of heroin working hard within their bodies.

Brian, almost the healthiest, stepped from the group and spoke.

'Ah, it looks a treat, luv. I haven't been to a party in eight years.' Brian lowered the east Sydney twang he normally used by a notch. 'It's not even my birthday.'

Brian and I found enough chairs in the warehouse so that we could all sit, and thus avoid a buffet. Those among us with enough energy took turns hammering the consul about our cases, while others sat quietly pocketing the plasticware.

A discussion began about the kidnapping months earlier of three engineers in Cambodia. Remnants of the Khmer Rouge had taken an American, a German and an Australian citizen into the jungle, and then made complicated demands for their return. Demands that carried the shriek of radical politics but an undertone of mercenary greed. The Australian man was highly regarded within his local community, and his suburban football club had raised $150,000 to have him freed. The plan stumbled at the door of the new Australian embassy in Phnom Penh.

'There were all sorts of odd characters arriving for the negotiations,' complained Campbell Broun. 'It seems to me the poor family were being very optimistic. In fact, the whole thing broke down.'

Brian had heard of the ordeal and wondered, 'Whatever happened to the bloke?'

'Sorry to say all of the hostages were killed.' Campbell finished constructing his sandwich from cold cuts. 'Beheaded. A brutal lot, those Khmers.'

'Did the Americans offer money, too?' I asked. 'Or the Germans? They usually pay up.'

Campbell replied that he wasn't there, didn't know.

I kept at it. 'The story was that the pay-off was actually blocked by the diplomats. Private money, private negotiators, but somehow the embassies dropped the lid. Anything to that?' I couldn't make my position with the Australian officials any worse than it already was. When a government is funding its policemen to fly to a foreign land to testify for the prosecution, you've got nothing to lose.

'Those people were terrorists – we can't negotiate with terrorists.' That was Dennis Effusius, the head of mission. In the first visit to a Thai prison by such a senior official, Dennis had been pretending to listen to a hopeless petition from Garth Greengills. 'When one starts paying, where does it stop?'

'I guess if it's a private arrangement, it stops when you get your dad back in one piece.' I looked at my fingers, as though figuring it out for the first time. 'I think everyone knew the kidnappers were ugly, not much point in asking them to prove it. Or was there?'

The head of mission looked to a chargé d'affaires for confirmation, and got it: Yes, this was the troublesome shit who would soon be dealt with. Dennis then said to the table, 'Indeed, a real tragedy.'

As the sun tilted in the sky, the cream sponge cake was cut, the pavlova meringue dished and every inmate was given a business-class toilet bag from Qantas. Campbell's two sons were nine and eleven and kept to themselves, even though most of us were now remembering an old ability to mingle. To the children, we prisoners must have seemed a freakish bunch. The majority of those standing in that walled garden were diplomats with clear, glowing skin, wearing clean, new clothes, the women with brightly coloured dresses accompanied by an easy manner. They could have been airlifted from any Sunday barbecue in Sydney. We on the fringes, like a growth, must have seemed more repellent to the children than the bizarre sights they would have seen on Asia's city streets. Most of us grey of skin, thin and diseased. Three with T-cell dropsy, now bedecked with mottled, patched blemishes, wasted bones and lingering carrion odours. Also one, emaciated and green-blue from impending liver failure, and another wheelchair-bound being eaten by consumption.

At the soft-drink table, I turned to Dennis Effusius.

'Been stationed in Bangkok long?'

Escape

'Oh, two years now,' replied the mission head. 'But strictly speaking, my sentence is over. I'm staying on for a bit.'

'Good accommodation?' I showed an interest. 'I think I'd live in a high-rise if I had to work in Bangkok, although I guess I'd always stay with friends if given a choice.'

'Can't do it. We'll soon all be living in the compound. Just built 35 villa units.'

'Security the issue?'

Dennis wrinkled his lips. 'Not really. It's the traffic. Just can't spend three hours travelling to work each day . . .'

And so it went on. Even though I was sure I had some angry things to say about the certainty that all the Australian captives were slowly dying, and about the policy of using these deaths as examples, we were talking here about the dangers of eating locally made pâté. I soon caught myself recommending the best place to buy thickened cream in the city. This professional talker had got the better of me. What's more, he managed the last word.

'Now, you don't look like you need fattening up with cream. Do quite well for yourself, I'd say.' Then, before I could respond, he said: 'Ah, there's my daughter, Violet. She's about to say something.'

'May I have your attention, everyone? My dad has asked me to distribute the gifts.'

Violet was a television actor, then just 21, and had played a young policewoman in *The Short Arm*, an Australian soap. But this day she was every inch the daughter of a missionary. Brave and warm in ash nainsook, professionally in control of the natural revulsion that had scattered Campbell's children.

Violet stood beside a large cardboard box under the canopy's shade. She effortlessly plunged her hands into the box to capture a dozen green travel bags, freebies intended to promote the Sydney 2000 Olympics. 'There seem to be some extras, I'm sure you'll find friends for them.' Violet let drop this polyurethane bounty on the table before returning to the box with a look of childlike wonder at what it might contain.

'Ah, books!'

Escape

'Ah, fuck!' muttered Dale Hollowcheeks.

Violet took a book from the box as she passed her eyes over a small card on which our names were written. She leaned towards Tim and read the book's title for the first time as she offered the much-read paperback.

'*Alive!* "The gripping story of survival following the Andes mountains plane crash." Now that's interesting.'

Emaciated Tim released the lock of his wheelchair and grabbed for the book just as Violet decided that this tale of cannibalism in the snow might not be suitable for him. Violet dropped *Alive!* back in the box, announcing, 'That one's a little dog-eared, I think', and looked for another title.

Tim's lunge forward on unfamiliar slopes had set his wheelchair rolling back, a retreat he attempted to correct by clutching for the table. His grip fastened on four slices of inconveniently placed Port Salut, and it was only the practised reflexes of an accountant from the embassy's chancery nearby that halted Tim's backward slide.

Violet closed a napkin around *Dr Ernesto's Golden Cummerbund* and set it beside Tim's plate.

'I know you'll like that, Tim.' Violet had become more selective. '"Love and magic under Ceauşescu's Rumania",' she read.

The other civilian and professional guests returned to talking among themselves as Violet read blurbs in the book box before offering them as gifts.

'You could have them all but we have to call at the women's prison next door before we go.' Violet set aside a diet book, a guide to Provençal cooking and several self-help books before giving Martin Sallowface a sports autobiography, *If Memory Serves*.

'I don't get a chance to play tennis often these days,' Violet chirped. 'Martin, you look like a sportsman, I'll bet.'

Martin took the paperback and tried reading it with each eye from under an airline eyepatch mask. 'Yeah, thanks', was all he could manage. That afternoon dealing with outsiders and the heavy food had combined to drain the effervescence of the Australian prisoners.

Escape

'Now, what have we here?' Violet held up an oversized grey paperback. 'The new one from Laura Dragoman Smith, *The Seven Portals of Pavlodar*. "A mystical journey through Kazakhstan." It's the best one, I think, and it's yours, David, for being so patient.'

Violet's bubbling performance ended neatly with, 'Well, I'm sure you all have little messages to give and to take before we pack everything up, and don't forget to take all of this food.'

As I'd been to three of these events that month, I'd come prepared with a wad of Ziploc plastic bags. Campbell, the vice consul, gave me a sharp look until he saw me dividing the plastic carriers between Brian and Dale Hollowcheeks. Letters were surreptitiously passed for posting, and cash given in envelopes. Most of this was against prison rules, and although it was easy to be cynical about the limits and stated premise of the embassy staffers' rule-breaking, it was impossible not to be a little charmed.

As I had no cash to collect, messages to entrust or requests of any kind, I stood aside with Dennis Effusius. I blathered idly about the mysteries of diplomatic immunity – mostly to avoid speaking about my case and the help the embassy was giving the Thai prosecution.

Dennis, trained against questioning, saw that I'd been trying to get some inside information and changed the subject.

'Not taking any of this food back?'

'Eh? Oh, I'm full. Still, I'll be taking something. Thanks.'

'I must say, you don't look in bad shape.' Dennis looked at the others before turning sideways in accusation. 'Considering the circumstances for everyone. I suppose it's not all the same in there.'

'You know everyone here will be dead before any make it home.' I was already cursing myself for rising to the bait. 'I'm just new here. Give me some time, and I'll look the same.'

Dennis didn't answer, and was hardened enough to stand next to me with serene tolerance before moving away.

As anvil clouds moved across the sky, the table and picnic canopy took on the appearance of a cavernous cellar where some madman has tied his victims to chairs while rats and cockroaches scurry over cake crumbs. The villain raises his glass to his long-dead and decomposing guests, then exclaims: 'You didn't listen to me, did you? Now we have all the time we need, and we'll be such good friends.'

The office was empty when I returned. Bo-Jai's helpers brought the usual steel canisters of food for the night, which was good as I found I was hungry after all. Stateless Arib saw me at my desk and began to sweep around my feet. I waved a hand at the floor, telling Arib that he could finish for the day.

Sten arrived, soaked with sweat from weightlifting, something he'd been doing twice each day in recent weeks.

'Enjoy your lunch?' Sten removed his leather mittens. 'Make any new friends?' He raised a doubtful eyebrow.

'One on medical transfer from Bangkwang. As if the hospital here is better. I give him four months, six if he gets on the hammer. The other, some Vietnamese kid – in for the long haul.' I was tired.

'Hammer?' asked Sten.

'Oh, right. Hammer-and-tack. Smack. Heroin. I've been with Australians all afternoon.' And had quickly adopted the slang once again.

Sten drank from a bottle of iced water and sat by the doorway. 'We start paying for this tomorrow.' He held up the plastic bottle of tap water. 'Water strike. Barely enough to drink. No showers— '

I sat up, about to protest.

Sten raised a hand. 'Don't worry, Jet's got a tap opened.' Sten stood to leave. 'He's getting our tanks filled in the room.'

'Anything else?' I queried.

'Since you ask, the chief wants a new air-conditioner, and the foreigners have to pay for some new covered kitchen but haven't any money, of course. Ah – your factory worker's in the *soi*, and your Chinese friends have been bushwhacked in the coffee shop. The chief sold it out from under them to the son of some rich guy who wanted to give his kid something to do in prison.'

Escape

'OK, then.' I took my keys to lock our cupboards. 'Another fine day in Klong Prem.'

'Yep. Oh, and one other thing. English Martyn was bundled to court this morning. He got 50 years, and he'll be off to Bangkwang tomorrow.'

Sten took a towel and moved out under the new drops of rain to cool himself. Looking across to the building entrance, I saw Jet struggling up the steps with buckets of water. Lifting our food canisters, I thought I must try harder to keep my friends.

CHAPTER NINETEEN

Dean Reed was lying well: offhand, casually, from-the-hip, even warmly – which was how he sounded at his best. The problem was, they weren't buying his stuff.

Dean sat in the purposely-low chair provided in the shuttered debriefing room of the American embassy in Kuala Lumpur. A man and a woman stood at the bare table without speaking. They were Dean's countrymen – officials – impossible to identify and difficult to bullshit.

'I just want a full passport. I'm entitled to that.' Dean wanted to take off his own jacket, to join them with their white shirts, but he thought they might suspect nervousness. 'Every time I renew my Thai visa, they ask about that cut corner on the passport. It's not easy to get the 90 days, you know.'

The woman interrogator wore her hair pulled back. She said, 'You weren't thinking of going home?'

'No! I've told you people in Bangkok – I've got no reason to go home, my *home* is in Thailand.'

'And not planning to travel elsewhere? Europe, somewhere outside Asia perhaps?' asked the man.

'No!' Dean whined in exasperation.

'Odd thing that, Dean.' The man sat on the edge of the table. 'Just yesterday you were in the Australian embassy trying to get a visa. They didn't think much of you either. Mind if we take a look at that Filofax there?'

Escape

Dean had realised that these two were not passport officials, and he felt foolish agreeing to this interview. 'Look at what you want,' he said. 'But I can't see what right you have. I've done nothing. Nothing.' This sounded weak.

'Who were you planning to see in Australia?' It was the woman's turn to ask questions. 'Someone in Melbourne? Yes?' No answer. 'The Australians wouldn't give you a visa, Dean. Not with a full passport, not with any passport – and not with your drug record.'

'Oh that,' Dean began dismissively. 'That's nothing.'

But the interview would not improve. Eventually, Dean gathered his bits, loosened his tie and left the embassy and the town.

Again, he would have to return to Thailand by train. The officials at Padang Besar would allow him only a 30-day visa. If nothing more, he could afford to take a plane from Hat Yai home to Bangkok.

Dean let himself into the neglected but palm-shaded house in a watery lane off Soi Ekamai. Fortunately, Tara was not at home. Later he would tell Tara a version of his failure when she returned from work. A version that blamed David and his friends. She had accepted his story about Swiss banking and currency manipulations to explain the cash he'd been spending for the last seven months. Yet she'd seen little of that money. And now it was gone. For now, Dean would draw the yellow blinds and turn on the television set. Play *Natural Born Killers* just one more time—

'*Natural Born Killers*?' Chas wondered where that came from. 'I don't know what Dean did when he got home. And don't interrupt – who's telling this story anyway? I thought *I* was!'

'And you are,' I assured Chas from behind the mesh at Klong Prem. 'It's just that I know Dean. That silly fluff was his favourite film. He once told me that he'd played it to death. It was his comfort video, would you believe. He'd be sure to watch it under stress.' I apologised for interrupting. 'Anyway, go on, Chas.'

'Right. Well, Tara didn't much like being broke. She was packing to go when I called by. She said Dean was on another visa run. Talked of their breaking up. No sign of him, not that I could see.'

Escape

'Did you believe her?' I'd never met Tara, an Amerasian born in Thailand, though she'd been with Dean for five years.

Chas smiled and held his hands out. 'Believe? Now, what would that mean?' Chas had been surrounded by true believers since he'd campaigned against the death penalty in the 1960s. He'd heard so much belief from all sides that he saw no need to add his match to the bonfire. 'I think she really was going somewhere for a while. Or maybe she doesn't eat fruit or use toothpaste.'

Not much of either in the house, I presumed. Chas thought the Swiss banking nonsense was something Tara would repeat, whether she believed it or not. He didn't see Dean as a smuggler of anything but the cash he might fleece.

'I suppose if he'd made it to Melbourne, he'd cook up another backhander-for-bail story,' Chas speculated. 'Not that he'd get anything from me. Michael might've felt differently.'

Michael would be new territory for Dean. He'd already taken my old friend Myca for $48,000, and would get no more. I was sure Dean would try to sink new wells by travelling the world filling a war chest from my friends. Big chest, no war. Chas knew that sometimes my schemes to misdirect the opposition could create too much disturbance, and had made his own investigations.

I said, 'Michael knows Dean's no smuggler. It's sad that Dean thought I would like the sound of that. Him smuggling drugs to raise the necessary funds for bail. Any idea what the spooks in KL got from Dean's Filofax?'

Chas raised his eyebrows. 'Let's just go out on a limb and assume that they got everything he had to give.'

This forced me to think of any stray bits of papers, notes, receipts left in Dean's hands. I'd taken some care that there shouldn't be much. 'Well, forget him, Chas.' The time had passed for such digressions. 'How did Charlie make out with my photo?'

'He'll be out to see you as soon as I leave. He wanted to show me some passport he seemed proud of. Hidden in a grooming kit. Charlie thought me terribly thick that I couldn't open the thing.'

Escape

I saluted Chas. 'And not even willing to try the catch, I'll bet. So no fingerprints there.'

Chas was nodding at the ground and paused before speaking. 'I'm sorry you're on your own. Here.' He looked up at the walls. 'It's just too much for those of us left. Too old, I guess.' Chas smiled, and I knew he wasn't speaking for himself.

Chas left me with a fresh credit card, more cash and best wishes before taking a taxi straight from Klong Prem to the airport. He took the first available flight from Bangkok carrying the same collapsible shoulder bag with which he'd arrived. A Kevlar-fabric bag impossible to line without easy detection. Chas didn't wish to think the worst of the authorities, but neither would he give them a chance.

A couple of days before the end of the month, a parcel arrived for me from Australia. Jet had excitedly called to me, 'Passadook! Passadook!', meaning parcel, as I sat digesting lunch.

Walking from Building Six, I joined the huddle of foreigners waiting in the courtyard in front of the KP post office. The Thai parcels would be opened first.

Between 50 and 60 parcels arrived for prisoners every day. These would be checked by a guard, who sat under a tree while the receiving prisoner squatted before his throne hoping for less damage than usual from the guard's inspection. With effortless mischief, the resentful guard would kick the torn boxes into position before vandalising the contents using a rusty knife.

For the Thais, their soap bars would be chopped to flakes, their honey left speckled with rust and clothing soaked in dirty water in pursuit of imagined narcotics. By contrast, foreigners' parcels were presumed free of drugs (pointless sending drugs *to* Thailand), and so ransacked sparingly. To save the Thai prisoners the humiliation of this disparity, we foreigners waited for the local carnage to end before presenting our goods for inspection.

Despite this distinction, the *passadook* guard Satrakorn would make a masterful inspection by holding our finery up to the light, maybe tapping our low-pH soap bars to listen for their acoustic properties, or scrutinising the labels of our condiments with feigned comprehension. Face was saved.

All this pretence was particularly good for me that day, as I saw that my parcel was from Michael, although he'd used a false name. This meant that almost certainly it contained – somewhere inside – the four tungsten-and-steel hacksaw blades I'd asked for. Michael had sent parcels before, although usually in his own name and always containing money and messages rolled tight and then sealed in small tins. We had a portable canning machine into which for years we'd packed our banknotes and frankincense. Applying labels such as Vitapooch and Pusschow, they'd take some spray-on dust before deep-corner cupboard storage away from seizing hands.

The sender's name on this package was Maurice Binder but displayed Michael's distinctive penmanship, so I should watch for more than the usual tins with outlandish brands. The hacksaw blades would each be over a foot long. Sten and I had abandoned the cell-door key project. The new-and-improved plan was straightforward in approach: cut through the window after midnight and scale the walls.

Waiting with the other foreigners beneath the shade of a tree, I was pleased to see Calvin amble forward from Building Two.

'Calvin! Good to see you.' I stepped into the sun. 'Another *passadook* from Hawaii?'

'Hiya, Dave. I dunno. A care package from my sister, I think.' Calvin had never taken to using even the most familiar Thai words. 'Dave, the chief's OKd my move this week. I've got to get out of Two. It's too much.'

'You're welcome any time. Remember, though, I did warn you that there might be some changes coming in Six. No details, but you won't like them.' I looked at Calvin's tattered shirt, with its rows of holes from cigarettes dropped during great noddings. His face was gaunt and grey, his shorts stained.

'Say, Cal – no need to dress up just to visit the post office. No formalities here.'

Escape

Calvin lit a cigarette and smiled. 'Yeah, I know. I haven't worn my tails since Jack's inauguration.'

'How's things in the American hut?' I was keeping watch on the *passadook* guard. He was tiring.

'Ah, Dave. It's all fucked. The stuff's everywhere, I can't get away from it. That's why I've got to get over to your place.'

'Where's your dedication, Calvin?' I chided absently. 'The dope's no fun without a raging habit. Anyway, you know it's to be found in Six.'

Calvin believed that the healthy atmosphere and calm inclinations of No. 57 would keep him from poverty and ruin. In the past decade, a quarter of the Western prisoners had died from infections contracted through sharing needles. Calvin wasn't using the needle – well, hardly. Even if I'd told him of our proposed escape, Calvin would have moved in anyway. Many foreigners spoke of escape. However much Calvin might try to imagine such a night, the dream would never overcome his fears to become real.

The Thai prisoners had now left with their goods: new leather sandals, dried fish and banana strips, strings of tamarind and copies of the gore-fest police slaughter magazine *191*. The foreigners' parcels were dragged forward, and I stood back from the others to let the guard set his pace.

Calvin squatted before Satrakorn, cloth sack in hand, scooping packets of American Marlboro as they tumbled from their torn cartons. He wadded the cigarettes down with new T-shirts and baggy shorts as the guard flicked them aside. Satrakorn then halted the spill of goods from the ruptured package to spread the pages of a fishing magazine, hoping to find pictures of bikinied women on beaches. Magazines revealing women were banned from entry. Seeing only bass and perch, the guard let the magazine drop from his fingers, and Calvin gathered the last of his winnings.

My large box was pushed forward. It was heavy, and the trusty gave a grunt to show irritation. I saw that through mishandling, a five-inch gash was torn from the side. I wondered about any damage inside, for I didn't know where the hacksaw blades might be hidden.

'That's a big one.' Calvin stood looking at the box. 'Must have cost a packet to send.'

'Mmm. Looks like it. Over a hundred on the stamps.' I then knelt and half-turned, keeping up a conversation with Calvin, hoping to give the guard a sense of free rein.

Packed for variety and distraction, Michael had spared little that gave colour or novelty. The now sluggish guard squinted at each item before pushing it clear with his short stick. Foods decorated the top layer, caught in glimpses as I looked for the blades. Duck-liver pâté, tinned Camembert, bubble-wrapped jars of marmalade, two stollens (too short to hide a file), larks' tongues in aspic, canned beef and ham, bags of dried fruit; spices: cumin seed, oregano, tannis root, basil and food acid 260 for pickling in a dark bottle. Then, three rolls of matt black gaffer tape lay curled among marshmallows, nougat, gummy bears and Callard & Bowser's liquorice toffee. Bunches of heavy nylon cable ties sprouted from the gaps between vacuum-packed plums and dates. A Rubik's cube nestled in the confectionery.

I skimmed a bunch of cable ties with my thumb. *'Good to keep the food bags fresh,'* I said in Thai to Calvin, who had the sense simply to nod.

The next layer in the parcel revealed boxes of muesli and Honey Smacks covering tubes of epoxy resin and wood fillers nestling against bags of almonds, pecans and macadamia nuts. Underneath sets of socks, jocks, shirts and a silk bathrobe with a red Chinese dragon there fanned a quintet of glossy-but-filthy magazines – guaranteed to be confiscated after a most thorough inspection.

Calvin gave me an arched *what-are-you-up-to?* look as the guard rose to the task of wide-eyed examination, with a leering trusty looped over each of his shoulders.

'No, no – no!' the guard announced without taking his eyes from the first image of something about which he'd only heard whispers.

Escape

Satrakorn barely glanced at a rolled parchment amid a scattering of toiletries, and pushed it aside with some books – an atlas, maps and travel guides. The handmade scroll was held by gold-lacquered rods tipped by teardrop knobs, one of which had broken in transit. Even though all the remains were safely in my hands, I unrolled the poster, for the guard was by then sliding some of the pornography under his chair. On the chart, I recognised Michael's fine hand within the calligraphy, scripting a parody of 'Desiderata'. 'Go silently amid the boys in haste . . .'

As Satrakorn had been tut-tutting with spittled clicks at some obscene act, he had not sensed the added weight of the scroll's supporting rods. He would never know that they contained four hacksaw blades concealed in carefully cut and refilled channels along the wooden staves.

Waddling away with my treasure in two denim bags, I believed then that I could have plucked a grappling hook and a stun gun from that box without discovery while Satrakorn was so diligently applying local standards to the 240-gsm full-colour porn.

The new plan was direct, but needed three rather than just the two of us. Sten and I might be able to assemble and carry the twenty-four-foot ladders over five walls, but not to keep watch, too. Our last best chance for a third man was someone who did not meet Sten's approval. I thought otherwise, so spoke directly to Luke, who that afternoon sat alone outside the umbrella factory.

'Luke, want to escape?' I dropped to my haunches and leaned against the brick wall of the factory, still hot from the afternoon sun.

'Say what?' Luke continued to roll his cigarette, taking un-necessary pains.

'Let's imagine everything's just fine,' I said, smiling with enough irony to back the whole thing into a joke. Not that serious caution was needed. Luke spoke to very few people, and I'd never heard him drop a name, place or date, even though we'd swapped some droll stories. 'Let's imagine we're all ready to go – the tunnel, or the rope, or the dynamite at the wall – whatever. All's ready. Would you want in?'

Luke lit his cigarette with a match. He was old-fashioned. And he was old; near 60, I was sure. His hair was a fine, grey fleece, and his eyes a hard glass. A black American from Philly, Luke had kept thin in the navy, even though he'd been a cook. He had a second wife in Charleston. They kept in touch, although his grown sons never wrote. Luke had trouble holding a name, too. In the Cure, he'd introduced himself as Jake, but was known in Klong Prem now as Yahya. Luke explained this change: 'When a black man's in trouble in a foreign country, he can forget about being an American. He can do worse than take one of those names.' Luke-Yahya meant names with an Arabic tone that suggested Islam. If there is any safety to be gained in pretending to be Muslim, Luke had chosen the wrong country, as many Thai Buddhists held suspicions of their Muslim countrymen even in the 1990s.

Luke had been raised among crooks, and learnt their ways so well that they'd accepted him easily. He'd held jobs as a driver, paint mixer and cinema usher before working nights as a barman. The world of gamblers and dealers was spread before him, available any time, for they all respected Luke. Yet he never forced himself in; he was too cool for that. He might tip everyone to some thin sounds or some fat weed, but he never overstepped. Luke was just too hip to step forward, and as flared trousers gave way to long coats he stayed on the fringe. Too laid-back to jump in the car as they waved invitations, those friends finally departed, soon to exchange their leather coats for heavy jackets. Luke slipped into the US Navy in the coolest way, too; uttering hardly a word and acting as a small stabiliser below decks. Still surrounded, though, by light crookery and a sense that everyone was getting away with it. Luke was shocked when the navy brass weren't cool enough to accept the casual theft of two gross of five-gallon tins of peas. A dishonourable discharge followed, and by then the brothers from his hometown were either dead or inside for life. Luke had been just too cool, and had missed it.

Escape

Luke then took work in the merchant navy. Lived port to port. A little hash from North Africa, or a few sheets of acid from Amsterdam. Then, the big move. Not to get too close, Luke took on two grown waifs from Ghana, then stranded in Yemen. He flew them to Bangkok and spent some time getting them plausible documents.

'But these guys were idiots, Dave. More than idiots!' Luke had told me, even though everyone could see at a glance. 'Morons. I couldn't even let them loose at the airport by themselves. They didn't even know what country they were in.'

All three were arrested in their taxi on the way to the airport by city police in the Sukhumvit area who had fallen over the operation. Luke had been crippled by his brace of albatrosses from that day to this. His boys followed him everywhere, trailing a few feet behind, carrying Luke's boxes and chatting happily to each other. As I spoke to Luke, the pair half-wittedly prepared Luke's evening food at the nearby charcoal-burner patch.

'Don't use plastic!' Luke called from his deckchair. 'It'll stink up the fish – use wood if there's no charcoal left!' He sank deeper into his already sagging chair.

'You see, Dave. They can't even feed themselves. Eighteen months here, and they think this is all part of the plan. I can't leave them. They're fucked as it is.'

'I don't know how you thought Yahya would be any good,' Sten said later. 'What were you thinking?'

I'd thought Luke might finally want to lift himself above all he'd seen, for he had the strength. Instead, he'd stepped back into this macabre adoption, wearing some battered noble hat.

'He's making peace with his makers, Sten. Nothing we can do about that. It'd be a mistake to try.'

Sten was not surprised. 'I told you.'

To give Sten some cheer, I announced that I'd thought of a way to use our bookshelf plank to overcome the crumbling tiles beneath our window. So far, we hadn't found a way to hold the

Escape

plank in place so that we could clear the two-metre awning.

'We don't need to build some massive siege-engine contraption inside the cell,' I explained. 'We've already got the strongest thing in the prison.'

'And what's that?' Sten leaned forward and looked around for something big yet in some way concealed in the office.

'The bars, of course. The strongest steel around. You could hang an elephant from any one of them.'

Sten sat back and held his chin. 'You mean the bars we're supposed to cut. Those bars.'

'OK.' I stood and opened a drawer, peeling a small sheet of paper from underneath. 'Look at this.' I pointed to the diagram I'd sketched – the window bars with two missing and three intact. 'The plank is seven feet. We need six-and-a-half out the window. I can make a special block – out of wood – that'll hold the plank tight in place between two bars and that flat bit in the middle, the strut, the spar – whatever you call it.'

Sten squinted at the paper. 'So, six inches or less of the plank between the bars, with us dangling 50 feet off the ground, all held by a little block of wood—'

'Actually, the middle brace of the steel, but—'

'With nothing to stop it sliding right out?'

'No.' I tapped my diagram for support. 'That little – ah, strong – pin there, at the end? That stops it sliding right out. And the plank is sideways, upended, you can see. That means it has the strength of an eight-inch thick log, not just a flat plank. It shouldn't bounce about.'

'Can we test this?'

Sten's question was fair. I knew he wouldn't like my answer.

'No. Not practically. But I've worked it out. I'm sure.'

'And numbers don't lie.' Sten folded the diagram and dropped it into the desk drawer.

I picked up the paper, unfolded it, nodded, did a pantomime of certainty, refolded the paper small and into my pocket, then winked.

Escape

'No one lives for ever, Sten.'

From the back room, Charlie Lao looked through a bead curtain to the shop. Small, with pale green walls, a cheap glass counter and three piebald maroon vinyl chairs. No other decoration beyond a dusty plastic bonsai-tree lamp on the counter, a calendar from the Xenshui Carbon Abrasive Factory No. 3 and a dozen faded Xerox enlargements of once colourful banknotes. The shop was empty, and few would imagine that this Chinese-run money exchange employed agents within hand-signalling range of the front window. If required, these men and women could arrive with over one million baht within five minutes' notice. Charlie turned from his chair to face his old friend, and then looked down to the photograph newly laminated into the British passport.

'This is a fine job,' Charlie said in Cantonese.

'As well as could be done,' replied the older man opposite. 'The original photograph was too small, so had to be copied and resized. You will find the entry visa is dated from Friday, and that all the passport details are now on the immigration computer. Naturally, we wish your friend well, but must say that we do not know of anyone who has yet been successful. The outcome may not necessarily be in your friend's best interests. He should know that he now has 27 days to leave the country. Do you think that is possible?'

Whatever answer Charlie might have provided to his moneychanger friend, he was later that day too tactful to repeat it as we met in the ambassadorial suite of the Klong Prem visits zone.

To the same question, I then answered, 'I think I can do it, Charlie, but there's not much time. Can that visa be extended? I've still got three or four court dates, and I don't want to rush.'

Charlie assured me that there would be no problem extending the visa. Since he was returning to Vientiane for two months, he would leave the passport in a small apartment he had rented in Lat Phrao.

'I'll put it in an envelope behind the bathroom mirror,' Charlie said. 'And I'll bring you the key to the flat before I go. That way, you'll be able to send someone to get it, if you need to.'

'Thanks, Charlie. And don't look so sad.'

Charlie spoke down to the table. 'David, I have to speak something. I do what you say, don't worry, but you have maybe 10 per cent, 15 per cent chance in this. That chance is not good. Don't worry, if you stay, I'll come to see you all the time. Help what you need.'

'Charlie, I just need to stand on the other side of that wall.'

The passport from Charlie was not the only one provided that week. Before Martyn had been taken to Bangkwang, he'd brokered a deal for the one passport still in private hands. It had been issued to a British citizen who had managed to keep it in Building Two. During his time, he'd become indebted to a Sri Lankan dealer in the building. Thursday afternoon, the Sri Lankan's servant arrived at our Building Six factory to deliver the passport with his master's compliments.

'It's in good condition, as you can see,' said the young Bengali as he was offered a drink. 'Only the staple marks from when it was in evidence.'

The passport had half a dozen Thai visas, entry stamps for Singapore and Hong Kong, and bore a face that might pass for me on a dark night, although the name was half-Italian. It would serve as back-up identification should I be delayed finding Charlie's flat.

'What's your name?' I asked the messenger.

'Karim, sir. I've been in Lardyao for four years.' Lardyao was an old name for the prison.

I'd been told some of this man's story before, and now wanted to hear more without filters. Karim came from a family that could be seen as middle class by his native Bangladeshi standards. Karim had rejected his parents' arrangements for a suitable marriage and had taken up with a girl who'd agreed to a love marriage. Apart from the cuff of disobedience, there remains in Indian ears something sinful and illicit in the phrase *love marriage*, even in modern times. To escape the shame, Karim and his bride had left their town for the capital, Dhaka. They had been disowned by their respective families.

Seeking better-paid work, Karim flew alone to Bangkok, one of the few places his passport could take him. Here, he found little work but did befriend some Pakistani thieves operating from Thailand. Karim said he was their cook. Perhaps he was. Within a few short meals, Karim was arrested by local police, who measured him for a handful of old shop burglaries. This was a housekeeping arrangement between the Pakistanis and the police.

The police had not been fussy in their preparations for the case and charged Karim with several burglaries that had taken place before he'd arrived in Thailand. Karim pleaded not guilty at his trial. He had produced his passport, along with a passport clerk from the Bangladeshi embassy, who testified that both passport and exit stamp from Dhaka were genuine. As I've said, the practice in Thai sentencing is to give the maximum and then reduce it for any mitigation such as a guilty plea. Burglary attracts an eight-year term. Karim left court with eight years.

'What did the judge say?' asked an incredulous Calvin, who had arrived at the office in time for some background.

I turned to Karim. 'Did the judge explain away the fact your passport said you weren't in the country at the time of the robberies?'

Karim was matter-of-fact. 'He said that criminals like me often keep other passports. That I might have come before.'

'Well, I suppose you must be out soon then, Karim?' I sympathised. 'Another year or two?'

Not so. While serving time in Klong Prem, Karim began working as a cook and gofer for the Sri Lankan in Building Two. Some two years ago, not long after Karim took his new position, his boss had had a dispute over payments with the guard who was supplying the dope. The guard worked in the visit pens. Twice each week, Karim would walk to the gate to collect the Sri Lankan's prison-shop food. This food is paid for by visitors, packed by outside staff employed by the guards and then issued by the guards themselves at the front gate. When Karim collected one of the shopping bags, a second guard stopped him for a search. Twenty grams of heroin were found stuffed inside a bread stick. As an object lesson for the Sri Lankan dealer, Karim was arrested.

'I'd give up being a cook, kid,' Calvin suggested. 'A dangerous game.'

Again, the police were not fussy with their preparations for the case, and there was no evidence that Karim had had any opportunity to touch the bread, which had been sealed at the prison bakery. Karim pleaded not guilty at his trial. He produced a receipt for the prison-shop bag bearing another prisoner's name and called a clerk from the prison to testify that prisoners did not select or pack the goods. The practice in Thai courts for sentencing is the same for all crimes, and possessing 20 grams of heroin attracts a 25-year term. Karim left the court with a further 20 years.

'Must've taken off five years on account he didn't do it,' suggested Calvin.

'I had a very top lawyer,' Karim mournfully tried to explain his stubbornness.

'Hired by his boss,' Calvin suggested to me as an aside.

The boy from Bangladesh nodded.

'Cheer up, fella. I've got some good news for you.' Sten had walked through the factory huts to our office. 'The queen's birthday amnesty reductions have just been announced. Robbers get their time cut in half.'

Sten sat on the edge of a table and put a hand on Karim's shoulder. 'If it wasn't for the fact that you're a drug kingpin, you'd be happy back in Bangla in a month's time.'

'You're in a good mood,' Calvin said with cautious sarcasm.

'Why shouldn't I be?' Sten squeezed the contents of a green Tetra Pak into his mouth with one crushing fist. 'Thanks to our wonderful Western embassies, we now get the same as murderers – only a seventh off our sentences instead of half.' Sten potted the empty carton into a distant rubbish bin.

Escape

Calvin was unaffected. 'I don't think it means anything on a transfer to the States.'

Neither Sten nor Calvin need have concerned himself. The now meaningless amnesties benefited only those prisoners who had been in Klong Prem for more than two years and had purchased the 'excellent behaviour' status of trusties. However, the lifers were pleased. Most had their sentences reduced to 99 years.

CHAPTER TWENTY

Since American DEA operations with the Nigerians had ended, far fewer airport cases arrived at Building Six. However, the rise of budget airlines had produced a cloudburst of anaemic, tattered foreigners charged with minor thefts, drunken aggression or feebly sordid acts of public disgrace. These newcomers, even whiter and trashier than most, were doing only what they did habitually in their own countries, but now during the northern winter even bums could take a vacation. Vacate, they could – stop being bums, they could not.

Fiorenzo Bustamenti had been at Klong Prem for two years, and was the most travelled professional beggar we knew. He'd begged in Brazil, scrounged in Seville, touched sleeves in Geneva, sponged in the Adriatic and optimistically cadged in Cairo. Fiorenzo could profile the alms-giving attitudes of 20 nations, and had a wardrobe tailored to meet every prejudice. Now serving 25 years for possessing a few grams of his personal supply, any begging Fiorenzo might work in the future would be in piteous circumstances. Yet he still had his pride.

'David, have you seen what they've just brought in?'

Fiorenzo was affronted by the amateurishly dishevelled newcomers. 'This man, English – this does not surprise me – was caught stealing whisky from a supermarket. *Disgraziato!*'

I located one of Fiorenzo's untouchables sniffing the laundry drying in the breeze behind the charcoal pits. A Scot, his name was

Escape

Sorley, and he'd come from Manchester, where he lived. Flying to Thailand was not just globetrotting for Sorley. He had planned to return to England with seventy-five grams of heroin, which he'd packed in three condoms before departure.

'Maybe I should've bought a six pack, you know,' Sorley considered. 'And I shoved them up a wee bit early, the day before – just to be safe.'

This security measure proved insufficient protection against a late night of chilli-sauced food and two *klom* (large) bottles of rice whisky. 'I had a call of nature come on before I could get back to me lodgings, and they're damned slippery things in the dark, I can tell you. I could paint you a picture.'

Sorley then provided enough detail for a large fresco – all of which I shall expunge other than to report that the repercussion of Sorley's spate was a complete loss of baggage. 'The fellas back in Manchester wouldn't be too happy me coming home empty-handed, as it were.'

Staking Sorley to a meal at the coffee shop, I heard that the Mancunians awaiting the dope were not hard men from some firm or wily subcontinentals but ever-so-slightly organised criminal friends of Sorley. By his account, there exists in Britain today a tramp network that curls its tentacles round any fast-earning enterprise that can be accomplished while drunk. Their success rate was exceptionally low, but repetition and numbers brought stories of occasional triumphs.

Before I could learn more of this hobo mafia, Calvin arrived, seated himself, and told me that one of the servants was looking for me.

'Which one?'

'I dunno, Dave. You know how I am with these names. The stringy-looking one who lopes around in the prison uniform. A bit fruity, if you ask me.'

I squinted in recollection. 'Has a head looks like wood?'

'Yeah. That's him, sure.'

'Lok's his name.'

'Right. What's he do, anyway?' Calvin asked.

'Jet hired him as a chimneysweep, so he said.' I had no idea, although he could have been a bed-warmer for the carpenter in the days when they both had all of their parts.

As we walked to the office, leaving Sorley to eat, Calvin and I stopped at the two stone lions at the entrance to the accommodation block. It was said that one of the lions would roar every time an innocent man walked past. Calvin pointed to a pair of new arrivals splashing at the water tank behind the cooking shed. 'I shouldn't point, but take a look at those two. How do you suppose that happened?'

The two men appeared European, and seemed healthy except for their legs. Both had limbs that had been broken and then set badly. More than that: broken in many places and not set at all, like crushed drinking straws unable to straighten.

Yet there was something oddly confident about their manner, despite the heavy chains around their ankles. I turned to Calvin.

'Any idea where they come from?'

'They're Israelis, someone said.' Calvin lifted his eyebrows, recognising this as unusual. 'Came down from Chiang Mai.'

As we passed, I saw that their chains' ankle rings had been welded fast. Never to be removed.

'What's the matter, Dave?'

'Nothing,' I said slowly. 'They'll be here for a while. We'll find out what they've got to say later.'

Welded chains meant one of two things. Either that the death penalty had been imposed – and that didn't square, as they were in the open at Klong Prem, not chained to a wall – or that they'd tried to escape, and had been caught. Inevitably, Sten would see these two before long. I wondered how he might react to the appalling sight of their misshapen legs.

Lok was still drifting around our office when Calvin and I arrived. He shyly asked if it was all right if he might give me something.

'For what?' I was puzzled.

'For your court tomorrow.' Lok lurched forward his hand, upon whose long fingers rested a minuscule packet made from leaves and bound with twine. 'For good luck with your punishment.'

Escape

While it was true that I was due in court the next day, Lok mistakenly believed that I was due for sentencing. I thanked our chimneysweep and locked the talisman in the cupboard with my court togs. I'd seen some of these little wraps before, and had opened one. It contained nothing but tiny pebbles and grit that had been prayed over. Perhaps some Asian compromise was shown by the chosen contents: in the event that prayer failed to move mountains, it might just dislodge a grain of sand. Still, it's worth honouring a gesture and a superstition if neither costs a thing, so I would take the tiny parcel.

The following afternoon I ran across Calvin as he was collecting some bread from the bakery outside Building Six. I was clanking back from court in my chains.

'Calvin – you finished there? Come with me while I get these off.' I tugged at the string supporting my chains. 'You know what the bastards have gone and done?'

Calvin dropped the spongy loaves into a canvas sack he carried. 'What's that, Dave?'

'Only gone and finished their case on me.'

Lawyer Montree had that morning been surprised too by the prosecutor announcing that he would not present the remaining eight witnesses on his list. Beyond doubt, five of those eight were mere scarecrows – names of foreign police to impress the judge – but calling time on the case seemed sudden. Lawyers rarely axe shows with guaranteed fees.

'Why was that?' Calvin asked as we approached the chain-levering machine at the steps of the administration building.

'Not sure. Someone must be impatient, asking for a result. They wanted me to give my defence today, but Montree howled. I'm back there in five weeks. Supposed to produce my witnesses.' I crouched to loop my ankle ring over the hooks of the machine. 'Cal, give that lever a tug, will you? I'm not going to wait for a trusty.'

'Have you got any?'

'Any what?'

'Witnesses. To speak for you?'

My ankle ring stretched open and clattered to the ground. 'No. Well, that would be a waste of time. Nope – I can make a speech if I like, and that's about it.' I positioned my other foot, and Calvin attached the hooks. 'And I've got a feeling that as soon as Montree stops talking, the judge will smash down with a verdict and sentence before the day is over.'

Calvin dusted his hands of rust from the old machine. 'Any idea what to expect?'

I stood, holding the now-open steel C-ring. 'I've never seen how they weld these things on. I heard they slip a bit of rubber sheet around your foot so's you don't get electrocuted.' I looked up at Calvin. 'It wouldn't pay to sweat.'

Walking back to Building Six, we again passed the bakery, now closed.

I said, 'You could have got Jet to stand in line for the bread – he would have sent one of his underlings.'

'It's OK, Dave. Gets me out of the place.' Calvin twisted the bread bag in his hand.

'Settling in all right?'

'Yeah. Good – better than Two.'

'Be a bit careful about scoring in Six,' I had to say. 'They catch on quick, and will use it against us. Now, please understand, it's nothing to me. Whatever— '

Calvin broke in. 'It's under control, Dave. I just had to meet someone here today to settle some old business. Nothing new.'

We banged on the steel doors of Building Six and waited for the gatekeeper.

Calvin rubbed the back of his head. 'You know, I got a bad batch not long ago in the American hut in Two. Overdosed or poisoned or something. Thought I was going to die.'

The smaller door opened, and we stepped inside.

'My whole life flashed before my eyes,' Calvin said. 'And, you know what? It didn't even hold *my* interest.'

* * *

Escape

Sten had cast aside painting, and now spent most of his time working out with an improvised weights-set made from wooden staves and concrete blocks. He would take breakfast at the coffee shop, call at the office for lunch and leave soon after eating.

'The carpenter wants to make you a desk,' I offered that week. 'It'd be rickety crap but maybe not a bad idea if one of us could be around mornings.' No response, so I added, 'I'm normally over in my old place, mornings. Better reception for the World Service, for some reason. Less metal, maybe.'

'Less metal? That's your theory, is it?' Sten sat finishing his macaroni, holding his plate in one hand.

So I thought I'd best get to it: 'You missed a good story with the Israelis this morning. You should have come.' I'd hoped Sten might've shown an interest in the breakdown.

'I can see their story in their legs.' Sten cleared his plate. 'Don't need any more sad stories this week.'

'Sad, but interesting,' I said, adopting a tone of academic curiosity. 'Entirely down to a lack of preparation on their part. And of all people here, you'd think they should have known better.'

Agarn and Benny had separately completed their service with the Israeli military before they had met when scamming water trucks in the West Bank. Returning to Haifa, they sold drugs on the coast until they'd saved enough for their first Thailand run. Agarn was the stocky, quiet one; Benny talked more. Still in their late 20s, both had lives complete with earlier tribulations, quirky adventures, infatuations and unexpected opportunities.

However, not one article in all that softens the folly of the path they chose after their arrest in Chiang Mai with two kilos of heroin. It was their fourth visit to the city. As other soldiers have so endured, they too woke after that first night of captivity, reluctantly rising through a black-water sleep to the seared landscape of statutory war. They resolved to fall back, retreat, but not retire.

Chiang Mai is a town of just over 150,000 people: small; provincial. Agarn and Benny were confined in the Central Prison

Escape

near Ratwith Road, in cramped but relaxed conditions, sharing a cell with a mere dozen. A consul had flown north to see them from the office suite that is the Israeli embassy in Bangkok. Having been contacted by police, he could hardly refuse. The visit was brief. They were told that they were a disgrace to Israel, and that they should expect no help. Unluckily for Agarn and Benny, this attitude was conveyed to the prison superintendent.

Through a combination of guile, tolerance to discomfort and the confusion among their keepers about their foreign ways, the pair managed to keep almost $15,000 about their persons from the police station to the jail.

When it became clear that they would spend the next 25 years in the very same cell, Agarn and Benny made their escape plans. They bought a dozen hacksaw blades and made ropes from blankets. The old Chiang Mai prison is almost in the centre of town. Every night, they could hear the sounds of the living through the bars. Benny had said that sleeping was difficult most nights before 1 a.m., when the traffic noise and fumes settled. One cool night, they paid off their cellmates and cut their way out, then bridged the three-metre gap to the wall with strips of bedding tied to rocks. They were free by 5 a.m.

Here then, arrived the moment. Agarn's and Benny's years in the army had taught them a certain amount of tough resourcefulness, but it had not given them perspective. Chiang Mai is a square of moats and walls, yet neither of them accepted that their easy climb from the central prison was only the first of many ramparts of a larger stockade. Seeking rest and comfort too readily, they sought out the guesthouse where they'd stayed on an earlier run. It was small and quiet, and the owner was a happy scoundrel who had scored gram bottles for Agarn before they'd found a major vendor. The innkeeper welcomed them back and gave them special rack rates for escaped prisoners, promising to keep quiet.

It took the guesthouse owner almost two weeks to leech just over $10,000 from the Israelis. The prison had posted a 50,000-baht reward for information, and tuk-tuks puttered like mad ants throughout the city with photocopied enlargements of Agarn and Benny pasted to their fuel tanks.

From the guesthouse, the fugitives tried to contact their major vendor, but he wouldn't come to the phone. Worse, their host never delivered on a promise of special transport, passports and disguises. Still, they were together.

The day after they told the innkeeper that they could pay no more, he reported them to the police. The raid, when it came, was all through one wooden door, so Agarn managed to crash through the glass door of the room's balcony to escape again. He was arrested at eight the following morning in the waiting room of the White Elephant Gate bus depot.

Legs were what the prisoners had escaped upon, so legs were what the prison guards took from Agarn and Benny when they were brought back to the jail. They were chained to a wall in a small cell and worked over with iron bars, then wedged with stones so that their breaks would set askew.

'They were tough, though,' I told Sten as he glumly spooned up some melted ice cream, a morning gift from the coffee shop in celebration of its return to the Chinese owners. 'They managed to move the rocks around a bit so at least they can walk again – as you can see. The story's funnier the way Benny tells it.'

Sten lobbed the paper cup and plastic spoon to our bin. 'So, how come they're in Klong Prem?'

'The Chiang Mai court gave them a quick 30 years, but the jail wouldn't keep them. Sent them down here to save having to look at them. Fourteen hours in a tin box on the road. It's quite timely, don't you think?' I was trying to make the best of this. 'A good object lesson for us – what not to do.'

'Well, I'd be fucked if I'd run into some poxy guesthouse.' Sten leaned against a cupboard and folded his arms. 'You know they were right next to a wall when they cut out?' Sten had evidently made his own enquiries.

'Near enough,' I agreed.

'What if they weren't? I wonder what they'd have done if they'd stood on a sleeping guard when they climbed down.'

'A couple of ex-army guys.' I was picturing Sten up against Agarn and Benny for some reason. A close thing. 'A sleeping guard – they wouldn't have had much trouble handling that.'

Sten stared at the ground. 'You ever think what would happen to Jet if we go?'

If?

But I said, 'I'll give him money. There's not much around here you can't do with that.' Not that I was so sure, nonetheless it was alarming to hear Sten take this position.

'You *do* care about what happens to Jet?' Sten asked. 'I mean, f'rinstance, you seem to care about keeping the cat alive.'

'The cat stays alive because everything in here is trying to kill it. I won't have that.'

Steady there, Westlake.

I ironed out a frown with the heel of my hand and then looked up, all fair and reasonable. 'Look, Sten. I know you're in a different position from me. Just tell me what you want to do.'

Sten wanted to stay. He did not speak of the dangers of night encounters, or a five-point ambush when stepping into some departure lounge. No words spoke of a life on the run, or some rehabilitation in Sweden. Instead, Sten spoke of keeping Jet safe from the worst reprisals of the guards. He assured me, however, that he would help me cut out of the cell. In my turn, I assured Sten that he would have enough money – then and later – to live well in Klong Prem.

So. I would be alone. It was out now. Quite a relief.

Jet sat before his easel at the factory wall under the carnival-blue tarpaulin where the light was better. Nearby, at a low table, our carpenter cheered his cronies with stories of the good old days when jail wasn't the soft palace it is today. Calvin was slabbed out unconscious on a bench, part of my old office. He was sleeping it off. Or *on* – for he was still vacuuming tootskies of No. 5 White on the sly. I didn't disturb him. Jet looked at me, and then at Calvin, wordlessly asking, 'Should I set the living mummies on him and have him chased away?' I shook my head.

'What are you drawing there, Jet?' I enquired. 'Childhood memories?'

Jet was applying some charcoal depth to a large sketch of an automatic pistol. He paused to show me the colour photograph from which he worked. 'It's for the new guard. He likes guns.'

A new guard had been sent to Building Six by the superintendent. This guard was enthusiastic and had ideas. He didn't fit in. Our chief saw him as a spy for an administration unhappy with its percentage of Six's profits. Our old carpenter, having seen it all, disagreed. Through a series of rainforest shrieks and treetop gestures, he argued that the new keen warder was simply a nutter no other building would tolerate.

He was probably right. That night the new guard, Ravvid, ordered his trusty to set up his bed and mosquito net in the smelly dining hall. As I doused our light in No. 57 at eleven, I stood high on our new end table to look down from the window. Ravvid was still fussing with the drapes of his sanctum. His night-time post was directly in line with our cell, no more than a tennis-lob distant, if served by our puny Miraj.

And I was sure this Ravvid slept lightly.

CHAPTER TWENTY-ONE

One Saturday, about ten days later, I began to feel some emptiness in the prison. Not so many around our factory, even though the numbers in Klong Prem were higher than usual. And those who were visible were more impoverished, too. More in search of food, and too busy to notice me. Their faces looked expectant, and their speech was hushed. All a misapprehension by me, I'm certain – except for the impoverished part.

My days had become studded with frequent brief walks around Building Six divided by long spells at the desk of my old office. This was located in a narrow gully between an inner wall and the shell factory. I can't recall much of what people said in those weeks, although the sounds were plain enough. The clatter of wide spoons on plates as our extended family ate and murmured, the sudsy splash of water from our laundry (I'd taken to having my clothes washed and pressed each day), the constant slap of sandals and flip-flops along the paths and the dull whine of padded angle grinders as workers polished royal portraits.

At my desk, I was lacquering a decorative tag attached to a key chain. The key was to an empty locker, but the flat, wooden tag concealed the key Charlie had given me to the apartment in which he'd hidden my passport. Whatever happened, I did not want to have to explain that key if I was caught before the wall.

Nor could I explain away most of my other preparations should they be seen around the office or in our cell. Some things, such as the wooden block assembly (to hold the plank that would jut from our window), I'd made in sliding parts, and would later conceal in No. 57 as a footstool. The old carpenter was much put out by my insistence on working by myself. I had been taking up to an hour after my morning runs modelling furniture and constructing panels. A new wall cabinet was now in place with pigeonholes for each of the cell's residents.

The underside of that cabinet was false. Inside, fifty metres of one-inch-wide, flat nylon ribbon was held by pins making an arm's-length skein. Building Six's army-boot factory kept coils of the green canvas-like webbing to stitch across the heavy boots. Kept in a locked steel cabinet that took 500 baht to open. I'd told Jet I planned to make a deckchair, crossweaving the ribbon into fabric, 'Just as you'll find on the best cruise ships, Jet.' I'd shown him a sketch with which he seemed impressed. I was keeping secrets from everyone.

Almost every piece of good mischief that fails does so because of talk. Talk amongst the corps, talk from the best friend to his next-best friend, talk that's called planning and drill, talk that's called reassurance. We're born to talk. We grin at our first words. Chattering and pointing. A single sighting of that rope in the wrong place would mean the end. Not just the end of the day and start again. The end. I wouldn't talk in my sleep. I trusted Sten with my life, but no talking meant just that.

Even now, years later, my temples throb a vestigial warning as I talk with this pen. There's more, but I'm not talking until the night. I'm sure I haven't told even you everything, yet. Who knows what could happen before then?

A few feet behind my desk rose four metres of the inner wall, for me an unintentional and enormous artwork, a mural rendered by nature's casual hand. Sunlight had turned a 20-year-old paint job to orange branflakes, through which slanting rain had nourished green drools of mould, producing a gallery of long swords petrified in stone. At my side cooled an untouched bowl of ant soup, the steam from this dark broth commingling with a nearly invisible cloud of shelldust from the factory.

Chang, our first and best cook in the Cure, had once fried some ants for us. Swiss Eddie had been the only one brave enough to crunch into the bitter exoskeletons. Chang was 63 then, and only now in Bangkwang had his sentence been reduced to 99 years. Assuming he gets time off for good behaviour, Chang would only have to cling on to life until his 140th birthday. Could happen. There're those Russian peasants gumming blini on their sesquicentenaries. Happened in the olden days, too. Bible tells me so. Old Chang could make it home on a 797 to Taipei; just about tottering across the tarmac to meet his great-great-grandchildren, only to have his brittle bones and paper skin blown to dust by a taxiing Lear jet.

These days, Eddie used his time industriously managing his intoxicants, I'd heard. However, the cost prevented him from eating at Chang's table. Unquestionably, a price too high, for Chang was still the best.

I'd had a report of English Martyn, too. Quite mad, they'd said: Martyn sitting blindfolded at his table wearing boxing gloves. Pummelling half-cooked peas (chick and garden) with his insensible fists, wailing, '*At last, a free lunch!*' Not mad, of course. Just misunderstood, with what I would see years later as a mimed description of an atom-smasher.

I'm sure this madness-in-chains hypothesis is oversold. A week earlier I'd passed the crazy Czech Karel Stendak as he was being escorted to his new accommodation in Building Two. The Czech government had allowed him to be a citizen again after establishing his Moravian birth. He'd paused at the gate and hefted his bedroll on one shoulder as he turned to me.

'David, I can fool some of myself some of the time, but I can't fool all of myself all of the time.'

Perhaps I'd been enlisting the wrong people.

Dean Reed had returned to Bangkok and was helping a German businessman retrieve some assets tangled up in the Thai courts.

Escape

Dean was having trouble keeping up appearances. He'd sold those bits of glitter that remained from the $48,000 he'd finagled out of Myca. Probably now regretted stashing my getaway clothes at the luggage depot rather than selling those, too.

Did I tell you that Sharon had visited just after Christmas? She'd spun down into the Klong Prem walled garden. Between shows, for her new band was doing well. There were only a few tables of foreigners at that time of year, so we were undisturbed. Sharon sat and sang 'Whatever Became of Me', and looked tired.

'You made me love you,' she'd said. 'You can't do that and just – just let it go.'

I gave reassurances about my affections, but as for my luck? The days had passed when I would present smooth excuses to vindicate my nosedive. Those implausible explanations I'd offer with beguiling worldliness as though lifting the lid of a burled humidor of Cuban cigars. Each had exploded before Sharon's simple virtue. Even then, she had an unassailable faith in my abilities. Every attempt to restrict hope and to issue warnings was met with bright, innocent protests and kisses. To smother Sharon's buoyancy seemed as cruel as bagging a kitten.

So I promised to be her keeper of the flame. She was wearing shorts.

There's some folklore – mostly credited to women – that men in prison are frequently driven to boy-chasing and madness by sexual deprivation. This is not so, for the boarding-school structure of the prison disentangles this little society to childishness. However, there is a deprivation, assuredly chemical, in banishment from the company and complex spells of women. Without contact of the most primal senses, women existed only as a collection of brief moments in memory: quick eye contact igniting a chance courtship on cool nights; a stiletto's spark at pavement; blonde sunflower girls whose folded eyelids soften their smiles. For some amongst us, a converse make-believe featuring shock-talking, low-note women with taproom pasts. Most of the views expressed by my fellow prisoners were oddly sentimental, considering the reputation of hardened criminals. Perhaps I was just in the wrong prison. I kept Sharon from appearing in my mind as much as those things can be held at bay. The prison was no place for her, even as a recollection. Even so, she appeared with sudden glances at the corner of my eye before I turned and those eyes were gone. *Soon*, I usually said, *soon*.

One quiet morning at the end of the week I was standing in the umbrella factory at the window that faced the coffee shop tree. Sten was sitting beneath it, on its concrete surround, examining his toes. He was alone.

I spent a few minutes talking with the top parasol man, detailing the size of the pop-up umbrella I wanted made. I then spent a few minutes more waiting for a runner to return with a can of black paint from the autoshop. When I left the factory, I saw that Sten had not moved.

An hour later, in our office, Jet stretched silently at his desk. His fingers were black with charcoal. From time to time, he would pause at his artwork and watch me paint. I'd finished one cupboard and had moved on to blocks of wood. I wore thick rubber gloves.

Jet stood and adjusted his shoulders. Purposefully, he wiped his blackened hands on his shirt to enjoy the contrast. Jet was man enough not to mind a little dirt on his hands.

'Pretty colour,' he caustically observed. 'Those blocks go nicely with the cupboard.'

The paintbrush fell from my awkward grip. Jet theatrically picked it up from the floor.

'Jet,' I protested. 'They're the only gloves I could get. If you were any kind of a thief, you'd steal me some doctor's gloves from the hospital.'

Sten arrived as I began work painting the laser-pointer pen I'd bought from Fiorenzo the beggar. Acquired, another Italian had told me, as he'd tearfully embraced his consular rep last month.

'Someone died I don't know about?' Sten rubbed his forearms as he looked around.

Escape

'I'm in the mood for matt black this morning,' I said. 'I'll get started on those picture frames of yours in a minute. Sit down. Take a load off.'

After Sten moved a chair, I asked, 'Had a busy morning?'

'Busy enough. I've been working out with Big John, the Nigerian.'

I nodded. 'Seen Calvin?'

'Yep. He's been over behind the toilets. Nose to the grindstone.'

'What is it about toilets and drugs?' I wondered aloud. 'They must be the least private places in KP.'

Jet left the office to wash his hands, and I set the newly blackened laser-pen on a stand to dry. I turned to Sten.

'From tomorrow, be a bit careful with the room shower screen. I'll be taking the hacksaw blades from their stash. Hiding them behind the wall of the shower.'

'Whoa there, Kemosabe.' Sten kept it low and leaned back in his chair. 'What's the bustle?'

'Nothing. I mean, soon – but no hurry,' I assured him. 'It's just that getting those blades out will be a job in itself. Won't have that much time on the night – whenever that is.'

'Fine.' Sten said no more than that.

Sten had not lived in Sweden for more than seven years. In his travels, he preferred the company of those who were strangers to his country. He was an outlander in Klong Prem, perhaps the man with the thinnest ties to country, tribe and commonwealth. An outlander, yes, but still earthling enough to keep both feet on the ground.

That night, as my cellmates covered waves of desolation with the foam of sleep, I carefully padded the steps of furniture built for silence to take my position at the high window. An observation deck. For weeks, I'd been watching the nocturnal activities of the guards. Or inactivities, really, for most would be in their beds: one in a factory garden, another on the floor of the chief's office and, infuriatingly, the new guard camped below our window at one end of the dining hall.

The new sentry, Ravvid, would fuss with his sheets and mosquito net and carefully arrange his water jug. Fool around opening and closing his bag of dried fruit like a squeamish bulimic at a horror movie. Go to bed; turn once, twice, thrice – get up, sip water, adjust the net, scratch ass, get back in bed, pick nose, get up, put three dates on a plate, go to bed – I passed my time inventing variations of a flying-fox wire from which I could scream down the sixty feet to his bed while wearing mountain boots fitted with six-inch, sharpened crampons. It seemed he worked seven days and nights straight before taking a two-day break.

Resting my chin on my folded arms, I looked beyond the wall to the red aircraft-warning beacons atop Bangkok's tallest buildings. So deep into the night had the haze settled that even the traffic fell silent. Ravvid was finally asleep. The stillness recalled nights at a hotel window 17 years earlier. Sleepless, I would imagine the higher ground where friend Myca had gone to raise our fortunes. The Triangle and Myca's perilous return journey south. From the slowly dissolving city, it then seemed our lives could turn on such small things: an angry checkpoint; a broken axle; some enthusiastic nobody. And now, so little had changed.

Suddenly, silently, Ravvid raised an arm to the net above his head. He flicked a finger at the net and set it in motion as a spider might test a web. No other parts of his body had moved.

I no longer cared. Let Ravvid and all his kind sleep or lie in wait. I would do whatever was necessary.

As a teenager, I had kept upon my wall a most detailed map of the Soviet Union. Its faded colours still pronounced the fine, veinous network of connecting roads from metropolis to village. The map remained on my bedroom wall until a wiser friend looked at the map one day. He lazily advised me that almost all of the positions of towns on Soviet maps were intentionally misplaced. When he saw that I was upset, he added: 'Of course, the KGB has special editions of these very maps. Only with theirs, you need ultraviolet light to read them. Shine some UV on a secret map and the real road network comes out.'

The next day, I bought an ultraviolet tubelight from a stamp-collectors' hobby shop. No special tracery appeared on my wall map, only spots of bleach in the paper. I concluded that my friend's KGB embellishment was probably a lie, but I took down the map anyway. For it was true that some cities were missing and others joined by fictitious roads.

I soon ended the long night-time vigils. I'd seen all I could. And in daylight hours, too, I had learned as much as I would in KP. There seemed nothing more of value to discover about my arrest or the courts, and should I continue to be curious about those around me, that unprofitable information would come at great cost. The time had come to yield control to those cognitive motorways formed in us all under a primeval light.

After my usual morning run, I nodded at Pornvid on the steps and ascended the stairs to our cell.

Approaching the cell door, I saw Ding the cat waiting for me, sitting with her paws tucked under her chest. With the cell keys in one hand, I scooped up the cat with the other.

'Dinger, young lady,' I scolded. 'Don't sit in the corridor. Some nasty man will come along and boot your head in.' One of our Building Six guards had a liking for kicking cats with his heavy shoes. Dinger's mother had been brained that way, and had delivered early.

In No. 57, I set the cat on a pillow and returned the keys. Once I was back, Ding watched me remove a cloth-wrapped roll of small tools that I'd had tucked in my waistband. Her eyes were wide, as a child watches television. Taking the scroll poster from its hook on the wall, I tore 'Desiderata' from its two supporting rods. Using pincer pliers, I split the rods enough to tear them apart with my hands. From the splinters, I removed the four hacksaw blades that Michael had hidden inside. I saw he'd wrapped each blade in the foil travellers use to safeguard their photographic films, and had then sealed the blades with wood filler. He must have used a radial-arm saw to cut channels in the dowelling. A delicate job, for sure. Removing the blades had taken 20 minutes and generated some noise. Noise that would be reckless at night.

After I'd hidden the blades behind the shower screen, I put the fragments of wood and torn pieces of the poster into a cloth sack that usually held my damp exercise clothes. Turning to the cat, I knelt at her side by my bed. With one hand, I encircled her tiny neck. She was so small that with the same hand I easily and gently pinched the scruff of her neck with two fingers. She began to purr as she always did at any touch. I could feel the throb on the palm of my hand. With my other, I took a small syringe from my kit and flicked bare an ultra-fine 29-gauge needle. Ding's purring was unaltered as I slid the needle into the furry arch of skin behind her neck, and didn't change for the next 30 seconds as I pressed the plunger home – injecting 200 milligrams of heroin. Then the purring stopped, her head flopped and she went limp. I held her body to my ear to listen for her heart while I capped the needle. At seven months, she weighed no more than a lady's kidskin glove. I put her body in the sack with the broken spars.

In Klong Prem, it is difficult to throw anything away, for there are always people poorer than the ones you see. I had to wrap the cloth sack in paint-splashed newspapers before throwing it into the deepest pocket of the rubbish dump.

Young Steve from Hampstead joined Sten, Calvin and me for lunch. In that last week, Sten and I raised occasional conspiratorial eyebrows but never the subject of the escape. This nodding acquiescence to each other's position was enough. During lunch, I let my guests do the talking. More than ever, their faces held the awkward camaraderie of deserting husbands.

In a perfect scheme, I should have helped with some good humour. Made jokes. But on that day, I couldn't join in the laughter of captive men at all.

CHAPTER TWENTY-TWO

On Sunday afternoon I finished my job as censor of the foreigners' post by sending the outgoing letters to the Klong Prem post office. I then turned to the fat ledger on my desk and removed every record of my limited use of official post.

The factory was almost empty. The sun, low in the sky, began to slip into the office as it usually did for 20 minutes when no one was there. Sten, Jet and Calvin had already begun the afternoon amble to No. 57. Miraj would already be in our room. In his corner.

As I had for the past five days, I set the padlocks of our cupboards to appear locked, although they were not. This was so I could unfasten the doors in silence at any time. All set, I went upstairs to dinner.

While we ate, we talked about other inmates' troubles and the latest jail outrages but I struggled, then easily gave up pretending to sound real. In my head the ticking of a countdown clock drained away the personality I'd borrowed for the past two years.

As Jet folded our picnic blanket, I stepped up to the shower to wash my hands. Pausing at the window, I saw that the new and troublesome guard's trusty had not prepared his master's bedroom below our cell in the dining hall. That meant he would not be on duty tonight; the only guard in this part of Building Six tonight would be Somchai, who customarily slept his nights on our landing.

Escape

Turning from the window, I briefly forgot where I was. I saw a cell with four men sitting on the floor. Dropping down from that far-away moment, I joined them, helping Calvin with a birthday card for his boy in Hawaii.

A few minutes before midnight I switched off the light to encourage sleep. The new ceiling fan whirred smoothly, allowing the sounds within Building Six to state their business. The disputes of dice players, some distant applause rewarding late-night storytellers. Then laughter and retorts. Someone in a private cell took a shower to take the heat from his skin. Outside, a guard responded to a trusty, sharing a joke through the bars.

Climbing to our window in four barefoot steps, I saw the guard turn away. Above his trousers he wore only a thin vest stretched over a heavy paunch, which he rubbed in contentment as he moved away. His bed was under a canopy in a distant garden.

As I returned to my place, I saw that Sten was awake, although his eyes were closed. I spoke quietly.

'Sten. You awake?'

'What's up?' Sten opened his eyes to the half-light, asking again, 'What's doing?'

'It's a nice day for a white wedding,' I said.

'Yeah?' Sten pulled himself upright.

I nodded to the window. 'It won't get any better.'

'You got everything set?'

'As set as I know how,' I said, to keep it short.

Sten hunched forward, his arms loosely folded around his knees. 'OK.'

Not long after midnight, Building Six became quiet. I sat in No. 57 beside the weak light from the corridor, unrolling 50 metres of army-boot webbing, a ribbon of green nylon. Sten was next to me, awake but silent – lying back, arms folded behind his head. A legionnaire at rest. Before me, Jet, a sleeping servant. At his side, Calvin, an ally by heritage. Then there lay Miraj, whose heart was a pea in a whistle, a squealer by uncontrollable nature.

Escape

Of the seven hundred people in Building Six, five-sixths were too far away for easy hearing and sight, but many had rooms that faced the path I would take beyond the bars. Of these 120 fellow prisoners, 119 would shriek in explosive alarm should I be seen passing. (In cell No. 71, the hundred and twentieth man was a crippled mute, so might do no more than rake the bars with his crutch.) Inside the accommodation block, the guard on our floor slept on his elaborate but temporary bed 60 metres from No. 57. Outside, another guard slept in the factory gardens, and a third on the floor of the chief's office. Beyond Building Six, five guards were at the central command post and set for a drinking session, while half a dozen more were spread among some of the eighteen guard towers, happy to be above the mosquitoes. Seven officers manned the front gate, playing cards. Next to this Klong Prem prison of Lardyao sat the Bangkok Special Prison, Bumbudt Remand Prison (the Cure) and Bangkok Women's Prison – each with its complement of staff.

Over and around the Klong Prem moat sat guards' residences, a live-in training college and the homes of the multitudes whose incomes relied upon the prison complex. In the nearby streets, predatory police cars trawled the night. In addition to those officials, there idled a society of institutional parasites ready to claim just reward for any service. Within this sub-city, there slumped a monastery stocked with monks. Among them those who had briefly comforted two inmates who had been jolted from the electric cables atop the north-east tower before falling to the ground. The monks had held them until the prison guards arrived.

Inside the cell I set the rope aside and began freeing the hacksaw blades from their groove in the shower screen. There was no point in waking Calvin and Jet. They would wake soon enough.

Returning to my bed for the last time, I turned to Sten, sitting alert in the darkness.

'S'go.'

Handing Sten one of the saw blades, I packed a soft but tough bag with the back-up passport, a penlight, two sets of keys and padlocks wrapped in cloth and a set of clothes including long trousers. Only civilians and guards were permitted to wear long trousers.

Sten stood up from his bed as I lifted my mattress to the wide table below the window, to muffle the sound of standing feet.

'I'll begin on the first bar,' I whispered to Sten before checking at the cell door for any movement along the corridors.

I could just see the outline of the guard sleeping under his net on our third-floor landing. He was still. I then eased out a nest of tables near the shower, creating steps to the high table beneath the window. Stepping up, I removed the window's flywire screen and set it at the cell door, where it could not be knocked over accidentally. Any sound from the cell had to be considered.

The plan was to remove two of the one-inch diameter bars from the window in four cuts, to allow an easy exit.

Pressing the saw blade lightly above the base weld of the first bar, I drew its teeth back in a long stroke. The blade's tiny teeth flaked away a dozen layers of paint covering the bar and shaved enough minute curls of steel to leave a half-millimetre notch in the shaft. The sound of the rasping vibration, amplified in the bars, had thrummed into the concrete surround. An alien call in the still night.

'Use the oil.' Sten was standing behind my legs.

'Soon. I'll go slow for now.'

Curling my left arm through the bars, I held the tip of the blade with a folded square of damp cloth, pulling it taut and giving sideways pressure with my other hand. I focused on direction, not wanting to snap the blade. After ten minutes, I'd cut a quarter of the way through the bar.

Stepping down from the table, I gave the blade to Sten with a warning: 'The oil will make it quieter but slower to cut, because it won't bite so well. These blades are brittle. I nearly snapped the thing when it stuck.'

'No,' Sten disagreed. 'The oil will make it cut easier.'

'OK.' This was not the time for disputes. 'We've got another three. We can lose two without disaster.'

Escape

As Sten stepped up to the window, the table's badly set legs groaned under his weight. Turning to the darkened room, I saw a forced rigidity in the limbs beneath the light blankets. All three were awake but so far following cell etiquette by ignoring all private nocturnal activity. This good form might not hold once they realised that this was no simple unsealing of a stash or the venting of some home brew.

I checked for any movement outside before taking Michael's phoney can of aspic delicacies from a shelf. I peeled off the lid and removed the Swiss army knife nestled within.

The cupboard above my bed was divided into nine pigeonholes, all painted black. One was less deep than the others. Using a short blade from the pocketknife, I cut through a false backplate made from balsa wood. The wood was soft and easy to slice. Breaking away the fragments, I removed the hidden contents quickly to the bag at my side. If seen, the contours of a large automatic pistol and bulky silencer would terrify at least three in the cell and surely distract Sten.

I hung my soft teardrop bag on a hook and turned to find Calvin awake, sitting up. With his blanket still over his knees, he picked at the wrapping of a soft-pack of cigarettes. I eased down on my haunches to speak.

'I tried to warn you, Calvin. Told you it wasn't a good time to come to Six.'

'Ah – yup.' Calvin kept his thoughts to himself.

He held a lighter to his cigarette, looking around the cell as though for the first time. He saw it for the crypto-launch platform that it was: the stepped tables leading to the window, the furniture made from three-inch timbers, the triple layers of sound-catching nylon mosquito screens covering the cell door, the heavy clasps that held the window's screen – now serving as handgrips. And across one wall, the bookshelf plank, so heavy it required five triangles of steel to support it, yet never firmly attached. Calvin looked from side to side, taking in the careful selection of roommates. He nodded to himself and made the most of his cigarette.

Escape

'It'll be best if you don't look like you're part of the show,' I whispered, gesturing to Miraj's blanket-lump in the corner.

Sten loped down from the window to tell me he needed to move the bench, so he could cut from a better angle. He looked down at Miraj. 'He'll have to move.'

Crouching before Miraj's quivering coverlet, I tugged at the fabric. Wide eyes appeared above the hem.

'Miraj. Listen now,' I said, assuming the tone of a field surgeon. 'Nothing will happen to you if you stay quietly in your corner. Don't make any noise.'

Miraj said nothing as he pushed himself to the corner with his feet, and then bundled his blanket to his stomach. Sten and I moved the bench to a more central position.

As Sten resumed his attack on the bars, Calvin stood and silently moved to the bench. He held its edge with both hands to steady its movement. Sten looked down to Calvin, and then couldn't resist rasping at Miraj.

'Not disturbing your sleep, are we?'

I thanked Calvin for his support, and told him it was unnecessary. 'The bench is on rubber mounts. It won't move.' There was nothing I wanted Calvin to do.

I saw Jet standing on his mattress, pedalling the sponge with his toes. As I moved to the cell door, I unstrapped my watch and gave it to Jet with a wink. In the corridor there was no movement, and almost no sound. From my bag, I took a cheap but nearly indestructible digital watch and strapped it to my wrist. It was already after 1 a.m. Pressing my face flat and against the bars of the cell door, I peered hard. I held my breath to listen for any sounds below the scrape of metal teeth against steel. From the other cells, the source of this sound would be difficult to locate.

Every ten minutes, I checked on Sten's progress before returning to my corridor vigil. After half an hour, I gave him a break, taking his place with a new blade. Progress was slow: this first bar still only at the three-quarter point. Working on without oil, I stopped a millimetre short of the final cut.

Escape

'Sten. I need to give my hands a rest.' I stood down and rubbed my fingers, trying to suggest that I wasn't very good at cutting bars. 'Sweat's running in my eyes.'

Within two minutes of Sten's renewed cutting, the bar sprang away from its welded base with a clean snap and a vibrating sprong.

'Well done, mate!' I was quickly up at the window with an armful of wet towels. 'One for you and the rest around the bars. The next cut will carry more noise. Whole building must've shifted over the years since that went in. Twisted the frame.' I tested the bar with a tug. It barely moved. 'Let me get started, Sten. Stop for a drink.'

By 2 a.m., after very little cutting by me, we were still on the second bar. And that no more than two-thirds cut. I would not spend any more time or energy here.

Some suggestions were voiced but I was listening only for sounds outside the cell. At 2.10, I called an end to the cutting.

'What about we leave it for tonight?' Sten recommended. 'We can start again tomorrow night.'

Pausing for a moment to give an impression of thoughtful consideration, I shook my head slowly. 'Let's try this. Grab the bottom of the bar – here, let me wrap it in a towel – bend it up, it might snap.'

As Sten climbed up and took a double-handed grip, I again looked at my watch, the only impartial adviser. I avoided looking at Miraj. If work were suspended, I had no doubt that after daylight, as soon as the cell door would open, Miraj would scamper down to the chief's office and spill. Once free of this cell, no threat or inducement would halt his instinct for self-preservation, and any promise he might make now would be meaningless. While Sten would remain stoic, Calvin would walk through the day zombified and seeking anaesthesia. Jet, however, might give the game away with some gleeful and nervous sharing. All these were needless speculations: Miraj would see me chained to the floor of a pit before I could finish breakfast. Even should he die during the night, there would be meddlesome enquiries. Considering the others' reactions, this was unthinkable.

Escape

Sten tested the two-foot bar with one hand on the window's ledge and the other gripping the bar. He pulled as though separating wild beasts. The bar moved only a few inches and sprang back.

Undeterred, Sten made two small notches either side of the existing cut with a blade, and then stood down. 'I'm gonna have to get up on this thing.' He meant the ledge. 'My feet on both sides. You stand behind me if it snaps and I fall.'

I arranged mattresses on the floor below the window and stood with Calvin, ready to catch Sten.

Sten breathed in and gripped. He steadied himself and levered with a controlled tension as if pulling for Sweden. The bar groaned, and the room seemed to shake. So did Miraj. His courage was failing him.

I crouched in front of Miraj and took his ear in my fist, drawing it to my lips. I said, 'Miraj. The only reason I don't end your life here and now is because it would upset the others. That's the only reason. Don't you give me any cause to look at you again.'

Sten was through toying with the bar. 'Right, you bastard,' he muttered.

With sweat dripping from his brow, he knotted his fingers around the bar, locked his shoulders and lifted his thighs. Things shook. Sten had 50 prison guards between his hands on a descent into hell. The bar strained upward, it curved, it bent – but it did not snap. Sten stood down, breathing heavily.

The now curved bar had partially returned, leaving a gap of six inches. More if Sten could hold it in place.

'That's good,' I said, patting Sten on his shoulder. 'That'll be enough.'

Sten was exhausted. My cellmates' adrenalin would be drained. They would soon rest and reflect on what tomorrow might bring.

'I won't get through there with my shirt on,' I said to Sten. 'And that oil might be needed.'

I took my shirt off and stuffed it into my bag before oiling my chest. I turned to clear the bookshelf and saw Jet standing in his corner.

Escape

'My teacher?'

Standing before me with a tremulous soldier's stance, Jet was wearing his best shirt and kids' commando shorts. A pair of stiff leather sandals – a recent family gift – and a white handkerchief folded in his card-sized breast pocket. Some photographs in one hand for luck.

'I go with you, my teacher. Everywhere.'

Before me, Jet appeared as my child.

Somewhere in the Barents Sea, a few drops of the ocean seeped through an icebreaker's hull. Jet's loyalty was something surely worth saving, too. Thoughts of carrying him through the next impossible hours attempted to form. Yet such thoughts, as with drops from the ocean, evaporated immediately.

'Jet, you can't come. It's very good of you to volunteer. You've got three years. Maybe four. Sten is going to look after you. Won't you, Sten?'

'Sure will.'

'Here, put this in your pocket.' I took 5,000 baht I'd prepared and slid them into Jet's top pocket. 'I'll write to you. Send you things.'

I'd given Sten most of my cash. The guards wouldn't mess with him the way they might others, and he'd buy Jet out of serious trouble. He'd need to – the money I'd given Jet would be taken by lunchtime. Jet sat on his bed. I turned to Sten.

'Try to stop them doing their worst,' I said quietly. 'Calvin will be OK. They won't slap an American around in a hurry. You – well, you're fucked. But you know that.'

I lifted my bag from its hook and pushed in a towel. 'But you also know that they don't hold grudges on principle if there's money to be had. And you'll have some of that.'

'I know.' Sten lifted the bookcase plank from its mounts.

I disassembled our shoe rack, refitting its wooden parts to make a block that just fitted between two of the uncut bars of the window. As Sten came to look, I added a warning about Miraj.

'Shithead will be spilling his guts in the chief's office before you can pull on your drawers.'

Escape

Sten wasn't troubled. 'I'll keep him quiet till morning. And then as late as I can.'

'Are you sure about this, Sten? Last chance Texaco?'

'I'll be OK.'

Sten and I lifted the plank to the window, but it was too long to manoeuvre without hitting the fan. We had to move the large table to the centre of the cell and switch off the ceiling fan. The plank was almost the length of the room.

Sten slid the upended plank to the window ledge. I fitted the wooden block between the uncut bars, leaving a gap the size of a vertical letter slot: just big enough to allow the plank to slide out of the window. After some difficult guiding, we had six feet of plank jutting into the night air, less than a foot remaining in the cell. It held.

After a last check with a mirror of the corridor and the ground below, I climbed to the window and turned to face the room. I made no farewells. Sten stood on the bench and levered the bar while I twisted my head under the gap. With my hands now outside the window, I set my shoulders in position. I lifted my weight. The sawn stump of the bar dug into my back despite the cloth I'd draped over its jagged edges.

'More,' I called upon Sten.

As he strained, I writhed through. The stump scraped along the flesh ridge next to my spine, but did not catch, and I twisted out from under the bar to air that was different. Still facing the cell, I found myself clinging to the bars, my feet perched on the ledge – a flying wyvern that had been drawn from the night by some odour.

My soft green bag appeared at the bars, and behind it, Sten's face.

'Break *both* legs,' he winked.

'Thanks.'

I lifted the bag's sash over a shoulder and looked down on the grounds of Building Six. No movement. The paths and gardens lit in small pools from some scattered bulbs. A greater light spilled from the cells' windows. Quiet. No masking wind, only the sound of 100 ceiling fans whispering low.

Turning back to the bars, cell No. 57 was almost in darkness. I saw shapes moving inside – people lost to me now. Four men locked in a stone and iron room. Captives I had known, so distant in an instant. I let go of the bars, gripping the upturned plank that jutted into the gloom. Its surface was rough despite some earlier work with sandpaper. Hand over hand, I eased away from the building until my feet left the window ledge. Dangling from the plank, I worked my way to the tip, collecting splinters. I looked down.

Beneath my toes, 15 feet below, the crumbling tile awning sloped between floors. And another below that. From pebble-drop tests, I knew that any touch of foot or scrape of knee on my way down would produce a cascading shower of broken tiles and concrete. The cell at ground level held a nest of unhinged trusties whose whistles would shred the night air, should I be detected.

Abseiling would require swinging into the wall, so only a controlled drop would do. Dangling from one arm, I thumbed a loop of army-boot webbing from my bag. The 50 metres of thick nylon ribbon had earlier been unrolled and folded in half. I hooked the loop over the top of the plank and then lifted the remainder from the bag. In three drops, I released the rubber bands holding the bunched rope. As the last band sprang away, the rope softly folded to the ground, its last dozen metres piling like green fettuccine.

I gripped a twist of rope in each hand. Although I'd earlier taken some leather gloves from the autoshop, I'd found them loose, and this next move needed full control, no matter the cost. I eased my grip a little to allow movement, but relaxing at all was too much. The ribbon rushed from my hands, and I plunged towards the ground. Tightening my grip steered me into the wall. The ribbon burned across my fingers and palms, and I braked enough to kick one foot into one of the safety loops I'd tied. My descent halted just above the first awning, and I swung into a wide figure-of-eight spin, the trailing rope brushing against the lip of the fragile overhang. As spin combined with my pendular swing, I was granted an unwelcome close-up of crumbling wall-plaster alternating with a panorama of the far horizon.

I had no safe option other than to wait until I stopped swinging. I passed the time by watching the loop attached to the plank overhead slowly writhe to its tip. Yet I'd got the measure of this rope by then and lifted a strip under my shoes with one hand before easing down the remaining 20 feet with the webbing rope's loose end twisted and bunched around my hands as some protection. The ground was soft, so I allowed myself a gentle sideways fall. I looked at my hands. The nylon cord had cleared my palms of splinters along with several layers of skin.

Stepping back from the building, I took up the rope's slack and gently fly-cast the loop from the tip of the plank. Sten had been dutifully at the rudder, and I watched the heavy plank slide back into No. 57 as the coiling rope fell into my arms.

On the ground, I socked on a T-shirt and folded the rope into my bag. I had just this one length, which had to see me over many walls yet. Padding along the matted weeds, I kept close to the building's wall until the corner. Then, ducking through a prepared gap in a picket fence, I threaded through the darkened factory to my office. It was 2.55. Not much after 6 a.m., Klong Prem would sniffle and shuffle to life.

Through the mesh screens around the office I could see the top of the mosquito net under which a guard slept. Although he was no more than 25 metres distant, he was a sound sleeper of regular habits.

Now, when it was not needed, a drunken wind fitfully poured from the city, rustling palm trees and cloaking remote footsteps – should there be any.

I removed the padlocks from the office cupboard and opened the doors wide. After guzzling some water, I pulled on some dark track pants before setting a small flashlight on a chair aimed at the cupboard's interior. Removing a false shelf, I took out my street clothes, four rolls of black gaffer tape and a bunch of thick cable ties. All of that went into my bag along with the collapsible umbrella that had been delivered from its factory just a week earlier.

More carefully, I stacked eight heavy picture frames upon an open towel and secured them to each other to muffle any rattling. Together, they weighed an awkward 30 kilos. I left the cupboards open.

Although there remained three major and two minor walls beyond Six, my first stop was the paper-box factory where I would construct the ladders. Carrying the towelled block of frames on one shoulder, I wound along the paths to the wide street alongside the main factories. The box-factory door was chained and locked as expected, but for months the factory boys had been climbing through the twisted window mesh on Sundays to keep out of the rain. Unfortunately, a week earlier some plywood had been nailed to the window frame to halt the intruders. Setting down my load, I saturated the nail points with machine oil from a small squirt bottle and waited 30 seconds before working out the nails with the bottle opener on the pocketknife. Despite the oil, two nails complained. This main street was a bad place to work. A corner each end – far enough away not to hear an approaching guard, and too distant to do much about those who might see me.

Inching my sack of frames, swollen bag and myself through the window into the factory in silence chewed up valuable minutes. Doing everything without making much noise was taking a lot longer than the test moves I'd timed during the noisy daylight hours. I would remember that.

The gritty factory floor was smeared with oil and dye, and littered with bunched paper and plastic bottles. The two long walls held rickety scaffolding upon whose beams rested thousands of five-metre bamboo poles – each four inches at the base, tapering to thumb width. Many were draped with sheets of yellow and red paper, drying in preparation for folding as offertory gift boxes for Chinese funerals. The 12 tiers of poles looked set to collapse.

Clearing some floorspace with one of the poles, I laid the picture frames in two rows before selecting poles to match. Holding the torch in my teeth, I found eight poles to make two ladders, taping the frames at intervals as rungs. Taking an extra pole for luck, I lugged everything to the end of the factory. The back wall of the paper-box factory abutted the autoshop. The autoshop was gated and never visited at night. Taking this route would be better than dragging a bamboo litter along Main Street.

My mouth had dehydrated from holding the torch, so I paused for a few seconds to drink and look at the next obstacle. The rear wall of the factory was corrugated iron and topped with mesh. I didn't like the slog, but I'd have to peel the holding nails from the mesh and go over the top. I would not look at my watch until I was in the autoshop.

Balancing on cross beams, I peeled back the ventilation mesh, but had trouble evicting the long, heavy ladders. I used the short one to climb down to the autoshop. The driveway was pooled with oil and staked with steel battens to hold car parts.

Standing on the driveway, I saw that the autoshop gate in my path had been chained. The gate was easily scaleable, but too jangling if touched. I'd have to slide the ladders underneath the narrow gap and climb carefully over the hinges. It was then 4.10 a.m. Sliding the ladders quietly and climbing silently took another 15 minutes. I stopped looking at my watch. That wonder-drug adrenalin would soon be demanding payment with dizziness and unsteady movements – but not yet.

After I reassembled my rigging, I looked to the next objectives. Beyond the rows of toilet stalls, clotheslines and cooking hearths was the first of the inner walls. This led to Building Seven and from there to the AIDS hospice. This route meant an additional wall but avoided the certainty of being seen by those few sleepless inmates moon-staring from windows. The 500 prisoners of the AIDS building were already at the porridge-fleshed, carrot-boned stage of their way to death, so mostly the strength for window-gazing would be no more than an anguished memory. From their untrodden gardens, the surrounding wall led to the final high barrier. Or so I thought.

Escape

At that moment, a familiar sound stroked my spine. The unmistakable scrape of a sandalled foot across gravel. Sinking behind a factory pillar, I looked left and froze. Sixty metres away, standing at a massive water trough, the pot-bellied guard Bonpan stood leaning over the slowly filling tank. Wearing only shorts and a vest, he appeared to have shuffled from sleep, seeking water.

In the darkness, I crouched to my bag and groped for the one device I'd hoped might save me from such an event: a bulky, black automatic pistol, its fat round-tipped silencer now attached to the front – a recognisable silhouette at any distance. Easing the final tube into clips at its bridge, I activated the laser that formed its sight.

As I waited, the red dot quivered with speckled iridescence low on the factory wall, describing the inclination of my grip. Bonpan, known to me, and a man of mostly even temper, sagged heavily at the trough's edge and splashed water on his forehead. I took a handful of cable ties and planted them at my back under my belt line.

Only I knew what the drowsy guard should not: that the macabre-looking automatic was a fake – nothing but the laser sight was true. The body and grip of the gun I'd sculpted from model-aeroplane balsa wood before gluing and painting it black in utmost secrecy. The matching silencer had been a bottle of skin cream, its domed cap severed to form the exit port. The laser was also a pen.

This charade was not ill-considered. The value of having a real gun seemed low in almost every scene I could imagine. To begin with, smuggling a silenced weapon and sub-sonic ammunition into Klong Prem would have carried deplorable risks. Even speaking to the type of locals who could find such a weapon would invite gossip. What's more, to fire even a well-made gun on a still night would be far from silent, much less the dodgy tool I might get. More importantly, a real gun would be almost useless. Any night, distant guards would be no threat for I could simply avoid them. Those behind me whom I failed to spot would either sneak away for help or shout to me at a distance. Shooting one on the turn at 60 metres was no job for a pistol. Even a hit would most likely result in the wailing wounded groping for his radio as I emptied my gun at a now more difficult target. Any real shooting would probably generate the sounds I hoped to avoid.

Conclusively, the only value in a gun would be its appearance. Should I turn from my ladder to find an advancing guard, the first impression must carry the moment. The sight of a red dot upon his heart combined with the lethal intent implied by a fulsome silencer would take his breath away. Before he could speak, I would issue calming instructions to hold him until I closed the gap between us. Gaffer tape and cable ties would then form the best silencer. Alternatively, I could round a corner to come face-to-face with some barefoot wanderer, and a gun would be unnecessary. Without the sensitivities of my roommates to consider, a guard could more easily be made still by hand.

At the tank, Bonpan raised himself from the water with some effort. He looked at the clouding sky, then turned and lumbered away. I moved to the factory corner to watch him return to his garden. It was not yet 5 a.m., so there was a good chance he would re-enter the semi-conscious drift that formed guards' sleep. I turned off the laser pen and replaced the fake pistol in my bag.

After collecting my ladders, I carried them balanced underarm beyond the water tanks to the first wall. The wind had settled, and I heard the dribbling chortle of water pipes as they filled the wash tanks. A sound that belonged to Klong Prem only at night, for in daylight hundreds of voices smothered all small things. Similarly, night changed the odours of even the worst places. During the day, clay stoves fuelled by rags, rotted furniture and empty plastic bottles soured the ground and issued microstring soot over the washhouse. Now, during the smokeless night hours, the smells of the cooking hearths blended and the earth breathed. On the lines, the laundry of the moneyed classes left oversoaped by their washermen perfumed the air and brushed my face as I made a hunched transit between sheets and sarongs.

Escape

The wall leading to Building Seven was topped by wide, flopping coils of barbed wire. These were held between steel posts and anchored by U-bolts. One ladder allowed me to the top to wrench out the U-bolts with pincers. Then, although I knew better, I tried to cut the wire with those beaver-tooth pliers. Not enough leverage.

From the ground, I taped a small coat-hook to the spare bamboo pole. The barbed-wire coils were now conveniently sagging between their supports, and I hooked the low point with the pole. I drew the wire well below the wall's rim, but it sprang up as soon as I released the pole. I could have sacrificed some of my rope to stretch the coils and tie them to the nearest laundry pole. Yet with time burning at my neck, I simply grabbed a table from the cookhouse, taped it roughly to the pole hook I'd no longer need, and so produced an ugly anchor.

Now with a clear approach, I put both ladders against the wall, my bag over my shoulder, then climbed, straddled the wall and hauled the smaller ladder over, followed by its big sister.

From my perch, I had a view of walls unseen from any window in Building Six. The thick, angled walls of Building Seven, the wire hedges between sections and a high ferro-concrete wall that obscured those beyond the AIDS compound. I climbed down to the marshes of Building Seven, hearing my breathing: exhausted, drained of ambition and even curiosity. Feeling contempt for something – I don't know what – I now had to make decisions as well as climb these cheap mountains.

So then, quite empty, I called upon unreasoning hostility. Yet by then, this usually reliable resource was puddled in torpor. I stood unmoved by images of flesh-grinding chains and dungeon rot that shadowed upon the stones from every angle; unmoved by my certain fate if caught now.

Fortunately, the night air told me that I was alone, and free to move alone among the 12,000. The air of freedom lifted me from my weakness.

Abruptly, I found myself sitting high again, now on top of the second wall of Building Seven, with my needless speculations left on the ground. I had taped the two ladders together and was moving between walls with my skinny castle-storming ladder balanced over my shoulders. Atop each inner wall, the ladder rose well above its rim, allowing me to climb quickly down as it seesawed over.

From an unfamiliar courtyard of dangerously open ground, I speared into an unexpectedly dense garden – squashing through its wet soil, seeking any path that would take the long ladder. Here, plenty of newness and freshness for someone confined to Building Six for almost two years, but I was a slave to time and the ladder, a runaway cross-country bus. The ladder's weight carried me forward.

The climb to the AIDS-sufferers' building brought a surprise: no tree cover. So, quickly down and over to the building's wall. Keeping low beneath the windows, pausing to check for sounds of others and continually adjusting my load to avoid strikes. No sound from the wards, only a cloying odour that seeped and held.

The next wall was comparatively low. An easy hurdle using the ladder to flatten three rows of barbed wire on top as I tilted from one side to the other. The gaffer tape was holding well, and the picture-frame rungs made climbing swift, while the bamboo settled quietly each time it touched ground. An advantage of using organic materials. Before me opened a wide-pathed quadrangle with weedy lawns just under half the size of a football field. High, bright lights illuminated two intermediate towers. This must have been an old prison left as an island when Klong Prem was enlarged. The towers were unmanned, but between them sat a darkened guards' hut.

Setting my ladder flat to the ground, I crept to the hut to hear faint evidence of a sleeping guard: an intake of breath; his body weight shifting against hemp cords from a charpoy bed. I would like to have known more, but the hut was edged with a gravel path. Footsteps on gravel would make another alarm. I retreated to my ladder.

Beyond this field rose the outer wall. Given the position of buildings, lights, towers and guards, going sideways was as dangerous as going ahead. And there was the hour. I could smell dawn.

As I loped across the quadrangle like a pole-vaulter's caddy, I wondered about the function of a row of three-metre concrete poles I could see ahead. Almost as I was upon them, I saw they held a near-invisible wall of barbed wire. Twenty or more taut strands from base to top. I turned my ladder in time to collapse in the mud beneath this unforeseen barrier.

It was simple but effective. Too muddy to dig under, too noisy and exposed to ladder over. Triple-stranded and too tough to cut.

I cursed heaven and earth in whispered Arabic – a language whose rich and satisfying obscenities I'd learned from some friendly Lebanese. Reluctantly, I cut loose one of the picture frames and wedged it upright between the barbed strands. After dragging my ladder and myself through the gap, I left the frame in the mud, as both it and my hands were too wet and slimy to grip fresh tape. The missing two rungs now made the ladder shake with a light rattle, but would not be missed when climbing.

Ahead stood the wall, the last wall. But before me still oozed the two-and-a-half-metre width of Mars Bar Creek, the internal sewer-moat that flowed below the outer wall. Although I was covered in mud, I would be damned if I'd wade through shit. People would smell me in the streets.

I slid the ladder across the turdal canal and then adjusted the angle to make an oblique crossing. I tied one end of the rope to the end I was leaving and scrabbled across holding the cord tight. This was because at the wall side there was less than three feet of path – not enough to drag the ladder across without tilting it into the fetid magma of Klong Prem. This ladder and I were pals by then. I would treat it with courtesy. After pinning my side of the ladder with a stick (I'd snapped off a finger of bamboo – I was less concerned with noise by then), I raised the rope to pivot the ladder across the moat like raising a drawbridge.

Done. Now, the last wall.

Escape

From my narrow belt of land, I could only raise the ladder by lifting one end and walking underneath while keeping my arms above my head, moving sideways. Finally raised, the ragged bamboo tips reached the wire atop the wall. I climbed.

The sky overhead was a glowing shroud of deep blue, yet I didn't look at my watch. As its figures would become visible, so would I. Here at the western wall, the nearest tower was unmanned. The corner tower was probably manned by a guard ready to wake. The ladder held its strength but wanted to bounce away from the wall as I ascended. I reached the top and opened my eyes to a view I had imagined for so long it had become a living memory: stars above an infinite purple-black horizon.

Instead a flattened rainbow of colour at the horizon flashed, where a deep orange was pressing against the forgiving deep blue. It was 5.45, with dawn just minutes away. I was breaking out in daylight.

Sliding and bumping to the ground back inside the prison, I threw off my muddy clothes and used the last of the bottled water to clean myself. I changed into the street clothes I'd kept in a plastic bag. Before climbing again, I put on the heavy rubber gloves to deal with the electric wire.

Once more at the wall's apex, I looked closely at the strands of wire I would need to climb. I'd quickly decided two things: to abandon Martyn's voltmeter (for no figure would alter my course), and to avoid swimming the moat. At the other side of the wide klong was a muddy field of reeds leading nowhere. I dropped the rope over the free side and attached the midpoint fold to the steel post that held the electrical cables. Touching the wire with the back of my gloved hand, I felt nothing.

As I lifted myself up to the post – leaving my faithful ladder for ever – I looked up once more. I was alone, floating above a free earth. A small, unbelieving human in this sudden and most-private world, I was inescapably touched by the red ball of the sun as if by the source of all creation.

Lifting myself to the tip of the steel post, I had to risk a rubber-soled foothold on the exposed wire. I felt a tingle of conductivity along my shin, not more. Easing myself over and turning, I repeated the foothold. A last surge of current, and then I was clear, taking the acrylic rope in both hands and sliding 30 feet to the ground.

I had landed on the narrow earthen footpath that surrounded the prison walls. Pulling the rope through, I bunched it up and threw it over the reeds. I felt like a civilian in my street clothes, but clouds had greyed the sun as its light rolled towards me, and I knew I was far from being just one among the morning crowds of prison staff who would be arriving for a day's rest.

I drew the black umbrella from my bag and popped it open. Only a few drops of rain fell over Klong Prem. The clouds were unconvincing and the skittish mists lifting, but I needed that umbrella's protection as I had a long way to walk.

Keeping an even pace, I kept close to the wall, walked to the first corner and turned. Another great wall before me and I kept the umbrella low – just high enough to see the path ahead. As I passed the last corner, I could not resist looking up to the guard. He held his rifle in the crook of his arm and looked down at the people arriving with early deliveries, and others opening their stalls at the front of the prison, some boiling water for a first coffee. As I passed below, he took an interest, so I lowered my black canopy upon my pale face. I held to that day's maxim: escaping prisoners do not carry umbrellas. I hoped the guard would conclude from my khaki trousers and brown shoes that I was one of his colleagues taking the side path, perhaps to avoid a boss.

'Luck, lucky, lucky,' I whispered to myself, for I could see nothing.

The footbridge crossing the moat was just to the side of the main gate, by then alive with voices and feet. From my webbed shield, I heard greetings and chatter, the sound of cars, too. Crossing the bridge, I had to lift the brolly's rim to avoid collision. I walked beyond the visitors' shops but kept to the driveways, despite the foolish temptation to head for open ground. Drivers have less time to focus, I thought, than those peering across an empty field. At the unmanned and open boom gate, I moved against the tide of arriving civilian Klongsters and cars hopping over the speed humps. A new Mazda belonging to a ruthless Building Six guard bumped high, and he gave me a most curious look. A *farang*? But his car drove on, and within two minutes, I was at the main road. Another long minute before a break in the traffic allowed me to cross this main artery and its dividing barrier without looking panicky. Finally, I could lower the umbrella that had been my staff and comfort.

I looked back to Klong Prem from relative safety. My first viewing other than as a chained prisoner in a steel bus. Looking at the vast expanse of huts and hovels spread across the parkland around the prison, I saw that to have passed this way at night might have been hazardous, or *fraught with no danger*, as we used to say.

I moved back and up a few steps of a pedestrian road bridge to look for a taxi. Several minutes passed. It was now late, but I would not stay in Thailand. Yet I hesitated, looking at the prison. Behind those walls remained the chained and the phantoms of the dead. I put away my umbrella. Now in the clothes of an outsider, I felt different – myself again. This was the world I had left, the place where I could take things in hand. Nearby, shops offered devices and objects never seen within the prison. Behind me, a building site held strong machines and steel tools, ready for work. And within reach lay a big city with all its wiles and magic. I thought of those inside cell No. 57. I thought of Sharon.

I took the few steps down from the bridge in time to flag the yellow taxi that was approaching.

'Lat Phrao,' I told the driver before he could ask. As the cab moved forward, I sat in the back seat and broke open the seal that held the key to Charlie Lao's apartment.

The first taxi took me to the small hotel near Charlie's apartment. I dodged the entrance to look for an isolated place to dump the cable ties, tape and phoney gun from my bag. The balsa-wood gun had already fallen to bits. Cheap stagecraft would not play in the greater world. A second taxi took me the few streets to the apartment. The traffic was thickening. Seven-fifteen.

After sliding the key into the lock, I was pleased to see it turn. Easing the door open, I saw a dark room. The door stopped on a chain, and I smelled human occupancy.

'Yo! Good morning. You awake?' Whoever you are.

Then, the sound of a couple of choking gulps, two or three uncoordinated foot thumps, and then a sleep-creased Chinese face at the crack.

'Who dat?'

'Me. David, Daniel. Charlie's friend.'

'Oh – ah, yeah,' followed by the boy's fumbling as he unchained the door. He then stepped backwards to plop on the bed. The flat was small.

'Sorry for calling so early,' I began and kept talking. 'The door was locked so I used the key. When that worked, I opened the door. Sensible of you to use the door chain, yes. Friend of Charlie, are you?'

'Yeah. Charlie say. Wha'?'

'Oh, you're too kind.' I dropped my near-empty bag on the floor. 'May I use your bathroom? Through here?' There was only one other door.

Inside, I closed the door. Turned the lock. A cubicle: toilet facing the shower stall, a small hand-basin with a mirrored cabinet above and a second mirror mounted on the wall above the toilet. This was it. Charlie had described the mirror behind which he said would be the doctored passport. Complete with an entry stamp and immigration card. If it were not there, I would have to stay in Thailand.

About this time, at Klong Prem, Building Ten guards would be wondering at the two taped ladders rising against the wall, and in Six, trusties would be staring at the twisted bars of No. 57, where inside, Jet would be hiding under Sten's wing as Calvin paced in a tight circle. Miraj would be prostrate in the chief's office, in full lava flow.

Escape

I looked at my face in the mirror.

'Charlie, old chum,' I said to myself. 'Are you the genuine article?'

Picking out the file tool from the pocketknife, I slid it behind the mirror. It halted at a paper something. A brown envelope. Quickly tapped and torn, I removed the British passport. Its original holder had crossed many borders and, according to a triangular stamp, had entered Thailand three and a half weeks ago. And there was I, smiling from the inside cover. I touched the passport to my head in salute.

I stepped from the bathroom to find the young man, still in his underwear, poking at a jar of compacted coffee granules with a spoon.

'Sorry I can't stay for breakfast.' I put the key on the dresser by the door. 'Give this to Charlie, and say hello for me.'

'You want coffee?'

'I'd like to, but I've got to take the bus to Pattaya this morning.'

Before questions could begin, I stepped out into a day that was warming rapidly. The next taxi took longer to find, and as I should have known, it took me straight back to Klong Prem. The V Rangsit Highway passes near the front of the prison on the way to Don Muang airport.

As we passed, I touched the belt I wore, from the dead Frenchman, and sank low in my seat. This was the third taxi with unnaturally soft seats. From the ledge of the taxi's side window, I looked at KP. The prison had not vaporised from the earth. I had merely left it.

At Don Muang, my driver finally accepted that, although I'd insisted on getting out at Arrivals, I did not want him to wait. I burrowed in to the stairways and then emerged at Departures. No special atmosphere. Just a working Monday morning. I could see no bad people waiting.

From a shirt pocket, I took hold of a thick Christmas card, gripped one edge and tore it apart. Inside – held between the glued layers – was a left-luggage receipt. Kept there safely in case I had been caught before climbing the wall. I walked to the long-term luggage depot. Presumably, this pick-up would be uneventful, as it had been a secret kept. I still had the receipt for the clothes that Sharon had given Dean Reed, which he had left at the Moh Chit bus terminal – clothes left for no other purpose than to lead my imagined enemies astray. I was convinced everything I'd shared with him had become noted and filed with the narcotics agencies. There'd be a warm welcome there for me if I stayed in town. Instead, from the card, I carried this receipt for parcel C589 in the name Cisco Pike for a bag deposited two months earlier by a Mr Walker. After collecting the in-cabin-sized bag, I found it contained two sets of clothes – labels removed – a bag of toiletries and a paperback. No-frills travel.

Staring up at the electronic departures-board, I searched among its cities for a temporary home. A long-haul flight would give me too many hours imagining incredible feats of detection by the opposition. There were three short-haul flights on offer, each with a full compass of onward connections: one, to Manila, FINAL CALL; then Hong Kong, leaving at 10.00; Singapore, flipping to NOW BOARDING as I watched. Over-the-counter tickets for immediate departure are not always cheap, so I moved quickly to a bank of ATMs.

Having dispensed most of my cash in No. 57, I was now dependent on two Visa cards, neither of which matched the name in my passport. The first card – the one that had kept Pornvid relaxed for over a year – was declined. At that, the previously blank-faced ATMs took on ugly personalities, but using the second card at the third ATM I was rewarded with a gurgling shuffle from its heart. Even so, I was lucky the flight to Singapore was an unpromoted Lufthansa hop that had originated in Frankfurt, otherwise I would have boarded penniless.

'You'll have to hurry,' said the clerk. 'I've one window seat left. Is that OK?'

'A window's fine.' I picked up the boarding pass and moved on to the immigration desks.

Escape

All the immigration officers appeared alert and intelligent. Not what I'd wanted. The hoped-for cross-eyed moron must've missed his bus to work that day. Propped against a trolley, I squinted at the passport from Charlie, forged a passable facsimile of a Gerald Griffin's signature on the departure card, and queued. I put myself in a line behind two girls who were digging into narrow handbags for documents as a tall, full-faced immigration officer watched. They were giggling as though they'd only just realised what the queue was for. Fullface found this charming, and fooled around with them for an extra minute. As they angled off, I stepped forward, shrugging my shoulders down as befits a tired European businessman defeated by wily Thais. I let him take the passport from limp fingers.

If Fullface's mind was still occupied with the vixens, he was not slowed at his terminal. He pawed the keyboard with one large hand and held the passport pinned to his desk with the other. Just a minute—

Did I really expect that the Chinese friends of my Chinese friend Charlie would do any more than bang a stamp in this stolen passport? That they'd take the trouble to meet with Thai contacts at the airport and find a quiet moment to enter the name, number and incoming flight details into the computer for a passenger who didn't exist?

I wondered if immigration clerks had a silent alarm button at their desks, or if they used a signal. A sound broke this unwholesome reflection: the thunk of an exit stamp onto paper before Fullface returned my passport and nodded farewell.

On board the Airbus, I downed a couple of glasses of too-cold water and waited in my seat. It was 10.20, and we were already late departing. I would later come to know that guards from Klong Prem had driven to Don Muang, arriving just after 10 a.m. to look for their missing *farang*. Aboard my plane, a Captain von Slagian announced, 'Ah – there will be a slight delay, I'm sorry. We are waiting for one passenger.'

As we waited, I entertained myself by staring rigidly at the back of the seat in front of me. Eventually, I heard the sound that is an angel's kiss to every smuggler, the *fwump* of sealing aircraft doors. I would later come to know that the guards of Klong Prem were at the airport by then, but too shy with real-world people to state their business and get beyond the check-in desks.

As the ascending jet banked into the clouds, I cast a final look at Bangkok through the port windows. I said nothing to myself, allowing the roar of the turbo-fans to do the talking.

At Singapore's Changi airport, the previously reluctant Visa card consented to whatever figures I keyed. I did this before passing immigration. At the transit-lounge shops I bought sunglasses, a radio and a pair of bathing trunks.

A floppy-haired immigration officer stamped my passport almost immediately, before casually flipping to the photo page. He didn't like something about my photograph. It was grainy. In a frozen moment, he held it before the UV tubelight, and I was back in Chinatown. British passports then included three invisible crowns edging the holder's photograph that only became pinkly visible under ultraviolet light.

The friends of Charlie Lao had been meticulous. After a moment, I had the passport back and was seeking a taxi outside the terminal.

Obeying the standard rule for airport arrivals, I made sure to take two taxis to break the connection to my hotel of choice before I checked in. I made many factual errors when completing the registration card.

Following a brief shower, I took a towel and left my room for the rooftop swimming pool. As it was noon on a workday, the small pool was deserted. Less than 12 hours had passed since I'd turned off the light for the last time in No. 57. There, another country, another name abandoned. In silence, I took three rapid steps to make a low dive into this so-transparent pool, spearing underwater from end to end. From the deep end, I expelled some air before

Escape

surfacing and in one movement lifting myself to the tiled edge. Still draining water, I stepped to the railing and rested, looking to the Panjang hills. There I remained for some time, watching a row of blackthorn shrubs straining inland with the wind, before turning and once again taking to the pool.

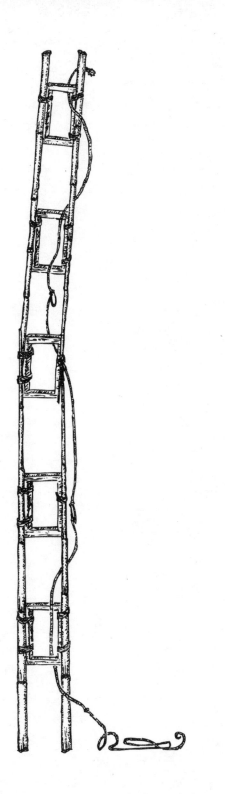

EPILOGUE

There is nothing more to say of the prison in Bangkok and the escape. Apart from memory, there remains only this collection of surviving communications to describe the balance of that year.

[To Connie Stanford, wife of Chas]
Friday, 23 August, Singapore

Dear Connie,

This might have taken a week or so to reach you – a friend in London posted it for me, as you can see from the envelope. I'm at the beginning of a long journey north. From here to central Asia, where I plan to stay with an old pirate friend.

After years of transit travel, this is the first time I've spent more than one day in this tiny state. And not just because a fellow can get strung up here for littering. Despite being one of the world's smallest countries, Singapore tenders the world's largest-value currency notes, the S$10,000 – worth about US$6,000! Making up for the country's small size, I suppose.

After a long, dreamless sleep on my first night in town, I had my first meal among strangers for quite some time. I found the waitress at the hotel as soulless as the city itself.

'Most girls in Singapore work to have the five Cs,' she said when serving me a bowl of tiger prawns. 'Cash, career, credit card, condominium.' That contrasts Confucian contemplations considered contentment in earlier times, eh?

I shouldn't have eaten that public food. I paid for it later. Made me ill.

After lunch, I walked through the wide suburbs surrounding the hotel, and didn't stop. I became a passenger aboard my legs, ignoring taxis and buses, counting hills till I stopped at some docklands. Point covered, I launched back towards the city centre in time to send some faxes, rent a post box and send a message to the Ghost[1]. I'll chance a brief call tomorrow.

Connie, I've found a little-known note in the basket of world currencies. Called International Floral Units, the exchange is ultimately to flowers. Interflora invented this borderless currency. I sent fifteen hundred IFUs. I know, it's utterly wet, but there you are! However, I won't call her until it's safe. Mr Plod will probably be all over Sharon's phones until they lose interest.

By the time I got down to Orchard Road, the cooler evening breeze had drawn people into this bright shopping street. Silver dials and coated lenses sparkled from the electronics stores, and the sounds of countless radios created strong machine froth. I see that the slinking kids have adopted the European fashion for T-shirts the colour of bain-marie peas. The smell of burning peanuts still mingles with the catspray, but some things have changed. Chinatown's been razed, and even Raffles is no more than a shell of depleted mystery. Foolishly, I ate at a busy chow-house on the main drag – hoping its brisk supply chain might limit the bacteria. (Funny, I can't remember being this phobic about food before.) Then walked two miles into exhaustion and back to the hotel.

Not too exhausted though to forget the precaution of taping my passports and money underneath a plastic chair on the balcony.

At breakfast, I saw a small piece in the *Straits Times*. No pictures, but it started me thinking about how some pestiferous investigators might get a lead. And if they did, I'd be stuck. Yet there's still one way to get tickets in names just different enough

---

1 Michael Sullivan

from a passport. So, I went out in search of a particular type of travel agency. The kind of place where they handwrite tickets. A place where the staff aren't too fussy. I found one within the cramped offices of some huge commercial block.

As I sat in the owner-manager's cubicle, I had a chance to take in the adornments. Behind his paper-strewn desk, this blubbery agent leaned in a weight-skewed black-vinyl recliner erupting with patches of pink foam. While one bunch of his beringed fingers gripped the handset of a blistered green phone with big buttons, those of his other hand kneaded the folds of his chins. There'd been several stillborn tries at a beard. He sweated under two layers of stretch wool – maybe to support the fantasy about working air-conditioners. On his desk, a Scotch-taped model Pan American stratocruiser nosed towards coffee-stained Venetian blinds, and a paper poppy drooped from a dusty Shalimar bottle. Behind his chair, the yellowing laminate of a world map had countries with names that are history. Ceylon, New Hebrides – even British Honduras. He was speaking to a client with chipper assurance, although his pauses became instant frowns as his eyes flew from a miniature, sun-browned Turkish flag to his overflowing trays for in, out, stuck, incontestable and irredeemable. The place was perfect.

A day later, I went back after our arrangements. He was on the phone again. We didn't speak much. 'Your ticket's there. All confirmed,' and pointed to the coupon under a puckered aluminium ashtray. 'You've paid, I think?' And then back to his caller.

The point of all this is that the handwritten ticket provided the means to have a booking made in the two Christian names of my passport. It's a common error in Asia. If the ticket works, you'll hear from me at my next port. If not – you'll hear from me much later!

I shan't dwell on it, but I'm lucky to be here. Just before take-off on my last leg, I expected a posse with nets and tridents to jump on board, and me with no defence other than a targeted spurt from a single-serve UHT milk portion.

More seriously, I owe a debt to my new friend from the Orient, Charlie. Chas might have mentioned he's soon to open a restaurant in Sydney. For those of us accustomed to a lifetime of triple-crossers, any promise fulfilled silently and at a distance remains a source of wonder. What is it that the evolutionary behaviourists say about friendship? That fidelity is no more than a trader's selective altruism, based on the soundness of reciprocal guarantees. Isn't that it? Or perhaps that wonder of friendship is not to be dissected – best left intact.

There were close moments, too, on the big night. One, halfway to morning, when all energy seemed spent. Although I wasn't going to surrender, I ask myself now: what it is that drives us on when fear and pain have been numbed by excessive application? A belief that there is another country beyond? Or some vainglorious need to prove a point? No, nothing noble, that's for sure. In the end, there's only that irresistible lure of opportunity. And maybe, just a little, to say something to all those doomwatchers in KP. Twelve thousand of them, and behind them ten times as many ghosts haunting the corridors. All sitting like children cross-legged in Sunday school receiving false instruction about absolute power. Not one wondering if he's listening to an absolute lie. In the darkness, with my bamboo poles, I did so want to call to them and say, 'You don't have to stay!'

Well, I say that now to clothe the naked stubbornness that I've had since my own childhood, my only real motivation. I'll tell you how it all went down some day when it's quiet. I suppose if I run through the 100 things leading to that night, it might seem as though it was easy, or just a process with an inevitable result. But holding to it all wasn't easy, and if any one of those 100 things had gone wrong, I wouldn't be here to write this.

It's only the living who get to tell their stories, so maybe all those survivors' stories added together seem like a picture of how things are. I can't see that as true – the real world is down there with the many who fail, whose histories are cut short or passed over.

My very best to Chas, to whom I'll write when I reach the land no one tribe has conquered.

Love,

D

Escape

26 August 1996

From: Phillip Keel, Fedpol, Canberra
To: T MacLean, Joint Taskforce Operations,
      Melbourne

Tom,

This is a transcript of a call intercepted
here at the bunker. One of your old targets,
I'd say. It's nothing official. Just another
'signal test' as we say here. Before you ask
where the call originated from, I'll tell you
we can't tell. International, yes, and the
originator shown is the USA. But our friends
say it's a bulk telecoms router. He probably
called a discount call line in the US from
somewhere and then used the service to re-
route the call.

The good news is that there's an effort to
cross-match all departures from BKK that day
against lost/stolen passports. That might give
us a name. When I say all departures, I mean
those with AUST/BRIT/CAN or US documentation.
The way it is now, you can forget European
cross-matches. Not likely though that he'd be
on anything too foreign. I'll let you know if
there's any joy.

Best wishes,
Phil

Escape

MS: Hello. Yes?

DMcM: Go placidly amid the noise and haste.

MS: Ah - It's you. You scallywag. Right. There was nothing on the phone display, so I hoped - Anyway, you OK?

DMcM: Yeah. Not used to being without my cook. Missing Chang.

MS: What the - fluck?

DMcM: I mean, fun's over. Flag planted, photo taken. Now, back to being pursued. Is this toy OK?

MS (referring to new mobile): Speaking its first words today, the little whippersnapper. Got it from an old lady who only phoned her bookie on Sundays.

DMcM: Sure?

MS: I swear by the eyebrows of Oscar Homolka. It's safe.

DMcM: OK. There's some messages for you down at the watery place.

MS: Watery?

DMcM: The print shop.

MS: Oh, right. Got you. So, you need anything?

DMcM: That little numbered edition still available? I'm feeling a personality disorder coming on.

MS: Yep. Still intact. You want it post or courier?

DMcM: Let it sit for now. I'll keep it for some fresh disaster. How tropical are you these days?

MS: Still smoking. They take an interest - from a distance. Don't collect overtime, as far as I can tell. You need money?

DMcM: Thanks. Not for now. I've got a tombkeeper from London to call Western Union. Look, I'd better end this. Usual reasons. Just wanted to hear the ghostly voice.

Escape

MS: OK. You have my pager number.

DMcM: Sure do.

MS: Take care, then.

DMcM: (Laughs)

MS: And watch out for exploding cigars.

NB We're sure the 'little numbered edition' refers to a hidden passport.

Escape

Friday, 30 August 1996, Karachi

Dear Michael,

Your package arrived just before I left my last rest-station. Thanks. Good to have music, and even better to have the freedom to listen to it. I never could stomach music in the Klong. I get your selection: Arvo P, Danny O'K, Górecki, Robbie R, *Hejira* – music for travellers who'll never reach home. Not a random grab, was it? Marc Jordan sounds less cynical these days. And is that a Fazzioli piano I can hear? Ach, what would I know – it's been a long time without air.

Landed in Karachi quietly. 'Welcome to Sindh province, Mr Peccavi,' said the immigration man, and I felt like an imperial agent, too. That's the last we'll hear of Mr Charles, Arthur. All ashes now. Any new editions will be locally modified. Not as bad as you might think. Here, there are set quality levels of forged documents – although we have to watch for spelling mistakes. Why would anyone want a third-rate passport, you ask? Well, they're not meant to work, they're only meant to convince the customer they might work, insh'allah!

I'll be ducking under the radar for a while. Staying with an old friend for a couple of months. However, you'll receive a SIM card and a phone sent from Europe by November. I can't bring myself to rely on the old wayz.

As ever,
David

Escape

Saturday, 21 September 1996, Baluchistan

Greetings Chas,

Seena has just brought my breakfast to the balcony as I write this. She is the daughter of my host, Mir Noor-Jehan Magsi, a tribal lord of the Magsi clan.

Seena tells me she is returning to school next week, and today she will go to Quetta to shop with her mother and a small entourage. She is shy and modest. As she left the tray on the table, her eyes brushed over a cool block of butter and a pot of marmalade. No one other than I appears to have eaten from either. A courtesy, as though it must be demonstrated that no one may meddle with the honoured Englishman's condiments.

This is N-J's heartland, the three-storeyed house the largest in a small town between the Arabian Sea and the big toe of Iran. My bedroom has this balcony from where I can breakfast in the shade and look over a sunblasted excavation of empty rooftops, for the town's houses all look like rocks. Scraped roads spike towards orange hills. It is dry.

His Lordship has just burst into the room. 'What's this? No one home?' before he waves aside the oddly heavy curtains. Although we are both wearing the shalwar kameez, mine is as close-fitting as N-J's tailor would allow. This morning, N-J appears as a small barque in full sail. Billowing white trousers and a shirt embroidered with jade silk. He fiddles with the fan-control box by the window and tells me we are off somewhere special today, and that he'd like me to dress English. Be a *gora* – a white man.

Before I can ask why, he switches: 'This fan is working well? You like the heat, eh?' I tell him I don't like the ceiling fan chopping over me when I wake. I offer tea & toast. Noor-Jehan declines and looks over the balcony. He is an early riser and would have eaten hours ago.

Escape

'So, today we travel to see friends. Kamran has the car ready.' Noor-Jehan speaks his native Balouchi, excellent Sindhi, commercial Urdu and almost no English. While he makes a concoction of words from his larder he thinks I'll understand, I often reply in mock-Fitzrovian, which N-J enjoys as the salute it's meant to be.

Chas, something I was looking forward to all that time in BKK was speaking English again to native English speakers. It hasn't happened, and seems it might not for a while. I don't mind so much at all. Even though I understand there can be no answer to this letter for who knows how long, I'm happy to be rattling on.

Sunday

Yesterday, we drove south to the coast road, turning east towards Karachi before reaching some beachside ship-breaking yards early afternoon. For miles, I could see nothing behind high patchwork fences that hide the goings-on: the business of dismantling the world's discarded tankers, liners and cargo ships. This is hugely profitable, so it was unsettling to find the surrounding junkyard township made of the scrap for which even the scrap-dealers have no use.

After the heavy chains and bolts of the seaside entrance were withdrawn by scowling sentries, we were escorted to a well-appointed office with uncommonly large windows overlooking what remained of the beach. The carcasses of three huge vessels had been drawn to the oil-clogged shoreline using bunches of linked anchor chains, the only remaining entrails of 100 digested ships.

At my request, our party moved on to the sand to be closer to the ships. We became small under the shadow of a nameless cruise liner. Her prow seemed to have been torn away by the jaws of some invisible, giant beast. Revealed from within her rust-stained carcass were sudden-drop gangways, a theatre of shattered cabins, unfloored corridors; even a dance floor slowly raining parquetry upon the eviscerated below-decks. Only the impacted boilers were holding out against dismemberment.

The teeth of the consuming monster became visible as I moved closer. A writhing colony of human workers, infesting every exposed pore and armed with little better than heavy hammers, crowbars and a few blowtorches. It looked as though this ill-equipped army, trained by injury, would win every battle, for their numbers are legion. To the liner's portside, a supertanker was being cleaved of its sheeting, and to her starboard a container ship had been halved. At perilous height at the tip of a freighter's mast, a lone worker struck out at the last fittings.

When I turned back towards N-J and his friends, I heard him laugh deep above the clang and sparks from the shore, but his Mayan walnut face crinkled at me with a conspiratorial wink – undoubtedly signalling that some villainy was being hatched. My job was to appear reserved, serious and deftly judgemental. I don't know what Noor-Jehan is plotting, and I don't much care. So, I arched my eyebrows and nodded at the group before marching back to the office. Using the binoculars there, I saw that my mast-worker was in fact a shattered antenna complex turning in the breeze, perhaps a warning to the dozen ships that lay at anchor awaiting the factory's attentions.

Now, don't worry, Chas, Mir Noor-Jehan is on my side. If any stranger came to our town asking about a foreigner within earshot of His Lordship's bodyguard, there'd be a game of head-polo set for the afternoon.

On our way home, we stopped at what I took for a fishing village. The car door opened, and air-conditioning met heat carried by the smell of 20,000 drying fish. The town is built right at the water's edge, on top of low rocks. The quayside buildings have

Escape

been constructed from those dead ships' finer interiors – but used for the outside. Stately wooden columns, curved banisters and bar-room panelling form the external walls of these thoughtful and accidental houses along the dock. Rare colours for this part of the world. This is a smuggling village – they just like to fish.

When we'd neared the village, we'd turned onto the first smooth-tarmacked road I'd seen for miles. It ran from the near-coastal road through scrubland and ended as if in error on the beach. I asked Noor-Jehan what was up. 'Who made it? I mean, who paid for it?'

'A big smuggler owns all this. His dhows sail from Oman every week.'

When I said something about this road looking a bit obvious, my protector drew his arms wide and grinned at the wonders, standing back towards the hills that, like N-J, resist all change.

Kamran had been playing music of the Sufi poets during our journey out. I hoped to please them in return with Coleman-Dudley's Victorious City songs. Everyone other than N-J appeared baffled at that Western homage to the East.

Tuesday

In a few days I must leave this calm zone to join my friends at the Frontier, so will post from Peshawar.

Today, I was allowed out with a car on my own (against the head-shaking of my guardians) and I drove back to stand with the steel bones of those discarded carriers at the shoreline. Something serene about the grand fleets of the West reduced to ignominy and scavenger food. Along the coast road towards Pasni I found a deserted pavilion weathering before the sea. In the style of a 1920s Brighton beach house, though I later learnt it is a remnant from the ambitions of the 1970s, when businessmen imagined this former sultanate might become what Dubai is today. The would-be Casino des Balouches entertained no ghosts, and its warped floors and crumbling plaster denied any odour of human occupation. Perhaps never used. Yet its taps ran water from a town that has yet to be built.

Drive inland from the coast and the weight of the land is pressed upon all travellers. It's hot. Beneath the disc of an implacable sun, the earth becomes a giant altar. A dry handful of earth may be held only temporarily; any tightening of the grip merely speeds its return to the ground. Biscuit crumbs too coarse to retain even a handprint. Here, there are unmarked graves where travellers – separated soldiers, thoughtless traders and simple strangers – are mummified in airless spaces not so very deep. The shoreline smugglers are intolerant of those who disturb. When jihadi pause here on their catastrophic pilgrimages, they may be served sweet tea, praise and blessings for their holy cause, yet be entombed by these sons of the soil, as the local tribesmen call themselves.

It is night now at Mir Noor-Jehan Magsi's. The menfolk are meeting in secret conclaves; servants crouch, sweeping the floors. Two of the dozen telephones of this township are in this house, and the one with the loudest and oldest ring is never answered. I've been thinking about muffling the bell. The family are watching TV. I set up a satellite dish to poach signals from space. The children are mollified, at least (they sleep where they will), and the elders sit similarly transfixed while silently mouthing dutiful condemnation at the colourful images of Western decadence.

On my bed lies my new documentation. Passports fanned out as a winning poker hand. We'll see. My Western clothes lie next to an open suitcase.

So, must close now,

With warmest wishes,

D

Escape

Sunday, 6 October 1996

Greetings D,

Good to hear that you are in high spirits despite the notoriously foul weather. Were you calling from Baker Street? I suppose your senses are still overloaded in the real world. That'll pass. We don't want you becoming overexcited. No need for names, no need to explain. You know that.

Your Swedish chum has been thrown in chains and sent to high security. Same place, though, according to his embassy. He's OK. Leave it to me. Reminds me – I read a quote in the *Post* from an Oz embassy drudge. 'There's always one who spoils it for everyone else.' That's a laugh. You'll have to let me know sometime about all the good stuff that got spoiled by your sudden departure.

No need to answer this. Our dispatch rider will carry all the news that's not fit to print.

Adios amigo,
M

PS I modestly draw your attention to the brevity and anonymity of the above.

Escape

Wednesday, 12 December, Annecy

Dear M,

I'm writing this from a curved window facing a frozen lake. The sitting room of a modest suite in an hôtel du charme below the Rhône Alpes. I'm not alone.

I left London three days ago, not wanting to leave the new house so soon – painters are still working, deliveries arriving and things to be installed. The agents say they'll supervise. I'm turning the garage into a workshop. No interest in a car. A car in London is a gift to the Forces of Darkness. Not that they'll know – I'm blissfully unknown there. Over 15 years now since the Heathrow thing. The mews house is more of a try at permanence than is usual for me, I'll admit. Don't read too much into that. Only that I can afford to buy and lose some ground as most of the biscuit tins were intact, although some needed the application of a sturdy tin opener.

The journey to France was to meet Sharon. Eurostar to Paris for me, and then to Lyons to wait. From Oz to Zurich for Sharon, and then a pick-up at Geneva. An old chum drove her across the border, just in case she had unwelcome company. None. Then to the lake. That was two days ago. Right now she's sitting on the floor, listening to music.

We walked around town today. Heavy, lined coats and a firm grip on each other. We'd just come from the patisserie, wouldn't you know. Walked over stone bridges and to the big hotel, not ours. Into the warmth, shedding coats to be thawed in the salon by brandy and firelight. Brandy's for the evening, I think. Too sad for the night. Too sweet. There was a black piano near our chairs, open for someone. We both looked at it, but shied away. Sharon's a singer, you might recall. The salon was wide, with tall ceilings. My mind was elsewhere.

315

Escape

As you'll soon find, we've business with a former captain of the PK army. Inexperienced – in our way – yet with contacts. In most ways, PK is all contacts. This afternoon, as Sharon and I sipped, we were silent, and I was thinking of my time in Baluchistan with His Lordship. I was watching a movie there, sniffed from Asiasat, TNT. Old, black and white: *The Santa Fe Trail*. Starring a future American president and a cryptic Australian. And Raymond Massey playing evangelical John Brown, fiercely calling up hellfire against those who would not see his vision of God. You'd know it; two generations of children have been chilled by that savage puss while sitting cross-legged, two feet from the tube on Saturday mornings. Massey's carved, dark features, glowing white eyes, untouchable beard and rock-breaking nose. Rather like some of the zealots I met near the border in that dry land. Deserts – do you think that growing up unable to take a relaxing bath produces religious headbangers? Well, they're of no account, although some will be our guides as we cross the tribal areas in the New Year.

Before I forget, there's no need to follow up on Dean Reed. I was all hot under the collar for a while, but Chas talked me out of it. As he said, it does everyone a little good to be conned every so often. Keeps us in touch with our inner selves, he said. And I guess Dean did something of a service to a few poor saps in the Cure. He gave them hope where there was none. Kept them away from the wheels of the sand trucks until the clouds lifted.

Sharon is humming under her headphones. She is stretching now – back arching, folding her arms over her head. Her toes wiggle in consensus. I'll not have long at this desk. She's likely to pounce.

On Friday, we'll hire a car in Lyons and drive back and on to Italy. She never asks about business – she's a tenderfoot in this, still. We'll keep to the surface, travelling north and on to London. Then peel off before Christmas. I'll be careful – I'm still superstitious about this time of the year – and, of course, I'll tread softly near the complete felicity of her heart.

Ouch! Didn't see that coming.

As ever,

D

Nor would I see coming those reversals of fortune that were being seeded in the North-West Frontier Province by people I'd yet to meet.

The closed communications above, and similar postings, remain the only written record of my times following the escape.

Only confinement and singular need allow any history to fall together and, from a distance, appear well defined. The David who was Daniel Westlake had, of necessity, been smothered in the Cure.

As Christmas passed with contentment and comforts anaesthetising my nerves, Daniel's spirit would reincarnate: an untroubled prospector seeking some imaginary country, a truster of destiny, and in coming back to life assure the inevitable consequences of such conceits. Yet first, I would have to become accustomed once again to all things too precious to lose.